The Cognitive Structure of Emotions

The Cognitive Structure of Emotions

ANDREW ORTONY
University of Illinois at Urbana-Champaign

GERALD L. CLORE
University of Illinois at Urbana-Champaign

ALLAN COLLINS
Bolt, Beranek, and Newman, Inc.
Cambridge, Massachusetts

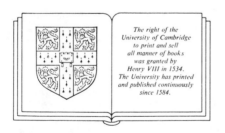

The right of the
University of Cambridge
to print and sell
all manner of books
was granted by
Henry VIII in 1534.
The University has printed
and published continuously
since 1584.

CAMBRIDGE UNIVERSITY PRESS

Cambridge
New York   New Rochelle   Melbourne   Sydney

Published by the Press Syndicate of the University of Cambridge
The Pitt Building, Trumpington Street, Cambridge CB2 1RP
32 East 57th Street, New York, NY 10022, USA
10 Stamford Road, Oakleigh, Melbourne 3166, Australia

First published 1988

Printed in Canada

Library of Congress Cataloging-in-Publication Data
Ortony, Andrew, 1942–
The Cognitive Structure of Emotions.
1. Emotions. 2. Cognition. I. Clore, Gerald L.
II. Collins, Allan. III. Title. [DNLM: 1. Cognition.
2. Emotions. 3. Psychological Theory.   BF 531 078c]
BF531.075   1988   152.4   87–33757

British Library Cataloguing in Publication Data
Ortony, Andrew
The Cognitive Structure of Emotions.
1. Emotions
I. Title II. Clore, Gerald L.
III. Collins, Allan
152.4   BF53/

ISBN 0 521 35364 5

To our wives,
Gillian, Judy, and Anne

Contents

Preface   *page* ix

1   Introduction   1
    The Study of Emotion   3
    Types of Evidence for Theories of Emotion   8
    Some Goals for a Theory of the Cognitive Structure of Emotions   12
    Summary   14

2   The Structure of the Theory   15
    The Organization of Emotion Types   18
    Basic Emotions   25
    Some Implications of the Emotions-as-valenced-reactions Claim   29
    Summary   33

3   The Cognitive Psychology of Appraisal   34
    The Appraisal Structure   34
    Central Intensity Variables   48
    Summary   58

4   Factors Affecting the Intensity of Emotions   59
    Global Variables   60
    Local Variables   68
    Variable-values, Variable-weights, and Emotion Thresholds   81
    Summary   83

5   Reactions to Events: I   85
    The Well-being Emotions   85
    Loss Emotions and Fine-grained Analyses   90
    The Fortunes-of-others Emotions   92
    Self-pity and Related States   106
    Summary   107

vii

6   Reactions to Events: II   109
    The Prospect-based Emotions   109
    Shock and Pleasant Surprise   125
    Some Interrelationships Among Prospect-based Emotions   127
    Suspense, Resignation, Hopelessness, and Other Related States 131
    Summary   132

7   Reactions to Agents   134
    The Attribution Emotions   134
    Gratitude, Anger, and Some Other Compound Emotions   146
    Summary   154

8   Reactions to Objects   156
    The Attraction Emotions   156
    Fine-grained Analyses and Emotion Sequences   167
    Summary   171

9   The Boundaries of the Theory   172
    Emotion Words and Cross-cultural Issues   172
    Emotion Experiences and Unconscious Emotions   176
    Coping and the Function of Emotions   178
    Computational Tractability   181
    Summary   190

References   193
Author Index   201
Subject Index   204

Preface

As cognitive psychology established itself in the 1970s, it became increasingly apparent that it was a "cold" approach to cognition, and doubts began to arise as to whether or not it could provide the machinery necessary to account for affect and emotion. In 1981, Donald Norman identified the topic of emotion as one of twelve major challenges to cognitive science (Norman, 1981). It was at about this time that the three authors of this volume decided to collaborate in an attempt to explore the extent to which cognitive psychology could provide a viable foundation for the analysis of emotions. Certainly, it was no problem for cognitive psychology, with the help of schema theory, to explain such facts as that the same thing can be perceived from different perspectives. This was already encouraging, because the capacity to view a situation from different perspectives struck us as lying at the heart of the fact that different people often experience different emotions in response to the same objective event.

Many emotion theorists have argued that cognitive appraisal is central to emotion, yet no one has been able to say anything much more detailed than that. This book is an attempt to give at least the outlines of an account of how such appraisals are made. In it we present many detailed observations about specific emotions, their organization, and the specific cognitive processes involved in their elicitation, but we would be satisfied if this effort succeeded in demonstrating only that a systematic and comprehensive account of the cognitive antecedents of the emotions is possible. Our goal is to convince our readers that such an approach is viable rather than that our particular version of such an effort is the correct one. We have, in fact, chosen a somewhat arbitrary stopping point for this enterprise. Further use of the same structural principles that we propose would allow one to continue to specify increasingly differentiated sets of emotional states. The more one does this, however, the more one becomes tied to the emotional system associated with a particular cultural view of the world. This, in turn, increases the risk that one will lose sight of the main agenda, which is to characterize the range of "psycho-logical" possibilities for emotions rather than to describe the emotions and emotion-related processes local to any specific time or cultural group.

We started collaborating on this project in the spring of 1980 when we began talking to each other about various emotions and the conditions of their occurrence. In the context of our common fascination with this problem, the differences in our backgrounds and interests made the end product different than it otherwise would have been. As a group we include a cognitive scientist interested in psychological, linguistic, and computational aspects of the study of mental processes, a social psychologist with interests in personality and in the influences of affect on social judgment, and a cognitive psychologist with interests in the formal modeling of human reasoning processes. As we started working out some of the ideas into a more concrete form it became clear that we were going to end up with a book – a book that we began to think of affectionately as *Principia Pathematica*. We saw ourselves as attempting to characterize some of the key principles governing the cognitive mechanisms underlying human emotions, so that title seemed to us apt and even a little humorous. After all, we tried to persuade ourselves, the Oxford English Dictionary contains the following (abbreviated) entry:

PATHEMATIC, *a. rare* [ad. Gr. *pathematicos* liable to passions or emotions, f. *pathema* what one suffers, suffering emotion, f. stem *path-*: see PATHETIC] Pertaining to the passions or emotions; caused or characterized by emotion.

However, many of our friends and colleagues were skeptical. The title we proposed would be incomprehensible to those lacking a classical education, they argued, and the book might well end up in the medical section of bookstores! Then again, there was the problem of hubris – was it not a little pretentious? We were eventually persuaded that discretion is the better part of valor, and settled on a title that, while maybe lacking something in panache, at least has the virtue of truth in advertising.

Thanks are due to a number of people and institutions for intellectual, financial, and moral support. In particular, we are grateful for the encouragement and helpful comments and observations of Bob Abelson, Gordon Bower, Jerry DeJong, Nico Frijda, Philip Johnson-Laird, George Mandler, George Miller, Robert Wilensky, and many colleagues at the University of Illinois at Urbana-Champaign, especially in Psychology. The ideas, criticism, enthusiasm, and hard work of the members of our research group, including Mark Foss, Terry Turner, Jerry Parrott, Steve Levine, and Susan Ravlin, were an indispensable aid to us. We also thank Katharita

Lamoza of Cambridge University Press for her tireless effort as production editor of this book. Thanks are also due to the National Science Foundation for the resources in the form of a grant (BNS 83–18077) that enabled us to explore some of our ideas empirically as well as theoretically, that allowed all three of us to get together, and that kept the project moving. In addition, we would like to acknowledge the support provided to some of our pre- and postdoctoral students through a training grant from the National Institute of Mental Health (MH 15140). We also want to express our gratitude to the Center for Advanced Study at the University of Illinois for granting two of us fellowships in successive years that allowed us to devote significant portions of our time to completing this book. Most of all, however, we thank our wives for putting up with us during years of obsessive discussions.

Andrew Ortony
Gerald L. Clore
Allan Collins

1   Introduction

Emotions have many facets. They involve feelings and experience, they involve physiology and behavior, and they involve cognitions and conceptualizations. There are important questions that can be asked about the expression of emotions, especially through the face, and the language of emotion constitutes an interesting research domain in its own right. In this book we are primarily interested in the contribution that cognition makes to emotion. The most general issue we shall address concerns the question of emotional differentiation – the question of what distinguishes one emotion from another – and our approach will be concerned more or less exclusively with trying to characterize the differences between emotions in terms of the different kinds of cognitions we take to be responsible for them. Taking the perspective of empirical psychology and cognitive science, we start with the assumption that emotions arise as a result of the way in which the situations that initiate them are construed by the experiencer. Our general plan is to try to impose some structure on the limitless number of possible emotion-eliciting situations. This is primarily an undertaking in theoretical psychology, although our proposals are intended to be consistent with existing data, as well as making their own empirically testable predictions. What we are trying to do, therefore, is to specify the "psychological" structure of emotions in terms of personal and interpersonal situation descriptions. Given these goals, we make no attempt to review the massive literature on the diverse aspects of the psychology of emotion. Such a review would only dilute our own efforts. Furthermore, we think it improbable that we could improve on the many excellent reviews that already exist (e.g., Frijda, 1987; Leventhal & Tomarken, 1986; Strongman, 1978).

The theory we propose is decidedly *not* a theory about emotion *words*. Indeed, our characterizations of emotions are intentionally cast in terms that are as independent of emotion words as possible, partly because we believe that the structure of the emotion lexicon is not isomorphic with the

1

structure of emotions themselves, and partly because a theory about emotions has to be a theory about the kinds of things to which emotion words refer, not about the words themselves. We consider the enterprise of mapping emotion words onto emotion structures to be quite separate from that of trying to characterize the structure of emotions themselves, and one that is better postponed until the structural questions have been resolved. Accordingly, we devote relatively little attention to the serious investigation of the relation between emotion types and the linguistic tokens associated with them. Nor do we devote much attention to other important aspects of emotion, such as the physiological, behavioral, or expressive components. This neglect is not because we think these aspects unimportant, but because we wish to start earlier in the causal chain. We think that emotions arise as a result of certain kinds of cognitions, and we wish to explore what these cognitions might be. The physiological, behavioral, and expressive aspects of emotions seem to us to presuppose that this first, cognitive, step has already taken place. Certainly, these aspects would be crucial to a complete answer to the question of what an emotion is, but we think they are less central to answering the question of where emotions come from.

Having emphasized that we are not attempting to define emotion words, we should also emphasize that we think our account is, in principle, capable of accommodating the fact that there are significant individual and cultural differences in the experience of emotions. Our claims about the structure of individual emotions are always along the lines that *if* an individual conceptualizes a situation in a certain kind of way, *then* the potential for a particular type of emotion exists. However, we do not attempt to specify the mechanisms that determine whether some particular situation will be conceptualized in one way or another. The question of how a situation is conceptualized in the first place, which we take to be the locus of individual and cultural differences, is a problem that is general for cognitive psychology, not one that is specific to the study of emotions. By attempting to be very specific about what emotions there are or could be, and about the particular factors that influence their intensity, we hope to achieve two goals. First, we seek to bring some semblance of order to what remains a very confused and confusing field of study. Second, we would like to lay the foundation for a computationally tractable model of emotion. In other words, we would like an account of emotion that could in principle be used in an Artificial Intelligence (AI) system that would, for example, be able to reason about emotions. Both of these goals require a level of specificity that has not been characteristic of previous work in the field. The degree to which we succeed in accomplishing them remains to be seen.

The Study of Emotion

Emotion is one of the most central and pervasive aspects of human experience. Normal people experience a wide range of emotions, from the quiet satisfaction of completing a relatively mundane task to the grief at the death of a loved one. Yet while emotions color, deepen, and enrich human experience, they can also cause dramatic disruptions in judgment and performance. Such disruptions can have profound and sometimes terrible consequences for individuals and society as, for example, in crimes of passion, suicides, and mental illness. This fact is clearly recognized by creators of literature, which thrives on the imagined emotions of its characters. The basic recipe is very simple: The writer describes a situation that readers recognize as being *important* to a character in the sense that it has important implications with respect to the goals, standards, or attitudes that the character is known or assumed to have. Then, the character is portrayed as correctly or incorrectly construing the situation as good or bad relative to these goals or standards or attitudes, and typically is described as having, or is assumed to have, a valenced (i.e., a positive or negative) *reaction* to the situation. Finally, the construal together with the reaction usually results in some sort of change in the character's judgment or *behavior*. Consider, for example, the main plot of *Othello*. We start with the assumption that the maintenance of Desdemona's love and fidelity is important for Othello. He then (incorrectly) construes Cassio's (presumed) actions as a threat to this goal and becomes consumed with anger and jealousy. The result is a dramatic deterioration in judgment and a correspondingly drastic action in which he kills both Desdemona and himself. As readers, a certain suspension of disbelief is required, but only up to a point. The essential ingredients have to be believable. If literature is a microcosm of the real world, it has to be recognizable as such.

It is apparent that writers can reliably produce in readers an awareness of a character's affective states by characterizing a situation whose construal is assumed to give rise to them. This suggests that writers use an implicit theory that individual emotions can be specified in terms of personal or interpersonal situational descriptions that are sufficient to produce them. Thus, writers do not always have to state what emotions a character is experiencing because if the described situation contains the *eliciting conditions* for a particular emotion, the experience of that emotion can be inferred. The fact that millions of readers, often over decades or even centuries, all infer similar emotions from the described situations suggests that this implicit theory cannot be too far wrong.

If the eliciting conditions of an emotion are to be effective, the experiencing individual must encode the relevant situation in a particular way. In other words, if an emotion such as distress is a reaction to some undesirable event, the event itself must be construed as undesirable, and because construing the world is a cognitive process, the eliciting conditions of emotions embody the cognitive representations that result from such construals. Perhaps one of the most obvious cases of the major contribution that cognition through construals makes to emotion is afforded by the reactions of players and fans at sports events. When one observes the reactions of the players to the outcome of an important game (for example, the final of the World Cup, or the NCAA basketball championship) it is clear that those on the winning team are elated while those on the losing team are devastated. Yet, in a very real sense, both the winners and losers are reacting to the same objective event. It is their *construals* of the event that are different. The victors construe it as desirable, the losers as undesirable, and it is these construals that drive the emotion system. The emotions are very real and very intense, but they still issue from cognitive interpretations imposed on external reality, rather than directly from reality itself. It is in this sense that we claim that there is an essential and profound cognitive basis for emotions.

Before we start, it is important to make clear that some emotions, (e.g., disgust), involve much less cognitive processing and structure than others (e.g., shame). Interestingly, however, those that involve relatively little cognition usually have metaphorical analogs that involve much more, whereas the converse is not true. Thus the emotion that one might experience in response to, for example, some totally inappropriate and unacceptable social behavior might well be called "disgust." On the other hand, it is difficult to imagine a cognitively impoverished analog of a social emotion such as embarrassment. We should also make clear at the outset that our claim that emotions always involve some degree of cognition is not the same as asserting that the contribution of cognition is necessarily *conscious*. To say that emotions arise from cognition is to say that they are determined by the structure, content, and organization of knowledge representations and the processes that operate on them. These representations and processes might sometimes be available to consciousness, but there is no reason to suppose that they necessarily are so.

Although we doubt that William James would have approved of our characterization of emotion in general, it is interesting to note that our claim that some emotions involve more cognition than others has a parallel in James's famous paper *What is an emotion?* (James, 1884). There, James restricted his discussion to emotions having "a distinct bodily expression" in which "a wave of bodily disturbance of some kind accompanies the perception of the interesting sights or sounds, or the passage of the exciting train of ideas. Surprise, curiosity, rapture, fear, anger, lust, greed, and the like, become then the names of the mental states with which the person is possessed" (p. 189). Emotions like these, James called the "standard emotions." He seems to have considered the "standard emotions" to involve little or no cognition, arguing that "in advance of all experience of elephants no child can but be frightened if he suddenly finds one trumpeting and charging upon him" (p. 191). However, James acknowledged that there can be more complex emotion-inducing perceptions, ones which, in modern terms, would have to be described as involving a relatively high degree of cognition, such as events having to do with the violation of social conventions: "Most occasions of shame and many insults are purely conventional, and vary with the social environment." In considering these as potential counterexamples to his theory, James goes on, rhetorically: "In these cases, at least, it would seem that the ideas of shame, desire, regret, etc., must first have been attached by education and association to these conventional objects before the bodily changes could possibly be awakened" (p. 195). James's answer to this apparent threat is to assert that the nature of the emotion-inducing perception is not the issue; rather, the issue is that, once triggered, the perception gives rise to the bodily response that is the emotion. However, like it or not (and James is now in no position to object), James had essentially characterized a range of cognitive content for the emotion-producing perception from low (e.g., a mother's delight at the sight of her beautiful baby) to high (e.g., the delight of receiving a national honor).

Modern theories of cognition have relatively little to say in the way of specific proposals about affect and emotion (Norman, 1981; Zajonc, 1980). It is quite possible that the root cause of the dissociation between cognitive theories and emotion theories lies in the emphasis that has been placed in recent years on the computer metaphor of "human information processing." This approach to cognition has been as noticeable in its failure to make progress on problems of affect as it has been for its success in making progress on problems of cognition. Given the abundance of psychological evidence that cognitions can influence and be influenced by emotions (e.g., Bower, 1981; Isen, Shalker, Clark, & Karp, 1978; Johnson & Tversky, 1983; Ortony, Turner, & Antos, 1983; Schwarz & Clore, 1983), the absence of a viable account of the emotions compatible with a general theory of cognition renders existing theories of both inadequate.

Just as few theories of cognition have much to say about emotion, so theories of emotion tend to be unacceptably vague about exactly what role cognition plays in emotion. Psychologists (e.g., Arnold, 1960; Lazarus, Kanner, & Folkman, 1980; Mandler, 1975; 1984) and philosophers (e.g., Lyons, 1980) frequently acknowledge that cognition plays an essential role in emotion, but for the most part they have not provided detailed proposals about exactly how this happens (but see, e.g., Abelson, 1983; Mandler, 1984). One of the clearer accounts is that offered by Mandler, who claims that what he calls "cognitive interpretation" or "meaning analysis" (i.e., *appraisal*) is the "cold" part of emotion. The "heat" is provided by *arousal*, which according to Mandler, is normally occasioned by the interruption of plans or action sequences. We find Mandler's account more attractive than other arousal/appraisal theories because of its specificity with respect to the appraisal aspect of emotion (see, for example, Mandler, 1982), and because of its explicit recognition of the importance of plans, goals, and knowledge representations. However, Mandler's account has little to say about specific emotions, especially positive ones, and it offers no systematic account of the relation among different emotions.

Another problem with the arousal/appraisal theories is that they offer no account of how arousal and appraisal interact to produce emotion. Our approach to this problem is to postulate an arousal-producing mechanism that, at the same time, registers valence. This obviates the need to postulate distinct mechanisms corresponding to arousal and appraisal, thus eliminating the need to explain how such mechanisms interact for the ordinary experience of emotion. We believe such an approach is viable even though, under special circumstances, it is possible to produce one in the absence of the other (e.g., Schachter & Singer, 1962). Our initial discussion of these issues can be found in Chapter 3.

From a global perspective, it seems that past research on emotion converges on only two generalizations. One is that emotion consists of arousal and appraisal (e.g., Arnold, 1960; Lazarus, Averill, & Opton, 1970; Mandler, 1975; Schachter & Singer, 1962). The other, emerging from the scaling literature (e.g., Abelson & Sermat, 1962; Block, 1957; Davitz, 1969; Engen, Levy, & Schlosberg, 1958; Russell, 1980), is that any dimensional characterization of emotions is likely to include at least the two dimensions of *activation* and *valence*. But, on closer inspection, even these two generalizations appear to be merely two sides of the same coin: The activity dimension can be viewed as the reflection of arousal, and the valence dimension as the reflection of appraisal. Many of the studies that have discovered such relatively simple dimensional structures have been based on judgments about emotion *words*. We suspect, however, that the uncritical use of scaling techniques with emotion words is inappropriate, or at least premature. The problem is that judgments about (the similarity between) emotion words depend on various, usually uncontrolled (and often uncontrollable) aspects of the stimuli – aspects such as intensity of the corresponding emotions, types of antecedents, types of consequences, and so on. Without knowing to which of these (or other) aspects someone is attending, judgments of similarity are largely uninterpretable. It is partly for this reason, no doubt, that the plethora of multidimensional scaling and factor analytic studies that have been conducted seems only to agree that the major descriptive dimensions of emotions are valence and arousal. We find this conclusion is as uninformative as it is unsurprising.

There have, of course, been numerous attempts to characterize the structure of emotions. They have been developed in different ways, often for different purposes. Theories have been proposed based on all kinds of variables; for example, biological/evolutionary variables (e.g., Plutchik, 1962; 1980), phenomenal variables (e.g., de Rivera, 1977), behavioral variables (e.g., James, 1890), facial expression variables (e.g., Ekman, 1982), and cognitive variables (e.g., Roseman, 1984). Authors have considered such variables to represent the primitive ingredients of human nature, and thus of human emotions. For example, some theorists argue that there is a fundamental opposition between fear and anger because of the underlying approach/avoidance difference. Notice, however, that this difference is rooted in the typical response to these emotions rather than in their causes; when viewed from a causal perspective there may or may not be reason to believe that they are opposed in an important way. An almost universal characteristic of these approaches to emotion is the postulation of a small number of *basic* emotions (typically fewer than ten). Our own view is that the search for and postulation of basic emotions is not a profitable approach. One of our many reasons for saying this is that there seems to be no objective way to decide which theorist's set of basic emotions might be the right one (for a more detailed discussion of this issue, see Chapter 2).

Apart from scaling and arousal/appraisal approaches to emotion, the other main approaches have studied the physiology of emotions and facial expressions. The visceral sensations accompanying emotions and the expressive manifestations of emotions are perhaps the two characteristics that most set emotions apart from other psychological states and events. This may explain why so much research has been concerned with them. The physiological research (see, e.g., Grings & Dawson, 1978; Levi, 1975) is valuable and interesting and may be important for understanding the functions of emotions. However, it does not address questions about the *cognitive* origins of emotions. Such questions are also finessed by the research on facial expressions, with which some of the most impressive research on emotion has been concerned (e.g., Ekman, Friesen, & Ellsworth, 1982). Insofar as such research is indeed concerned with the *expression* of any particular emotion, it presupposes that the emotion already exists, leaving unaddressed the problem of how it came to be there in the first place.

Types of Evidence for Theories of Emotion

There are four kinds of evidence to which one might appeal in attempting to understand the emotions. First, there is the *language* of emotions, which comes replete with ambiguity, synonymy (or near synonymy), and an abundance of lexical gaps and linguistic traps. Of course, emotions are not themselves linguistic things, but the most readily available nonphenomenal access we have to them is through language. Thus, in order to specify the domain of a theory of emotion it is difficult to avoid using natural language words and expressions that refer to emotions. However, a theory of emotion must not be confused with a theory of the language of emotion. Considerable care needs to be taken in the use to which natural language is put in developing a theory of emotions. Not all distinct emotion types necessarily have associated words in any particular language, and not all the emotion words that refer to emotions in some particular language necessarily refer to distinct ones. The absence of a word in one language to designate the particular emotion that might be referred to by a word in another does not mean that people in cultures using the first language cannot and do not experience that emotion (Wierzbicka, 1986). Such linguistic gaps can be filled through catachresis and metaphorical descriptions, although the latter are often used even in cases where the language does provide a word for the particular category of emotion, but where one seeks to communicate the particular *quality* of an instance of the category (Fainsilber & Ortony, 1987). For some categories of emotions, a language like English provides a relatively large number of tokens, thus reducing the need for metaphorical descriptions of emotional quality. In such cases, it becomes necessary to identify one of the words in the category as the unmarked form or category label. For example, *fear* has lexical realizations that mark special cases such as very strong fear ("terrified"), very weak fear ("worried"), typical fear-induced behaviors ("cowering") and so on. Thus, it may be helpful to think of the word "fear" as a relatively neutral word for an emotion type, fear. In other words, one can view the word "fear" as designating a distinct emotion type (whereas the word "terrified" does not). This is quite consistent with a subsequent fine-grained analysis that might examine what exactly the different tokens for the same emotion type do distinguish, and why. However, our ultimate goal is not to *define* emotion words such as "fear" but to specify, in as language-neutral a manner as possible, the characteristics of distinct emotions. Language, therefore, is a source of evidence that has to be used with considerable care. We will assume that the words in our common language reflect a number of important distinctions, that they reflect a number of not so important distinctions, and that sometimes they fail to reflect important distinctions at all. Some of these issues will be discussed in Chapter 9. We have also discussed them at length elsewhere (e.g., Clore, Ortony, & Foss, 1987; Ortony & Clore, 1981; Ortony, Clore, & Foss, 1987).

The second kind of evidence is evidence from *self reports* of experienced emotions. There is as yet no known objective measure that can conclusively establish that a person is experiencing some particular emotion, just as there is no known way of establishing that a person is experiencing some particular color. In practice, however, this does not normally constitute a problem because we are willing to treat people's reports of their emotions as valid. Because emotions are subjective experiences, like the sensation of color or pain, people have direct access to them, so that if a person is experiencing fear, for example, that person cannot be mistaken about the fact that he or she is experiencing fear. This is not to deny that the person might be mistaken about some relevant aspect of the world that is the *cause* of the fear (for example, about the threat that the feared event poses), or that the person may not be able to express the emotion in words (as in the case of a small child frightened by a dog). Yet, in normal cases, we treat self reports of emotions as valid. To be sure, we sometimes evaluate the reported emotions of others, but when we do, we evaluate them as being appropriate or inappropriate, or justifiable or unjustifiable, not as being true or false. Furthermore, these evaluations are invariably based on our own intuitions about the conditions under which different emotions can and do normally arise. Consequently, in the scientific study of emotions it is not unreasonable to appeal to our intuitions about what emotional states are typically produced by situations of certain kinds. Clearly, it is possible to determine whether or not such intuitions are shared by others, even if verifying the empirical accuracy of such intuitions, widely shared as they may be, is more problematical. In some cases, therefore, one has to take note, albeit cautiously, of shared intuitions about emotions. Of course, if a person does not share the consensual meanings of emotion terms, or is emotionally abnormal, or is simply being deceitful, then his or her self reports may well be invalid, but such exceptions presuppose a background of reliable reporting for their relevance.

This raises the question of the difference between scientific and folk theories of emotions. It might be argued that just as people's naive theories of certain physical phenomena bear no necessary relation to the scientific theories that account for those phenomena, so the folk theories of emotion that underlie our evaluations of the emotions of others bear no necessary relation to a scientific theory of emotion. However, the study of emotions is not like the study of physics. The phenomena that naive physics organizes are phenomena external to the judging system, but the phenomena that a folk theory of emotions organizes are subjective experiences that are part of the judging system – their veridicality is not an issue. A person who is afraid ordinarily knows that he is afraid, and he ordinarily knows that his fear is caused by the prospect of some sort of threat. That is what fear is in our culture. If this is a naive theory of fear, it has a quite different status from, for example, a naive theory of motion, an example of which would be the belief that a projectile emitted from a coiled tube will continue in a spiral trajectory that gradually straightens out (McCloskey, 1983). The status of the fear theory is different not merely because the fear theory is essentially correct while the motion theory is not, but because its correctness is guaranteed in much the same way as is the correctness of grammaticality judgments of native speakers of a language. Linguists and psycholinguists assume that native speakers have a *tacit* knowledge of the grammar of their language that is difficult or impossible to articulate. An important part of the linguist's job is to discover the grammar by making explicit the implicit principles embodied in the normal linguistic experience of native speakers. Similarly, we maintain that an important part of the psychologist's job is to discover the "grammar" of emotions by making explicit the implicit principles embodied in normal emotional experience.

So far, we have reviewed two kinds of evidence available to emotion theorists: language and self reports. We turn now to the third kind, namely, *behavioral* evidence. We shall play down this aspect of emotions for reasons that relate to the nature of our goals. Perhaps initially stimulated by William James's claim that the emotions *are* the bodily responses, research on emotions during the behaviorist and postbehaviorist era has been dominated by approaches based on the characteristic behavior associated with the emotions. Our view is that although it is important to identify characteristic behaviors associated with individual emotions, it is not often that these behaviors actually *constitute* an emotion, although, as has been observed by other theorists (e.g., Frijda, 1987; Lang, 1984), in many cases action *tendencies* might be properly construed as part of a total emotional experience. We prefer the view that actual behavior is a response to an emotional state in conjunction with the particular initiating event. All kinds of factors, many having little if anything to do with the emotions, determine whether some particular behavior actually occurs. For example, people often reject possible courses of action in response to an emotion if they believe that the intended goal will not in fact be achieved by them. On the other hand, we consider it important to emphasize that emotions are important determiners of motives. Since, ordinarily, there is a nonrandom connection between motives and behavior, our theory ought to be capable of accounting for certain classes of behaviors in terms of certain emotions (together with other determining factors). This, however, is not the same as predicting specific behaviors in connection with specific emotions. In general, the problem with concentrating on behavior when considering the emotions is that the same behavior can result from very different emotions (or even from no emotion at all), and that very different behaviors can result from the same emotion.

Whereas we see serious problems associated with the general use of specific behaviors as evidence in the study of emotions, we are more sympathetic to the notion (e.g., Arnold, 1960; Frijda, 1987) that different emotions involve different associated action *tendencies*. However, we remain unconvinced that this is a characteristic of *all* emotions, and if it is not, then action tendencies would turn out merely to be concomitants (albeit high frequency ones) of emotions. Our reservations over the necessity to incorporate action tendencies as part of emotions is that we find the analysis quite strained in the case of many positive emotions (e.g., happiness, relief), and even in the case of some negative ones (e.g., grief). We should make it clear that we do not intend to deny that, for example, smiling frequently accompanies happiness, or that weeping frequently accompanies grief. Our point does not pertain to involuntary reflexlike expressions of emotions but rather to the more voluntary actions that follow on the heels of emotions. We think the attention to action and action tendencies is a legacy from treating anger and fear and their associated reflexes of fight and flight as prototypes of emotions. In the general case, we think that action tendencies are neither necessary nor sufficient for emotions. We think they are not necessary because emotions (such as admiration) that are rooted in standards, for example, rather than in goals are not coherently characterized in terms of action tendencies in relation to changing goal priorities. We think they are not sufficient because it is perfectly possible for there to be action tendencies without associated emotions. For example, realizing that a house plant needs to be watered may lead to the action (tendency) to water it, but the antecedent perception is hardly an emotion. Our conclusion, therefore, is that action tendencies may be typical, and for some emotions even normal, but they cannot be constitutive of all emotions.

The fourth kind of evidence is *physiological*. Our view is that whereas the physiological concomitants of emotional experiences are of indisputable importance, they throw relatively little light on the cognitive components of emotion, which is the focus of our work. Thus we do not feel obliged to take sides in the debate about whether there is a unique pattern of physiological activity (of the sympathetic nervous system) associated with each specific emotion, because patterns of physiological activity are not directly relevant to the cognitive antecedents of emotions. There may or may not be unique patterns; the issue remains an open and empirical question (see Lazarus, Kanner, & Folkman, 1980). To believe, however, that the importance of the cognitive determinants of emotions is in any way contingent on the final resolution of this issue (should there ever be one) is to misunderstand the nature of the cognitive claim.

Some Goals for a Theory of the Cognitive Structure of Emotions

We share Abelson's (1983) view that an analysis of emotion must go beyond differentiating positive from negative emotions to give a systematic account of the qualitative differences among individual emotions such as fear, envy, anger, pride, relief, and admiration. One way of assessing the various approaches to emotion is to determine how adequately they accomplish this task. A number of interesting studies have focused on individual emotions or on small groups of emotions. For example, Averill (1982) studied anger, Mowrer (1960) looked at hope, fear, disappointment, and relief, and Epstein (1967) and Spielberger (1972) represent but two of the many who have studied anxiety. Such accounts, however, tend not to consider the emotions they investigate in the context of a larger, more comprehensive system, and they have not led to widely accepted conclusions about emotions in general. The more system-level arousal/appraisal theories (e.g., Arnold, 1960; Lazarus, Kanner, & Folkman, 1980; Mandler, 1975; 1984) have a better chance of success but generally tend to be weak when faced with the problem of differentiating distinct emotions. Furthermore, they are often based on a narrow range of (frequently only negative) emotions. However, such problems are not, we think, endemic to system-level approaches. Indeed, our own theory is essentially an arousal/appraisal theory, yet we think it does not suffer from these limitations.

One of our main goals is to present an approach to the study of emotion that explains how people's perceptions of the world – their construals – cause them to experience emotions. We consider two questions to be central to this enterprise. The first is "What is the cognitive structure of the emotional system as a whole?" The second main question is "What is the cognitive structure of individual emotions?" Our approach to the first of these questions is to try to show the relationships that exist among the individual emotions in groups of related emotions. The general answer we propose is that the emotions are best represented as a set of substantially independent groups based on the nature of their cognitive origins. Our response to the second question is based on the assumption that the particular emotion a person experiences on some occasion is determined by the way he construes the world or changes in it. Thus we attempt to specify both the eliciting conditions for the distinct emotions and the variables that influence their intensity. Insofar as a definition of emotion presupposes a theory, the adequacy of the definition we propose will ultimately depend upon the adequacy of the theory. Our working characterization views emotions as *valenced reactions to events, agents, or objects, with their particular nature being determined by the way in which the eliciting situation is construed*.

We believe that our two key questions concerning the overall structure of the emotion system and the nature of the individual emotions are related in important and hitherto unexplored ways. In order to address them, it is important to distinguish between those affective states, and other mental conditions, that are genuinely emotional and those that are not (Clore, Ortony, & Foss, 1987; Ortony, Clore, & Foss, 1987). This issue is neglected by most existing theories, perhaps because it is not appropriately considered as part of a theory of emotion as such. Be that as it may, we consider a treatment of the issue to be essential for any theory of emotion because it delimits the range of phenomena that need to be explained.

We have structured this book in a way that presents first the ideas that constitute the core of the theory that we are proposing. Thus we start in Chapter 2 with a presentation of the overall structure of the theory. We argue that there are three broad classes of emotions that result from focusing on one of three salient aspects of the world – events and their consequences, agents and their actions, or objects, pure and simple. Having laid out this general structure we turn in Chapter 3 to a discussion of the appraisal mechanism. This requires us to make some proposals concerning the macrostructure of people's knowledge representation. In particular, we discuss the nature of an organization scheme that might allow one to distinguish three major ingredients of appraisal. These are goals, standards, and attitudes, and they constitute respectively the criteria for evaluating events, the actions of agents, and objects. Because our analysis of individual emotions involves specifying the variables that influence their intensity, the second part of Chapter 3 and all of Chapter 4 are devoted to a discussion of the key factors that we see as affecting the intensity of emotions. This is an important issue for us because a major part of our claims about the overall structure of emotions is that groups of emotions tend to have the same variables affecting their intensity, and that many of these variables are local in the sense that they do not affect the intensity of emotions in other groups. Having provided the background concepts, Chapters 5 and 6 are concerned with our detailed analyses of the Event-based emotions, that is, of the emotions for which the underlying appraisal is based on goals. Chapter 7 is devoted to the Attribution emotions, namely those that attribute responsibility to the agents of actions in terms of standards, and Chapter 8 provides a brief survey of some of the issues surrounding the Attraction emotions, which are ultimately rooted in attitudes. Finally, Chapter 9 attempts to provide some criteria for the question of what is to count as an emotion and discusses a number of implications of the theory including, in particular, a discussion of how our proposals might, in principle, be formalized into a computationally tractable model.

Summary

Our goal is to construct a cognitive theory concerning the origins of the emotions. In particular, we want to specify the global structure interrelating different emotions as well as the characteristics of individual emotions. The global analysis breaks emotions into three general classes: reactions to events, agents, and objects. The analysis of individual emotions specifies the eliciting conditions for each emotion and the variables that affect the intensity of each emotion.

There are four main kinds of evidence about the emotions: language, self reports, behavior, and physiology. The latter two kinds of evidence concern the consequences or concomitants of emotional states, but not their origins, which we think are based upon the cognitive construal of events. For this reason we largely ignore behavioral and physiological evidence, focusing instead on language and self reports. Although we do take linguistic evidence into account, our analysis of emotions is not to be taken as a theory about emotion words. Rather, it attempts to specify different types of emotions. In many cases ordinary language has several words that refer to different aspects of the same underlying emotion type. For example, English has many words that refer to different levels of intensity or to the behavioral consequences of fear, but ultimately, all refer to the same underlying emotion type. Our account of emotions is in terms of classes of emotion types, such as these, and not in terms of specific words. It is an exercise in theoretical psychology, but one that we think can be tested empirically.

2   The Structure of the Theory

In discussing the merits and dangers of using linguistic evidence, the last chapter introduced the notion of an *emotion type*. An emotion type is a distinct kind of emotion that can be realized in a variety of recognizably related forms. The example we gave was of the emotion type, *fear*, which can be manifested in varying degrees of intensity (marked in English by words such as "concern," "fright," "petrified," and so on), and for which there can be various subtle shifts in emphasis (for example, an emphasis on a particular kind of associated behavior is captured by the word "cowering," and an emphasis on the object of fear as being psychological rather than physical is captured by the word "anxiety"). This notion of an emotion type is central to the theory. In order to provide a coherent account of the emotions, it is essential to reduce somehow the infinitude of phenomenally possible emotions to manageable proportions. We do this by focusing on the distinct emotion types rather than on the multitude of discriminable emotional states. The question that we then have to address is: What are the distinct emotion types and how are they related to one another?

It seems to us that the distinct emotion types cannot be arranged informatively into any single space of reasonably low dimensionality. Rather, we suspect that the emotions come in groups for which the intragroup structure is quite simple even though the intergroup structure is not (Fillenbaum & Rapaport, 1971). We shall therefore proceed by trying to identify and characterize representative groups or clusters. Each group is structured so that the definition of each cell in the group provides a specification of an emotion type that incorporates the *eliciting conditions* for the emotion in that cell. That is, it incorporates a situational description of the conditions under which the emotion can be triggered.

The groups of emotions that we identify have two important characteristics. First, emotions in the same group have eliciting conditions that are structurally related. For example, one of the groups that we propose, the

15

"Attribution Group," contains four emotion types, each of which depends on whether the attribution of responsibility to some agent for some action is positive or negative, and on whether the agent is the self or some other person (see Chapter 7). The eliciting conditions for each of the four emotion types are thus structurally related, involving only different bindings of the variables for identity of agent and valence of attribution. The second important characteristic of emotion groups is that each distinct emotion type represented in them is best thought of as representing a family of closely related emotions. The emotions in each family are related by virtue of the fact that they share the same basic eliciting conditions, but differ in terms of their intensity and sometimes in terms of the weights that are assigned to different components or manifestations of the emotions (e.g., behavioral components).

Another aspect of the theory is that the characterization of each emotion type includes a specification of the principal variables that affect its intensity. These variables are local to particular groups, and have to be distinguished from what we call "global" variables, which can influence the intensity of emotions in all groups. An important guiding principle in developing the theory was that it be sufficiently specific to permit empirical testing. Although we shall not discuss them in this book, there are two general methods of testing that we use. One involves the use of experimental studies relying primarily on evidence from self reports. The other involves the use of computer simulations. Experimental studies allow us to determine the validity of the groups that we propose. They allow us to determine whether, as they take on different values, the principal variables represented in the eliciting conditions really do give rise to phenomenally distinct emotions, and they allow us to determine whether or not the local intensity variables that we hypothesize as being related to individual emotions really do affect the intensity of those emotions. Many of the studies that we conduct to investigate these issues are studies in which we tap people's intuitions about the emotions they would expect others to experience under various conditions (e.g., Clore, Foss, Levine, & Ortony, in preparation). In such studies we systematically manipulate the underlying characteristics of the described conditions and the variables thought to influence intensity and then look for intersubject agreement about which emotions they think would be experienced, and with what intensity. It is relatively easy to collect data on a full range of emotions using such techniques because it is not necessary to create or wait for appropriate real-world situations to arise – for some emotions, such as grief, there are other factors that mitigate against using real-world emotions. However, it is clearly desirable to show that the proposed theory also describes adequately the emotions of individuals *as they experience them*. To this end some of our investigations have explored emotions under conditions that are ecologically more valid.

Two particular lines of our empirical research have been concerned with the emotions experienced by individuals as opposed to the emotions they impute to others. One of these uses an automated diary technique. In one application of this method (see Turner, 1987), subjects responded on an almost daily basis for two months to a detailed computer-administered questionnaire about emotions experienced in the preceding 24-hour period. This enabled us to examine a wide range of questions about variables affecting the elicitation and intensity of over 40 emotion tokens. A second approach investigates the experienced emotions of fans witnessing sports events. In these studies we ask subjects to identify the emotions that they are experiencing from time to time while watching basketball games. We also solicit from them information about the intensity of their reported emotions and about factors that we predict ought to be influencing what particular emotions they are experiencing, and with what intensity. As the data from such studies come in, it is quite possible that we shall find ourselves being forced to change certain aspects of the theory, and to the extent that this is so, we do not view what we present in the following pages as the last word. It may well be that the theory will require serious repair, or even that it will have to be abandoned. Yet, we think that even in this worst case, it will have been worth presenting. The point of what we propose is not that we think it is the right answer, but rather that we think it is the right approach. There must be some cognitive principles underlying the experience of emotions, and we are simply proposing an approach to thinking about what they might be.

A quite different technique for exploring the validity of the kind of theory we are proposing is to employ the tools of Artificial Intelligence in an attempt to model the theory. The point of such an enterprise is not to create machines with emotions–we think that such an endeavor would be pointless and futile–but to create a computer model that can "understand" what emotions people would be likely to experience under what conditions. Such a system should be able to predict and explain human emotions, not have them. To the degree that the predictions and explanations of a computer system match those of humans one can have confidence that the system embodies a reasonable model of the cognitive origins of emotions. Another virtue of exploring a theory such as ours through the use of a computer model is that one can experiment with the model by manipulating its parameters and examining the consequences of such manipulations to see whether or not they are reasonable. This degree of control is difficult and sometimes impossible to achieve in experimental laboratory settings.

The Organization of Emotion Types

In presenting the overall structure of our account of emotion types, we start with the least contentious assumption that we can, an assumption not about emotions as such, but about the ways in which people (at least in our culture) can perceive the world. The assumption is that there are three major aspects of the world, or changes in the world, upon which one can focus, namely, *events, agents*, or *objects*. When one focuses on events one does so because one is interested in their consequences, when one focuses on agents, one does so because of their actions, and when one focuses on objects, one is interested in certain aspects or imputed properties of them *qua* objects. Central to our position is the notion that emotions are valenced reactions, and that any particular valenced reaction is always a reaction to one of these perspectives on the world. We are perfectly willing to admit that different organisms, or people in different cultures, might carve up the world in different ways. If they do, then there would be corresponding changes in the emotion types that they could experience. Thus if, for example, certain animals are biologically and cognitively limited to attending only to events and their consequences, then the only emotion types that they will be able to experience are those associated with reactions to events.

Before discussing the overall structure of the theory, it will be helpful to clarify what we have in mind in distinguishing agents, objects, and events. Our conception of events is very straightforward – events are simply people's construals about things that happen, considered independently of any beliefs they may have about actual or possible causes. Our notion of focusing on objects is also quite simple. Objects are objects viewed *qua* objects. This leaves us with agents, which are things considered in light of their actual or presumed instrumentality or agency in causing or contributing to events. Agents are not limited to people, even though they are the most usual manifestations. Agents can be nonhuman animate beings, inanimate objects or abstractions, such as institutions, and even situations, provided they are construed as causally efficacious in the particular context. When objects are construed as agents, they are just that – objects *construed as* agents. So, for example, a person who buys a new car that turns out to be a constant source of trouble might blame the car for his series of misfortunes. In doing so, however, he would be treating the car as though it were an

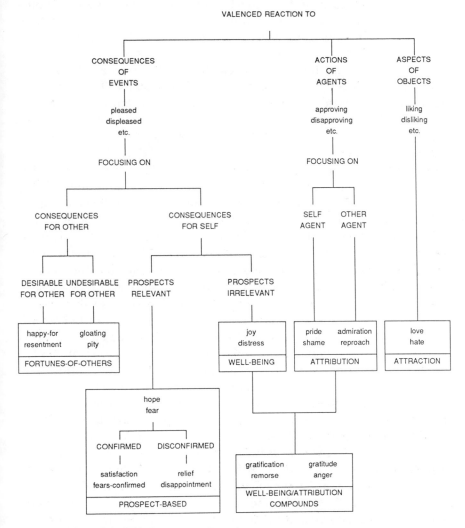

Figure 2.1. Global structure of emotion types.

agent, rather than simply as an object. In treating it as an agent, he could disapprove of it. Were he to treat it only as an object, his affective reaction to it would be one of dislike.

The overall structure that we propose is illustrated in Figure 2.1, where the three main branches correspond to the three ways of reacting to the world. It is important to realize that this structure is intended to be interpreted as a *logical* description, not as a temporal one. Each branch, that is, each of the three kinds of things to which one can have valenced reactions, is associated with a broad class of affective reactions. Whether or not these affective reactions are experienced as emotions depends upon how intense they are, which is one of the reasons why it is important to know what factors affect the intensity of what emotions. This issue is addressed in detail in the second part of Chapter 3 and in Chapter 4. The first broad class comprises all the emotion types indicated in the left hand branch of the figure. This general class of affective reactions we have indicated as those of being *pleased* and *displeased*. We should say immediately that the choice of these words here (and of comparable words elsewhere in the structure, indicated in lower case letters) is not critical. They are intended only as convenient reminders for the corresponding locations in the structure. Thus, they really serve the function of technical terms that are defined by the role they play in the proposed structure. For example, the particular words "pleased," and "displeased," simply represent the best we can do to find relatively intensity-neutral English words that refer (only) to the undifferentiated affective reactions one can have to events and their consequences. These affective reactions arise when a person construes the consequences of an event as being desirable or undesirable, so that judged *desirability* (including undesirability) is the most important, or the *central*, variable that affects the intensity of all these Event-based emotions. This means that desirability (which, as will be discussed in Chapter 4, also has to be taken as a technical term) is the main criterion for evaluation. The second general class of affective reactions is shown in the middle branch of the figure as being those of *approving* and *disapproving*. When these reactions are sufficiently intense they lead to a group of emotions that we call the Attribution emotions. These are caused by reactions to the actions of agents, when they are viewed as being either praiseworthy or blameworthy, making judged *praiseworthiness* (which we take to include blameworthiness) the primary basis for evaluation. Finally, the third general class comprises the essentially unstructured affective reactions of *liking* and *disliking*. The associated emotions here are the Attraction emotions, which are caused by reactions to objects, or aspects of objects, in terms of their *appealingness*. As mentioned above, we are using a broad sense of "object" here, a sense in which an object can be animate or inanimate, concrete or abstract.

To see how, in general, focusing on events, agents, and objects leads to different classes of emotional reactions, we shall consider a highly oversimplified example of the reactions a person might have upon learning that his neighbor is a merciless child-beater. If such a person focuses only on the neighbor's role as the *agent* of child-beating, judging it as blameworthy because of its violation of certain standards, his valenced reaction towards the neighbor could be realized as an Attribution emotion such as reproach or contempt. The person could also focus on one or more aspects of a child-beating *event*. If he focuses only on its undesirability it might cause him distress. He could also focus on the plight of his neighbor's children and experience pity. Finally, the person might focus on his neighbor *qua* (unappealing) *object*, giving rise to an Attraction emotion such as hatred. Clearly, this *is* a highly oversimplified picture. In reality, the person is likely to experience a mixture of emotions resulting from considering the situation from these different perspectives at different moments so that some of the resulting emotions may cooccur and some will occur in sequences. However, we have presented this example only in order to explicate the effects of focusing on different aspects of an emotion-inducing situation. It was not presented for the purpose of analyzing exactly what emotions would occur in what mixtures or sequences.

We can now return to discussing Figure 2.1. In interpreting the figure, notice that some of the labels are in upper case and some in lower case. Labels in upper case represent structural elements, whereas those in lower case represent emotional, or potentially emotional, states. Individual groups of emotion types are enclosed in boxes with the name we have chosen for each group indicated in the panel at the bottom of each box. Representative names for the emotion types are shown in lower case. In all cases where we have indicated emotion types, the particular words have been chosen only as suggestive labels for entries for that position in the structure. Thus, the structural descriptions that they represent are not intended to be taken as definitions of them.

We start by introducing the distinctions and associated emotions relating to reactions to events and their consequences. This branch includes emotion types that can be loosely thought of as *pleased* and *displeased, joy* and *distress, hope* and *fear, relief* and *disappointment, pity* and *resentment*. All of these emotions, reachable from the CONSEQUENCES OF EVENTS branch, are reactions of the experiencing person to the implications of events for the person experiencing the emotion. This branch of the emotion tree in the figure is the most complex. The first potentially emotional states to be encountered are shown, before the branch divides, as being *pleased* and *displeased*. Thus being *pleased* and *displeased* are intended to refer to relatively undifferentiated affective states that are nonspecific in the sense that they are nothing more than valenced reactions to *events* (as opposed to *agents* or *objects*). A consequence of this is that all emotion nodes below the *pleased/displeased* node are differentiated instances of being pleased or displeased. Being *pleased* and *displeased* seem to be rather pale when considered as labels for emotions. One reason for this is that they lack the specificity that is characteristic of typical emotional states. A second reason is that we have purposely chosen rather neutral terms to indicate these states – that is, terms that do not strongly imply a particular level of emotional intensity.

The structure that falls below the *pleased/displeased* node divides first according to whether the person who experiences the emotions is reacting to the consequences of the focal event with respect only to himself, or also with respect to some other person. This distinction is represented by the two main branches labeled CONSEQUENCES FOR SELF and CONSEQUENCES FOR OTHER. Consider first the CONSEQUENCES FOR SELF branch. This branch leads to two groups of emotions. For one of these groups the consideration of the *prospect* of an event is crucial and for the other it is irrelevant. The emotions for which the consideration of the *prospect* is irrelevant are simply those that result from positive or negative reactions to the events that affect one. They reflect upon one's well-being, and are in fact simply default cases of being pleased and being displeased. Such emotions are usually referred to in English by words like "happiness," "joy," "unhappiness," "sadness," and "distress." However, as will be discussed in Chapter 5, where these emotions are dealt with in detail under the rubric of the "Well-being" emotions, the situation is somewhat more complicated than this. Specifically, a number of emotions will be assigned to this category that are quite particular in content – emotions such as grief and regret. The reason we consider such emotions to be specific kinds of distress is that they appear to differ from distress only in that they involve more specific events about which the experiencing person is displeased. So, for example, grief is not just a generalized form of being displeased at an undesirable event; the undesirable event is a more specific one comprising the loss of a loved one.

The branch marked PROSPECTS RELEVANT includes first the emotions of *hope* and *fear*. These emotions result from reacting to the prospect of positive and negative events respectively. Four additional emotions arise depending upon whether the prospect of a positive or negative event is believed to have been confirmed or disconfirmed. These four emotions are shown as "satisfaction," "disappointment," "relief," and an emotion that for want of a better name we call "fears-confirmed." This entire group of six emotion types we refer to as the "Prospect-based" emotions. They are discussed in detail in Chapter 6.

The final group of emotions that we propose under the Event-based emotions are those appearing under the CONSEQUENCES FOR OTHER branch. These are emotions that result from reacting to the consequences of events when focusing on the consequences for others. This group of emotions we refer to as the "Fortunes-of-others" group, and it contains four distinct emotion types. The emotions represent the reactions to events that a person can have when the events are desirable or undesirable relative to the goals and interests of another person. The branch marked DESIRABLE FOR OTHER leads to emotion types that we refer to as "happy-for" and "resentment," while the branch labeled UNDESIRABLE FOR OTHER leads to "gloating" and "pity." Thus, for example, under suitable conditions, when an event is undesirable for some other person but is for that reason desirable for the person experiencing the emotion, that person can experience the emotion of gloating, or *Schadenfreude*, whereas if the experience of that undesirable event by the other person is (also) undesirable for the experiencer, the possibility of the emotion of pity arises. The way in which the figure should be interpreted with respect to, for example, gloating is that gloating is the valenced reaction to an event characterized by being pleased that some event is undesirable for another person. This illustrates the way in which we view the emotions below the *pleased/ displeased* node to be differentiated cases of being pleased or displeased. All the emotions in this Fortunes-of-others group are discussed in detail in the second part of Chapter 5.

The second main set of emotions are those emanating from the middle branch of the figure. This branch, labeled simply, ACTIONS OF AGENTS, represents emotions having to do with people's reactions to the agency that they attribute to agents. Basically, these emotions are differentiated forms of the affective reactions of *approving* and *disapproving* of an agent's actions. The figure shows these "Attribution" emotions splitting into two, depending on whether the approval or disapproval focuses on the self as agent (labeled SELF AGENT) or on some other as agent (OTHER AGENT). When the formal agent is the self, the emotion types of *pride* and *shame* can arise. When some other person is the formal agent, the emotion types of *admiration* and *reproach* can arise. A crucial aspect of these emotions has to do with the way in which the notion of the self is conceptualized. In order to account for the fact that Attribution emotions, such as pride, can result from the actions of others, an extended notion of the self is required in which the self can be the formal agent while the actual agent is some other person with whom one views oneself as being in a cognitive unit (Heider, 1958). This issue, and others concerned with the Attribution emotions, is discussed in detail in Chapter 7.

The rightmost branch of the figure shows a structureless group of emotions resulting from reactions to objects *qua* objects. These emotions, which we call the "Attraction" emotions, are all variations of the affective reactions of *liking* and *disliking*. Thus, they represent undifferentiated affective and aesthetic reactions to objects, for which *love* and *hate* are good examples. We do not wish to imply that objects construed in this way are necessarily construed independently of their agency, but rather that it is the object *qua* object, not the object *qua* agent, that is the focus of the evaluation. In fact, because of the psychological difficulty of separating agents from their actions, there is a strong tendency for Attraction emotions such as hatred to cooccur with compatible Attribution emotions such as contempt. It is important to emphasize at this point that we view the Attraction emotions as being *momentary* in nature, rather than enduring dispositions towards objects. Our intention is to focus on the momentary *state* of, for example, loving or hating somebody or something. The way in which dispositional evaluation is constructed out of individual experiences is primarily a problem to be handled by a theory of impression formation and personal attraction, not by a theory of emotion, although we do discuss it briefly in Chapter 8.

The figure also shows a branch leading out of the Well-being emotions and a branch leading out of the Attribution emotions both converging on a group of emotions labeled "Well-being/Attribution compounds." These compound emotions include those labeled as *gratification, gratitude, remorse,* and *anger,* and they have the property that they arise from simultaneously focusing on both the action of an agent *and* the resulting event and its consequences. We call them compounds because they involve more than the mere cooccurrence of their corresponding constituent emotions. Gratitude is not simply the cooccurrence of admiration for an agent and happiness at a resulting desirable outcome. It is a unified emotion in which the constituents need not necessarily be independently experienced. A detailed discussion of these emotions is presented in the second section of Chapter 7.

A major feature of the scheme that we have outlined is that some of the factors that affect the intensity of emotions are specific to particular groups of emotions. In general, as we shall discuss in more detail in Chapter 4, progress down the structure shown in the figure tends to result in the introduction of variables that affect the intensity of all the emotions lower down (see Figure 4.1). We mentioned three such variables in introducing the three main branches when we said that events and their consequences are evaluated in terms of their *desirability*, actions of agents in terms of their *praiseworthiness*, and aspects of objects in terms of their *appealingness*. Desirability, praiseworthiness, and appealingness are all variables that influence the intensity of all the emotions below the point at which they are introduced, so that, although each is central to a distinct class of emotions (Event-based, Attribution, and Attraction emotions, respectively) their effects are local to collections of emotions. At the same time, as will also be discussed in Chapter 4, there are a number of variables such as *unexpectedness* that have global rather than local effects on intensity.

One final aspect of the overall structure that we are proposing is that there seems to be an interesting tendency for emotional reactions to develop in a left-to-right manner with respect to the structure shown in the figure. To the extent that this is true, it might be because the most salient initial experience is that some event transpires; this would constrain the emotional reaction to an Event-based one. At the same time, however, one may seek to understand the causal origins of the event, so that an Attribution emotion becomes a possibility. Finally, because inferences about the properties of (animate) objects are made on the basis of their actions, Attribution emotions may give rise to momentary reactions of liking or disliking of agents *qua* objects. A more detailed discussion of this conjecture is presented in Chapter 8.

Basic Emotions

Although we embrace the notion of emotion types, we are inclined to reject the idea that there is a set of "basic" emotions such that they, together with their combinations, account for all the emotions (views aptly referred to by Scherer, 1984, as "palette theories"). At first sight, the thesis that there are basic emotions is not an implausible one. Surely there are too many emotions for all to be distinct and equally basic. As in the physical world of, say, chemical elements versus chemical compounds, it would not be unreasonable to suppose that the phenotypical emotions are based on a smaller number of genotypical or primary emotions. Such a conception seems parsimonious. Having said that, however, one has to be able to answer a number of difficult questions. First, it is by no means obvious what the claim that there are basic or primary emotions is supposed to mean. Does it mean that such emotions are universal? Does it mean that they form emotion compounds or blends, or emotion mixes? Does it mean that they should appear developmentally before other (nonbasic) emotions? A second problem is that whatever answers one might propose for such questions, it does not follow that one needs a concept of basic emotions. Some emotions, such as happiness, sadness, anger, and fear, could perfectly well be (and probably are) found in all cultures, without their being basic in any other sense (toe nails might be found in all cultures too, but that would not be sufficient to render them anatomically basic). Such emotions could also combine with other emotions without that necessitating that they be basic, or they might appear early in development, and that too would entail nothing about their being basic.

What we are suggesting is that talk of "basic emotions" is unacceptably vague. This vagueness manifests itself in another problem having to do with the manner in which basic emotions are supposed to be related to the other, nonbasic, emotions. Most theorists appear to take a combinatorial view. Plutchik (1962), for example, speaks of "mixed states," and of "dyads" and "triads" of primary emotions. One of his basic postulates is that a small number of primary or pure emotions can be mixed. Similarly, Averill (1975) argues for compound emotions based on more elementary ones. There are, however, several possible models of basicness and combination. One model, suggested by both Ekman (1982) (emotional blends) and Plutchik (mixed states), is that emotions mix. According to such a model both constituent emotions should be observable in the mixture, just as grains of both sugar and salt are observable when mixed together. The view suggested by Averill's term "compound," by contrast, is that the more basic emotional elements will not be observable but only the resultant compound state. Neither oxygen nor hydrogen are observable when compounded into water. The former model is clearly easier to test than the latter.

The distinction between basic or primary emotions and other emotions appears to be based on two kinds of analogical cases. One is the example of color, and the other the example of chemical elements. However, the empirical bases for the idea with respect to emotions is not analogously well-founded. Certainly, there is a remarkable diversity of claims about which emotions are basic, as can be seen from Table 2.1. This diversity is hardly consistent with a coherent notion of what it is for an emotion to be basic. In fact, we suspect that the search for and postulation of basic emotions is in reality motivated by an illusion. We think that the illusoriness arises from the fact that certain emotions are subjectively very salient, especially when they are intense. For example, extreme cases of fear arise in situations that are potentially damaging to the organism so that one thinks of fear as an important emotion. Similarly, anger may seem basic because the associated action tendency is difficult to resist and is potentially catastrophic in its consequences to the organism if carried out (or not carried out). So, one source of the illusoriness is that when they occur, many of the postulated "basic" emotions seem to be important for the organism and its survival. There are other sources too, however. A second source is that emotions that are proposed as basic tend to be salient because they occur frequently (relative to other emotions). Frequency augments importance in making them salient. A third source is the ease with which one may be tempted to impute to animals many of the emotions that are

Table 2.1. *A selection of lists of "fundamental" or "basic" emotions*

Theorist	Fundamental emotions	Basis for selection	Reference
Arnold, M. B.	anger aversion courage dejection desire despair fear hate hope love sadness	relation to action tendencies	Arnold (196)
Ekman, P.	anger disgust fear joy sadness surprise	universal facial expressions	Ekman, Friesen & Ellsworth (1982)
Frijda, N.	desire joy pride surprise distress anger aversion contempt fear shame	forms of action readiness	Frijda (1987, and personal communication)
Gray, J.	rage/terror anxiety joy	hardwired	Gray (1982)
Izard, C. E.	anger contempt disgust distress fear guilt interest joy shame surprise	hardwired	Izard (1972)
James, W.	fear grief love rage	bodily involvement	James (1884)
McDougall, W.	anger disgust elation fear subjection tender-emotion wonder	relation to instincts	McDougall (1926)
Mowrer, O. H.	pain pleasure	unlearned emotional states	Mowrer (1960)
Oatley, K., and Johnson-Laird, P. N.	anger disgust fear happiness sadness	do not require propositional content	Oatley & Johnson-Laird (1987)
Panksepp, J.	expectancy fear rage panic	hardwired	Panksepp (1982)
Plutchik, R.	acceptance anger anticipation disgust joy fear sadness surprise	relation to adaptive biological processes	Plutchik (1980)
Tomkins, S. S.	anger interest contempt disgust distress fear joy shame surprise	density of neural firing	Tomkins (1984)
Watson, J. B.	fear love rage	hardwired	Watson (1930)
Weiner, B.	happiness sadness	attribution-independent	Weiner & Graham (1984)

Note. Not all the theorists represented in this table are equally strong advocates of the idea of basic emotions. For some it is a crucial notion (e.g., Izard, 1977; Panksepp, 1982; Plutchik, 1980; Tomkins, 1984), while for others it is of peripheral interest only and their discussions of basic emotions are hedged (e.g., Mowrer, 1960; Weiner & Graham, 1984).

taken to be basic. For example, it is tempting to suppose that animals experience fear. However, such attributions are typically based on observations of *behaviors* (aggressive behavior or avoidance behavior), which turn out to be dissociated from the emotional states to which they are presumed to be linked (e.g., Mineka, 1979). As we have already discussed, we think that great care needs to be exercised in considering the role of behavior in emotion. In particular, neither we nor animal psychologists are willing to equate, for example, aggressive behavior with anger. It would be a relatively straightforward matter to program a robot to exhibit aggressive or avoidance behavior toward certain objects or classes of objects, yet, if having done so one were to claim that one had produced the emotions of anger or fear in the machine, one would be scoffed at by the scientific community, and rightly so.

A final argument that is sometimes used in favor of the claim that some emotions are basic is that some emotions appear at very early ages. For example, Campos and Barrett (1984) suggest that anger, which is the first-mentioned emotion in a list of examples of basic emotions that they present, is clearly evident by 4 months of age.[1] They use this "fact" to argue against the kind of structural proposals offered by Roseman (e.g., Roseman, 1984), proposals that include the claim that anger involves some sort of violation of a notion of legitimacy. Even if we grant that such young infants are indeed experiencing anger (as opposed, say, to distress) the fact remains that the early appearance of some emotions relative to others does not endow them with any special status vis à vis their being basic unless one can also show that emotions that develop later are somehow compounded out of those appearing earlier – a supposition for which, to the best of our knowledge, there is no evidence, especially in the case of anger.

While we eschew the notion of basic emotions, we do treat some emotions as more basic than others, and we do have a compounding hypothesis for certain emotional states. We claim that some emotions are more basic than others because we can give a very specific meaning to it, namely that some emotions have less complex specifications and eliciting conditions than others. Thus, insofar as the eliciting conditions for being displeased are part of the eliciting conditions for, say, resentment, we can say that being displeased is more basic. Furthermore, as will be discussed in more detail in Chapter 7, we believe that the simultaneous occurrence of the eliciting conditions of, for example, a Reproach emotion and a Distress emotion yields an emotion best described as "anger." In this sense, reproach is more basic than anger, a result that is in sharp contrast to the proposals of basic-emotion theorists, for nearly all of whom anger is a prototypical example of a basic emotion. However, to say as we do that one emotion, say reproach, is *more* basic than another, say anger, is not to say

1 In fairness, we should note that their exact claim is that "anger expressions are clearly observable by 4 months of age." (p. 248). However, it is difficult to imagine how they could believe on the one hand that the expression is an expression of anger, and on the other that there is no anger of which the anger expression is an expression.

that one *is* basic and the other not. The underlying principle inherent in the structure of our theory is not that of elements and compounds, but of successive differentiation, and this principle is as applicable to the constituents of compound emotions (e.g., reproach) as it is to the compound emotions themselves (e.g., anger).

Thus, in general, our view is that the complexity of an emotion is determined by the degree to which it is a more differentiated form of a simpler affective reaction. This means that the distinctiveness of an emotional state stems in part from the particular form of affective reaction that it is. Thus, our proposal is for a more hierarchical kind of structure in which, at the top level, there are two basic kinds of affective reactions – positive and negative. Valenced reactions are the essential ingredients of emotions in the sense that all emotions involve some sort of positive or negative reaction to something or other. When additional factors are brought into consideration increasingly differentiated emotional states may result. As already discussed, the most important of these factors is the nature of the thing (event, agent, or object) to which the valenced reaction is a reaction. Thus, according to our view, if there is any sense at all in talking about basic emotions, it is only in the rather nonstandard sense of "basic" in which there are two general kinds of affective reactions, positive ones and negative ones. In this respect, our position bears some similarity to that of Spinoza (1677/1986) who reduced all emotions to one form or another of pleasure or pain. Pleasure he held to be a transition from a lesser state of perfection to a greater one, and pain, vice versa. However, we prefer to think of the two kinds of affective reactions (positive and negative) as the most undifferentiated forms of emotions. In other words, rather than contrasting basic emotions with nonbasic emotions, we prefer to think in terms of levels of differentiation. We have no objection to thinking of less differentiated affective reactions as being more basic than more differentiated ones; on the other hand we see no particular virtue in this way of talking.

Some Implications of the Emotions-as-valenced-reactions Claim

A corollary of our view that emotions are valenced affective reactions is that if some putative emotion can occur in the absence of a valenced reaction, it cannot be a genuine emotion, and this provides us with a principled way of distinguishing genuine emotions from non-emotions. Consider in this connection the state of *being abandoned*. Since it is possible for someone to be abandoned without experiencing a valenced reaction, being abandoned cannot be a kind of valenced reaction, and therefore, according to our view, it cannot be an emotion.[2] Being abandoned is merely a description of some real-world, objective state of affairs (Ortony, Clore, & Foss, 1987). It is a state that, although often evaluated negatively by the person in it, does not necessarily involve a valenced reaction. In other words, being abandoned, as well as not being an emotion itself, does not necessarily produce emotions. A person can be abandoned and not know it (as Moses was) or, even if he does know it, he may not care. Of course, this is not to deny that being abandoned is generally considered to be a negative state, but only that it is not *necessary* to so construe it. Nor is it to deny that *feeling abandoned* is an emotion. We are merely claiming that being abandoned does not necessarily and independently give rise to a valenced reaction. In fact, even if it were always the case that it did, this would not make being abandoned an emotion (as opposed to the *cause* of an emotion), any more than being mugged is an emotion just because of the inevitable valenced reaction that it causes. A more extensive discussion of the distinction between emotional and other kinds of states is presented in Chapter 9.

The logic underlying our conclusions about the relationship between non-emotional states and situations – such as being abandoned – the undifferentiated valenced reactions, and particular emotions is illustrated in Figure 2.2 below. Any non-emotional state that is experienced can, in principle, give rise to a valenced reaction, as shown by the arrow leading from the circle marked "non-emotional state" to the circle marked E_0. In fact, of course, a non-emotional state can also give rise to other non-emotional states (being abandoned might lead to curiosity as to why). This possibility is indicated in the figure by the arrow leading from the circle labeled "non-emotional state" back to itself. The circle marked E_0 in the the figure represents an undifferentiated valenced reaction, experienced as a general positive or negative feeling. Specific emotion types are indicated in the figure by the nodes marked E_1–E_4. It is important to emphasize that the relationship between the undifferentiated state of a valenced reaction, E_0, and more specific emotions, E_1–E_4, shown in the figure is a *logical* relationship, not a temporal one. The node E_0, the undifferentiated state of a valenced reaction, is normally realized in one or other of its differentiated forms, E_1, E_2, E_3, E_4, etc. So, to continue with the same example, a person who is abandoned is in a non-emotional state that can (but does not neces-

2 In fact, we are not aware of any emotion theorists claiming that *being abandoned* is an emotion. However, there are many published lists (e.g., Averill, 1975; Bush, 1973; Dahl & Stengel, 1978) of emotion words that include the word "abandoned," presumably because it is assumed that *feeling abandoned* is an emotion. For present purposes, we are only interested in using this example as a way of elucidating our valenced-reaction criterion for emotions.

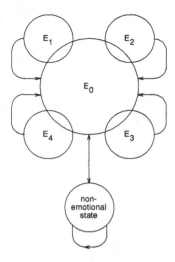

Figure 2.2. The relation between non-emotional states, undifferentiated affective reactions, and specific emotion types.

sarily) lead to a valenced reaction. In its undifferentiated form (E_0) this reaction is simply a (presumably negative) feeling. Ordinarily, however, the more detailed construal of the non-emotional state of being abandoned is likely to lead to some more differentiated emotion or emotions (E_1, E_2, E_3, E_4, etc.) such as distress, resentment, reproach, or anger. In this way, the person's being abandoned is potentially capable of giving rise to a valenced reaction, in which case the abandonment has come to be construed as an emotion-inducing situation, which is, of course, quite different from saying that *being abandoned* is an emotion. However, the particular constellation of emotions that the person may experience, coupled with the knowledge that the initiating event was that of being abandoned *is* well captured by describing the resulting emotional condition as that of *feeling abandoned*. In other words, to *feel abandoned* is

"to experience the feelings typically associated with being abandoned," and . . . this is "to experience the emotions one has when one believes that one is (has been) abandoned and cares that one is (has been) abandoned." And this suggests that the emotional content of *feeling abandoned* is contained not in the *abandoned* part, but in the *feeling* part, presumably by virtue of the inferences about *caring* that it licenses. (Ortony, Clore, & Foss, 1987, p. 347)

There is one other important feature of Figure 2.2, namely the fact that the emotion nodes themselves are shown as feeding back into the node that represents the undifferentiated valenced reaction, E_0. What this means is that the same kind of analysis as was given for non-emotional states can be applied to emotional states. Specifically, it means that emotional states can themselves become emotion-inducing events and lead to new emotions. For example, a person in an emotional state such as anger can construe that state as a negative situation which could itself give rise to a valenced reaction, and thus perhaps to another differentiated emotion such as shame. In general, any valenced reaction to an object or event can give rise to emotions, so that psychological states themselves (including emotional ones) are candidates for emotion-inducing objects and events, thus leading to the possibility of chains of additional, new emotions. In fact, some of our research has focused on naturally occurring sequences of emotions, and has led us to the conclusion that emotional experiences probably occur in complex sequences much more often than they do in isolation.

Whereas few emotion theorists have considered states such as being abandoned in their analyses of emotions, most have considered *surprise* (e.g., Ekman, 1982; Plutchik, 1980; Scherer, 1984; Tomkins, 1980; Wood-worth, 1938). Our view forces us to reject surprise, pure and simple (i.e., *unexpectedness*), as an emotion because surprise can arise in the absence of a valenced reaction. People can be surprised while being affectively neutral about the surprise-inducing situation. Contrary to the claims of some disso-nance theorists (e.g., Aronson, 1968), we do not believe that surprise is intrinsically negative (or for that matter, intrinsically positive). Rather, we believe that surprise in isolation refers to a cognitive state having to do with unexpectedness, which is quite independent of valence (Iran-Nejad & Ortony, 1985). Thus, for example, one might well be surprised, but indiffer-ent, at discovering that the temperature in Fairbanks, Alaska, reached 90°F one January day. When the surprising situation happens also to be per-ceived as positive then one may refer to it as a "pleasant surprise," and when negative, as an "unpleasant surprise" or "shock." We view *unexpect-edness* as a global variable that can modulate the intensity of any emotion (see Chapter 4), so that we view shock, for example, as distress modulated by high unexpectedness, with the focus on the unexpectedness.

If surprise is not an emotion, what is it? Our answer to this question (which we shall elaborate in Chapter 9) is that states like surprise are *cognitive* states (see Clore, Ortony, & Foss, 1987; Ortony, Clore, & Foss, 1987). Since such states can be valenced, they can be affective, but since they are not necessar-ily valenced, and, more importantly, since affect is not focal in their referen-tial structure, they are not emotions. The eliciting conditions for genuine emotions such as anger or hatred presuppose the existence of a valenced reaction toward something. If a state lacks what we earlier referred to as this "essential ingredient," then it cannot be an emotion.

Summary

The distinction between reactions to events, agents, and objects gives rise to three basic classes of emotions: being *pleased* vs. *displeased* (reaction to events), *approving* vs. *disapproving* (reactions to agents), and *liking* vs. *disliking* (reactions to objects). These three basic emotion classes can in turn be differentiated into a number of distinct groups of emotion types. Reactions to events breaks into three groups: one, the Fortunes-of-others group, focuses on the consequences for oneself of events that affect other people, whereas the other two, the Prospect-based and Well-being, groups, focus only on the consequences for oneself. Reactions to agents are differentiated into four emotions comprising the Attribution group, and reactions to objects lead to an undifferentiated group called the Attraction group. There is also a compound group of emotions, the Well-being/Attribution compounds, involving reactions to both the event and the agent simultaneously. In fact, there may be a general progression that operates such that differentiated emotions tend to be evoked in order: first reactions to events, then to agents, and finally to objects.

Many emotion theorists have claimed that some emotions are basic and others are not, but there is no agreement in the literature either on what the basic emotions are, or on what it means for an emotion to be basic. While we eschew the term "basic emotion," it is the case that some affective reactions in our system, such as being pleased, approving, and liking, have simpler eliciting conditions than the more differentiated emotions, such as reproach or pity. It is also the case that some emotions, such as anger, which have usually been treated as basic emotions, are treated as compound emotions in the system, because they have eliciting conditions from both the Event-based and Agent-based branches of the system.

Finally, the theory differentiates emotions from non-emotions on the basis of whether a valenced reaction is necessary. Non-emotional states, such as being abandoned, can give rise to undifferentiated emotional states, such as being displeased, which in turn can give rise to more differentiated emotional states, such as resentment, reproach, or anger.

3   The Cognitive Psychology of Appraisal

One of the most salient aspects of the experience of emotions is that they vary a great deal in intensity both within and between people. This means that a theory of emotion must address the question of what determines intensity. Our general view is that the intensity of emotions is influenced by a number of variables, all of which are present in the construal of the situation that gives rise to the emotion in the first place. Thus, in order to address the question of intensity, we first need to consider the mechanism whereby emotion-inducing stimuli are appraised. This will provide us with the background we need to properly approach the intensity question. In the first part of this chapter we discuss the macrostructure of the knowledge representation system that we assume in order to deal with the appraisal issue. This we call the "appraisal structure." In the second part, we use this system to show how the three central intensity variables of the theory can be explained. These variables are *desirability, praiseworthiness*, and *appealingness*, and they correspond to the three foci of valenced reactions, namely, events, agents, and objects.

The Appraisal Structure

Most of the things that people do are motivated. People rarely engage in random actions devoid of goals and purposes. In some sense, therefore, people must have a structure of goals, interests, and beliefs that underlie their behavior. It is in the elements of such an underlying structure that value inheres, and it is the value associated with these elements, often inherited from superordinate ones, that is the source of both the qualitative and quantitative aspects of emotion-relevant appraisals. However, it does not seem reasonable to suppose that such a structure is a permanently stored representation of everything to which a person aspires or which a person believes, from the most general to the most specific. Rather, it seems more sensible to view it as an implicit or "virtual" structure. People behave *as if* there were such a representation. In fact, we suspect that many of the goals people have are constructed as and when needed, presumably as a result of inferential processes based upon relatively high-level, abstract aspirations, and relatively specific, local considerations. Be that as it may, for our purpose here it is sufficient to answer the general question of what kind of knowledge representation is needed to account for appraisal by postulating the *theoretical* existence of an integrated structure of goals (to support appraisals of desirability), standards (to support appraisals of praiseworthiness), and attitudes (to support appraisals of appealingness). We shall discuss this structure first in terms of goals, and then move to a discussion of the other key elements that need to be represented – namely, standards and attitudes.

The Macrostructure. What might a person's "virtual" goal structure look like? It seems likely that the structure is more complex than a simple hierarchical tree structure. It is probably better to think of it as a more general lattice structure, even though its overall shape is probably treelike with far fewer nodes at the highest (most general) level than at the lowest (most specific) level. The high-level nodes represent fairly abstract goals that might better be characterized as aspirations or general concerns, while at the lowest level are the more concrete immediate goals. Each node in such a structure can be connected to other nodes in a variety of ways. Except for the currently highest- and lowest-level nodes, all nodes have both incoming and outgoing connections to other nodes. Incoming connections represent those goals whose achievement can be affected by the achievement of lower-level goals from which the links come. To see how all this works, we shall take as an example a woman who wants to become a concert pianist. As can be seen from the diagrammatic representation (Figure 3.1) of part of such a person's virtual goal structure, one of the incoming connections to the BECOME-CONCERT-PIANIST goal would be from a GET-AGENT (i.e., someone to represent her professional interests) goal. This same connection would, of course, be an outgoing one for the GET-AGENT goal. It is in this sense that the structure is a directed one, that is, it embodies a representation of the presumed causal flow with links from causes, or enabling conditions, to their effects.

In general, goals can have multiple incoming and outgoing connections. Furthermore, the connections can be of different kinds. When a goal has multiple outgoing connections it means that the attainment of that goal can directly affect several other goals, all of which are only one link away. So, for example, attaining the BECOME-CONCERT-PIANIST goal might affect not only a HAVE-IDEAL-JOB goal, but also a KEEP-PARENTS-

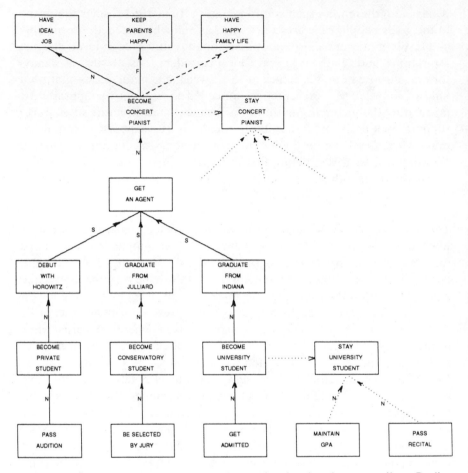

Figure 3.1. Imaginary example of part of a virtual goal structure (from Ravlin, 1987).

HAPPY goal. The situation is a little more complicated when we consider goals with multiple incoming connections. This is because outgoing links are usually conjunctive, that is, when there are many *consequences* of attaining a goal, those consequences are usually not mutually exclusive. However, typically, there are both conjunctive and disjunctive incoming links. Disjunctive incoming links simply represent alternative ways of achieving the goal in question. For example, the aspiring pianist might believe that the GET-AGENT goal could be achieved either by debuting with a famous concert pianist, or by graduating from a famous conservatory, or by graduating from a university well known for its music school.

These would then represent three disjunctive subgoals. However, many goals have more than one precondition for their realization. For example, suppose the woman achieves the BECOME-UNIVERSITY-STUDENT goal. The figure shows a STAY-UNIVERSITY-STUDENT goal associated with it, and this goal is shown as having as conjunctive subgoals MAINTAIN-GPA and PASS-RECITAL. Both of these goals would have to be achieved for graduation, and they can be considered as independent of one another.

There is another way of thinking about disjunctive and conjunctive links, a way that is preferable because it is more general. Consider first the case of disjunctive links in which there are several alternative subgoals, any one of which, if achieved, will lead to the achievement of the goal it serves. Each of these subgoals can be considered to be to some degree sufficient for achieving the goal, but no particular one of them is necessary, although it is necessary that one of them succeed. Thus, one might think of the links as being *sufficiency* links (marked with an **S** in Figure 3.1). In the conjunctive case, the links are all to some degree *necessary* (marked with an **N**), with no one of them alone being sufficient. The virtue of thinking of the links in terms of the degree to which they are sufficient or necessary for achieving the higher-level goals to which they are connected is that it is based on a representational system that readily permits other kinds of labels to be attached to links. Specifically, one can also represent links that are neither necessary, nor sufficient, but that are nevertheless positively *facilitative* (marked with an **F**). That is, some goals, when achieved, increase the probability that a higher level goal will be achieved even though they do not guarantee it. For example, if the aspiring pianist is enrolled at Indiana University, then getting an A on a course might facilitate the attainment of the MAINTAIN-GPA goal without it being either necessary or sufficient to attain it. Furthermore, we can now introduce *inhibitory* links (marked with an **I** and shown as a dashed line) in exactly the same way. For example, let us suppose that as well as wanting to be a concert pianist, the woman in our example also aspires to a settled family life. These goals might well be incompatible in the sense that she believes that if she succeeds as a pianist she will be traveling so much that it is likely to interfere with her aspirations for family life. Thus, while the attainment of the BECOME-CONCERT-PIANIST goal would be neither necessary nor sufficient to guarantee the failure of the HAVE-HAPPY-FAMILY-LIFE goal, she might well view it as reducing the probability of attaining it.

A crucial aspect of the representation of goal structures is that the representation is constantly changing as old goals are realized or abandoned and as new ones are introduced. Such changes are not limited to just the addition and deletion of nodes or branches from the structure, rather, the entire configuration can change. A particularly important aspect of this is that the nature of the links from a subgoal to a dominating goal can change. For example, given that the pianist entertains three possible ways of getting an agent, each way can be represented by a sufficiency link. Now if the necessary preconditions for two of the three paths fail, the associated branches will have to be pruned, with the result that there will now exist only one path. However, this means that the surviving path may no longer be merely sufficient. Depending on the availability of new alternatives, it will become increasingly necessary, and perhaps even absolutely necessary. In our efforts to build computer models of processes of this kind, we associate subjective transition probabilities with all intergoal links. These too have to be constantly updated as a result of achievements or failures in goal attainment. Finally, the attainment of goals often brings about a new situation or a change in status for the person, with the result that new goals may be established to maintain the new status. So, for example, if the pianist attains the BECOME-UNIVERSITY-STUDENT goal, her status will change to that of a university student and this new status will necessitate the creation of new plans and goals (such as maintaining an acceptable grade point average, and passing her recital) to satisfy the new STAY-UNIVERSITY-STUDENT goal. We have included a couple of examples of this in the figure. They are shown as new goals connected by dotted lines to their related goals to indicate that they only come into existence upon the attainment of their related goals.

Processing Assumptions. So far we have described what might be considered as a small part of a much larger general structure of goals and plans. Clearly, people do not think about and actively pursue all of their goals at once. In order to account for this, we need to superimpose some processing assumptions on top of the structural ones. The simplest way to do this is in terms of a spreading activation mechanism (e.g., Collins & Loftus, 1975; Ortony & Radin, in press). Let us suppose that some particular goal becomes activated as a result of some internal or external event. For example, suppose our would-be pianist comes to think about being a concert pianist. This amounts to saying that the BECOME-CONCERT-PIANIST node becomes the (currently) most active node.

We now assume a graded spread of activation from that node in the structure to other nodes. It is important to note that although the structure is directed in the sense that it contains a representation of the direction of causal flow, the spread of activation is not constrained by this directionality. In the example we have used, the most immediate nodes that could receive activation from the newly activated BECOME-CONCERT-PIANIST goal are the HAVE-IDEAL-JOB goal and the HAVE-HAPPY-FAMILY-LIFE goal (both of which are "above" it), and the GET-AGENT goal (which is "below" it). These nodes, in turn, will activate nodes that are adjacent to them, and so on, with decreasing strength on every cycle. If one also assumes, as is conventional in spreading activation models, that there is some threshold of activation that has to be reached before a node can transmit activation to other nodes, then there will come a point at which no more nodes are affected by the initially activated node. We now have a situation in which some (relatively small) part of the total network is active in the sense that the activation levels on the nodes have been increased. Notice, however, that there is no guarantee that all of that part of the network one might consider *relevant* to the originally activated node will be activated. The part of the network that one might consider as relevant is the part that is semantically or *informationally* related, whereas the part that is activated will be a subset of the relevant part whose boundaries are determined by how far the activation spreads.

The distinction between that part of the structure that is *relevant* to some particular goal and the part that is *activated* by it has an interesting consequence in terms of the *reasons* or justifications a person might offer for wanting to attain the goal in question. Consider again the pianist. Suppose she were asked why she wanted to maintain an acceptable grade point average at Indiana University. In terms of the structure we have proposed, one might imagine that she would have reasons available all the way up the structure: She wants to graduate, she wants to get an agent, she wants to be a concert pianist, she wants her ideal job, and so on to wanting life satisfaction. However, only the first one or two of these would ever be offered as reasons. She would be unlikely to justify the desire to maintain an acceptable GPA in terms of her desire for life satisfaction. We would explain this by saying that acceptable reasons are constrained to activated parts of the relevant structure. The activated parts comprise the *explicit* goals in whose service the originally activated goal is being pursued. The unactivated, but relevant parts comprise only *implicit* goals or reasons.

Goals. The example of a goal structure that we have just described was intentionally highly oversimplified. Yet, hopefully, even this simple example illustrates that one cannot think of goals as being merely well-defined target states that are actively pursued. A much more general notion of goals is going to be required if we are to do justice to the complexities of human action, cognition, and emotion. The nearest thorough analysis of the kind that will be needed is the one proposed by Schank and Abelson

(1977) who distinguished several different kinds of goals, including (but not restricted to): Achievement goals to *achieve* certain things, Satisfaction goals to *satisfy* certain (biological) needs, Entertainment goals to *enjoy* certain things, Preservation goals to *preserve* certain states of affairs, Crisis goals to handle *crises* when Preservation goals are threatened, and Instrumental goals whose only purpose is to be *instrumental* in realizing other goals. Impressive as their analysis is, it turns out that for our purposes it cuts the pie the wrong way.

Ordinarily, one thinks of goals as having at least two defining characteristics. First, they are the kinds of things that can be pursued. Second, they are the kinds of things for which one believes that one can develop a plan for them to be realized. In fact, we need to think of goals in a more general way than this because there are cases in which these characteristics are not present (Mandler, 1985), which is one of the reasons we prefer to talk about them as "goals" rather than as "desires." For example, some goals have a degree of independence from superordinate goals. They are attained not because their achievement is motivated by some higher goal, but because they are independently initiated by patterns of external stimulation; that is, some of the things people do, they do not because they "intend" to, but just because particular situations can trigger action sequences; the question of intention does not arise. An example of such an automatic action sequence would be the procedure one ordinarily goes through when one gets dressed in the morning. It is of course true that when one goes through one's morning ritual of getting dressed one does so because one *wants* to get dressed; however, the goal of getting dressed need not be consciously available.

The more important cases in which goals fail to satisfy what appear to be the typical characteristics are those in which the person has relatively little control over goal-relevant outcomes. For example, a fan of a football team may want his team to win, he may be pleased when it does, and displeased when it doesn't, yet he probably does not believe that there is anything much that he can really do to affect the outcome.[1] So having his team win cannot be considered to be a goal in the usual, restricted, sense. However, it certainly can be thought of as an interest or concern of the fan, and, as

1 Interestingly, if fans really do believe that they can in no way influence the outcome of a sporting event, there is a sense in which they may be wrong! Greer (1983) reports a study showing statistically significant decrements in performance of visiting teams coupled with increments in performance of the home team in response to sustained crowd protests such as booing. The interpretation of spectator-effect on performance was preferred over the interpretation of compensatory bias in referees' rulings. Notice, however, that just as in voting behavior, such effects are group effects and any particular individual may still (correctly) feel that his or her own contribution is inessential.

such, it plays an important role in determining behavior and in evaluating events. Furthermore, such interests can differ in the value that they have for the person. Even the most obsessive sports fan would probably agree that his interest in the fate of his favorite team is less than in the well-being of his loved ones, even though, in many situations, he may be relatively powerless to facilitate either.

In our discussion, we shall restrict ourselves to three kinds of goals, *Active-pursuit* goals, *Interest* goals, and *Replenishment* goals. Active-pursuit goals (A-goals) include Schank and Abelson's Achievement goals, Entertainment goals, Instrumental goals, and Crisis goals. In our view it makes good sense to lump all of these together. This is because Crisis goals can be viewed as just a special case of Instrumental goals, namely goals that are created merely as a means of averting threats to Preservation goals. In this sense they are instrumental in realizing other goals. Instrumental goals themselves are actively pursued, just as Achievement goals are. Finally, we see no difference in principle between Enjoyment goals and other kinds of Achievement goals. Thus, we group all of these goals together as A-goals, which, as a group, represent the kinds of things *one wants to get done*.

The second class of goals that we consider we call Interest goals (I-goals) of which Schank and Abelson's Preservation goals are a special case. Whereas A-goals represent the kinds of things one wants to get done, I-goals represent the kinds of things *one wants to see happen*. This is not a sharp, categorical distinction because, while I-goals differ from A-goals in that they are not themselves the kinds of things that are normally actively pursued, largely because the person who has them does not believe that he or she can exert a great deal of influence over them, it is possible to engage in activities that are designed to further the interests in question. Occasionally, however, I-goals spawn A-goals designed solely to further the interests they represent. Interestingly, when an I-goal is treated like an A-goal, the resulting plans and associated behaviors often appear to have an obsessive quality. Interest goals represent interests such as that one's friends should prosper, that people should get what they deserve, that one's favorite sports team be successful, and that one preserves one's good health. Preservation goals are a special case because they represent one's interests in preserving certain valued states of affairs. For Preservation goals the default situation is the status quo in which the situations to be preserved are preserved. These situations include the maintenance of one's good health, one's position, or one's property. When a Preservation goal is threatened, the person may well establish subgoals to deal with the situation but, once achieved, the Preservation goal remains even if the subgoals are abandoned.

The third class of goals that we consider important to distinguish comprises achievable goals that are not abandoned when achieved. Many of Schank and Abelson's Satisfaction goals have this characteristic, and they are marked by their special cyclical characteristics. These goals become more insistent as the time from their last realization increases. Unlike A-goals, they cannot be discarded once they have been realized. All that happens when such goals are satisfied is that the urgency to realize them drops temporarily to zero. For this reason, we prefer to think of them as Replenishment goals (**R**-goals) and to include in them not only biological needs but all goals that have this cyclical nature (e.g., filling one's car with gasoline, receiving one's regular paycheck). We should note that while the distinction between **A**-goals and **R**-goals is theoretically important in the sense that **R**-goals persist, albeit with less insistence, immediately after they have been attained, we shall not make use of the distinction in our account of emotion, treating them, for expediency, as special cases of **A**-goals. Nevertheless, it is probably the case that emotions that implicate **R**-goals involve time in a unique and critical fashion.

One can think of goals as having lives; they are born when they are set up or established, and they die when they are realized or abandoned. Different kinds of goals tend to live for different lengths of time. Active-pursuit goals are highly variable in duration. Some, because they represent aspirations to possess valued objects or social positions, take a relatively long time to achieve and thus have long lives. For example, a person who has decided that he wants one day to own a Rolls Royce or become President of the United States is not likely to have such a goal realized in a matter of minutes, days, or even months. Such goals can take years to achieve, if they are achieved at all. Because their realization often takes a long time, high-level **A**-goals tend to be far removed from the majority of everyday activities, thus they are are usually implicit rather than explicit. Lower-level **A**-goals, on the other hand, tend to be explicit and shorter-term when they are active because they are more likely to be the immediate conscious causal origins of behavior. Replenishment goals tend to be explicit much more often than **A**-goals, and they tend to have long lifetimes. At the same time, they may have quite small periodicity because they pertain to the satisfaction of frequently arising needs such as for food, sleep, and sex.

If goals are ever immortal, **I**-goals are the best candidates because so many of one's interests are not and cannot be finally attainable. The most obvious example of an **I**-goal is one's own well-being, a goal that ordinarily persists from early childhood to death. Because of its longevity, such a goal is rarely explicit, although it becomes explicit when one has to make major decisions such as whether to change jobs, get married, have children, or take up jogging. One's interest in one's own well-being (or the well-being of others, for that matter) also becomes explicit when one perceives a threat or potential threat to it, in which case, as already indicated, the response is often the establishment of relatively short-term A-goals such as going to the dentist when one has a toothache. Such short-term A-goals are set up merely to enable the realization of some other goal. So, for example, in order to be treated by a dentist one may have to make an appointment. Making an appointment has no value in and of itself, It merely satisfies a precondition for the achievement of an A-goal of having one's tooth fixed, which, in this particular case, is only in the service of restoring a situation that is part of a higher-level I-goal. It would seem then that the frequency and duration of the explicitness of a goal is inversely related to the longevity of the goal, so that a short-lived goal tends to be explicit and active for most of its life, whereas a long-lived goal is only occasionally explicit.

Virtual goal structures are highly dynamic, and the different kinds of goals interact in different ways. We have already alluded to the fact that I-goals can sometimes spawn related A-goals, and that A-goals, once attained, can spawn related I-goals. The example we gave of this latter case was of the creation of a STAY-UNIVERSITY-STUDENT goal on attainment of the BECOME-UNIVERSITY-STUDENT goal. Also, of course, when R-goals become active, they become temporarily A-goals, the difference being that upon attainment, the A-goal is abandoned, but the R-goal remains. There are other important issues that we shall not discuss here having to do with the effects of goal or subgoal attainment on the overall structure. In general, one has to suppose that goal priorities and structures are constantly changing in response to changing prospects of goal attainments or failures. Issues such as these are not really important in the present context; a more detailed account of them can be found in the AI literature on planning (e.g., Chapman, 1985; Stefik, 1981; Wilensky, 1983).

The complex network that we consider to be the virtual goal structure can either be considered as unrooted with several top-level goals, or conceived of as having one top-level goal such as that of maximizing or maintaining well-being, or even some "dummy" node at the root. In either case, any lower-level goal can be related to two or more quite different, unrelated, higher-order goals. For example, a businessman, in taking a prospective client to an expensive restaurant, might be contributing to the satisfaction of an R-goal (to become "unhungry") and of A-goals of having a good time, eating fine food, and impressing his client. Some of these goals would be in the service of a higher-level A-goal having to do with obtaining the client's business, and so on. The most dominant (top-level) goals are often quite general, abstract goals. They are mainly relatively permanent A-goals and **I**-goals. This is why one might choose to view the virtual goal structure as having only one top-level goal such as the **I**-goal of furthering one's well-being. In contrast, lower-level goals are more specific and transitory. A subgoal of a substructure in a person's implicit goal structure might be necessitated by one high-level goal and yet be incompatible with another (see Wilensky's 1978 discussion of goal conflicts). We presume that weights associated with goals contribute to the determination of priorities and selections between incompatible and competing subgoals.

To conclude this discussion of goals, we need to introduce one more important distinction, namely, that between *all-or-none* goals and *partially attainable* goals. Suppose a young couple decides that they want to find a house to buy and they set about searching for one that they can afford. This would be an example of establishing an all-or-none **A**-goal. They will either attain it, or they won't. It is not possible to "partially" attain the goal of finding a house even though it is perfectly possible for certain events to transpire that may increase or decrease confidence that it will be attained. Now compare this with a case in which one wants to mow one's lawn before dusk. The goal of getting one's grass cut is a partially attainable **A**-goal – it can be attained completely, or only partially. The same distinction can be applied to **I**-goals. Suppose a person has an interest in seeing a Republican president elected. This would be a case of an all-or-none **I**-goal. The victor either will or will not be a Republican. In contrast, many **I**-goals are partially attainable, and some are only partially attainable. Indeed, the most important **I**-goals are almost all partially attainable **I**-goals that are superordinate to (particularly) all-or-none **I**-goals. So, for example, the all-or-none **I**-goal of having a Republican president elected is presumably supported by an (only) partially attainable **I**-goal of wanting a Republican government. More obvious examples of the limits on partially attainable **I**-goals are provided by such interests as that one should be in good health and that one's friends and loved ones should prosper. Notice that we are making a distinction here between **I**-goals that are partially attainable in the sense that it is possible to attain them *to some degree* and **I**-goals that are *only* partially attainable, by which we mean that they can never be totally realized. At the same time, it should be recognized that whether a goal is an all-or-none goal, a partially attainable goal, or an only partially attainable goal appears to depend on how the goal is formulated, but this is not an issue that we shall pursue further here.

Standards and Attitudes. So far, the representational system that we have outlined has been characterized exclusively as a structure of *goals*, namely, states of affairs that one *wants* to obtain. However, if such a representational system is to serve as the substrate for the appraisal mechanism, it must contain more than goals. In particular, it has to include representations of at least two other categories of knowledge, namely *standards* and *attitudes*. Standards concern the states of affairs that one believes *ought* to obtain. Standards need to be included because they represent the beliefs in terms of which moral and other kinds of judgmental evaluations are made, and attitudes (including tastes) need to be included because they constitute the basis for the appraisals of appealingness that are the foundations of liking. As far as standards are concerned, what we have in mind are the kinds of standards to which people typically appeal when they are explaining why they approve or disapprove of what someone is doing or did. For example, we have in mind the kinds of standards that underlie such admonitions as "You ought to be more careful," "You ought to have tried harder," "You ought not to do things that upset other people." One might call these *moral* or *quasi-moral* standards. In addition, there are standards of behavior and performance. Standards of behavior include conventions, norms, and other kinds of accepted regularities governing or characteristic of social interactions. Standards of performance include more specific role-based norms. For example, although one would expect a lifeguard to attempt to save a drowning child, one would not expect a paraplegic to do so. Thus, to some extent, one's beliefs about what is an acceptable, normal, or expected way to behave are determined by the role in which one casts the agent. Similarly, there can be personal standards of performance, based on expectations derived from one's own model of one's self. For example, a world-class long-jumper who jumps less than, say, 27 ft in some particular competition might consider his performance to fall short of his standards of an acceptable performance by a world-class athlete. In other words, he would evaluate his performance in terms of expectations generated by his own model of himself as an athlete. Of course, others of us would feel that our expectations had been surpassed were we able to jump 10 ft, or even to jump at all!

In general, standards involve a quite different set of considerations than do goals. Many are socially learned, and involve norms and consensus. They frequently relate to the manner of behavior as much as to the content, and their ultimate justification is often in terms of social, or socially determined, considerations rather than in terms of personal ones. This means that the source of value of standards is quite different from that of goals. The value of a goal can be thought of in terms of the potential contribution it makes to the attainment of the highest-level goal or goals in the goal structure, whereas the value of a standard seems better thought of as being intrinsic, or at least, inherited from some superordinate standard whose value is intrinsic. It seems unlikely that standards are organized in a very elaborate structure, although there surely is some degree of hierarchical structuring. Thus, some of the standards that a person subscribes to (for example, that people ought not to inflict needless pain on others) probably are subsumed under other, more general standards (for example, that people ought to do what is right and not do what is wrong). Furthermore, it is important to realize that very general standards are generative in nature, so that a standard such as ONE OUGHT TO TAKE CARE OF OTHER PEOPLE'S THINGS can generate specific instantiations such as ONE OUGHT TO TAKE CARE OF OTHER PEOPLE'S CARS. One is hardly likely to store the infinitude of possible instantiations of the general standard. Finally, there is no more reason to suppose that all of a person's standards are internally consistent than there is to suppose that all of a person's goals are. Since our purposes here are not those of moral philosophy, it is not important that we enumerate what these standards typically are. Rather, the point is to acknowledge that there must be such standards.

Whereas we have distinguished standards from goals, they are related in such a way that an alternative approach would have been merely to identify standards as a special kind of goal to be maintained. We prefer not to think of them this way, partly because we think it important not to lose sight of the difference. However, if, as we do, one postulates the existence of some very abstract high-level goals, such as MAINTAIN SELF-ESTEEM or PRESERVE GOOD HEALTH, one has to acknowledge that the standards in terms of which one judges actions are likely to be connected to at least one such high-level goal, specifically, an I-goal representing one's interest that the standards to which one subscribes be upheld. Thus, if one violates a standard one holds to be important, it will tend to interfere with such a goal with the result that the violation of a standard will not only constitute an occasion for blame, but that, construed as an event, it can also be judged to be undesirable relative to goals. Much the same is true of attitudes, which we view as the *dispositional* liking (or disliking) one has for certain objects, or attributes of objects, without reference to standards or goals. At the same time, one of the differences between attitudes on the one hand and goals and standards on the other is that some attitudes, especially those that we call "tastes," do not have, and are not expected to have, justifications. If someone likes caviar and dislikes Berlioz, that is that! The person's tastes might change with maturation or even instruction, but tastes do not have the kind of underlying logical or propositional structure that goals and standards do.

As we have already emphasized, it is not necessary to suppose that every single goal, standard, and attitude that can play a role in appraisal has to be a permanently stored representation. Two considerations make this unnecessary and unlikely. First, it is reasonable to suppose that most of what we have stored are high-level, relatively nonspecific goals, standards, and attitudes, all of which have powerful generative capabilities. For example, if one has as a standard that people ought not to inflict needless pain, one also has implicitly (and sometimes explicitly) a host of instantiations of this standard such as that one ought not to harm animals, and so on. Similarly, if one has as an abstract goal that one wants to attain a great deal of general knowledge, one also has implicitly (and on some occasions explicitly) instantiations such as that one wants to read widely. Second, it is neither useful nor necessary to suppose that every experienced situation makes immediate contact with the appraisal structure. It makes better sense to suppose that people propagate inferences about the implications of specific situations, and that sometimes these inferences make contact with elements in the appraisal structure, and sometimes they do not. When no contact is made, the situation is not construed as being relevant to a person's concerns – it has no implications for his goals, standards, or attitudes. On the other hand, sometimes goals, standards, or attitudes are activated as a result of inference propagation. When this happens, the situation is seen by the person as being relevant to his concerns and the possibility of an emotional reaction arises.

Together goals, standards, and attitudes constitute the major ingredients of an integrated structure, with any one of the three types of representation being able to interact, in principle, with any other type, sometimes in a facilitating manner and sometimes in an interfering manner. The values of goals, standards, and attitudes have to be calibrated in such a way as to permit the possibility of, for example, a goal conflicting with a standard so that the subjective value assigned to one might outweigh the subjective value assigned to another. Therefore, we do not conceive of the structure as having three separate components – one has to suppose that it is perfectly normal for it to be (or become) a goal of a person that he upholds certain principles or standards. Freedom fighters who are willing to die for the liberation of their country, or highly moral people who are willing to suffer rather than to violate a standard they deem to be important, are real-world testaments to this fact. In such cases, we might suppose that one of the highest-level I-goals would be something like MAINTAIN A CLEAR CONSCIENCE rather than PRESERVE OWN LIFE, and that important moral and quasi-moral standards inherit their value from it.

Central Intensity Variables

We have just sketched the basic outline of an appraisal structure that has three interwoven components – goals, standards, and attitudes. We are now ready to relate these three notions to the three foci of valenced reactions that we described in Chapter 2. Associated with each of these three foci is a primary variable that affects the intensity of all emotions involving that focus, and central to the evaluation or appraisal is one of the three components of the representation system we have just sketched. The variable associated with reactions to events is *desirability*, which is computed with reference to *goals*. The variable associated with reactions to the actions of agents is *praiseworthiness*, which is computed with reference to *standards*, and the variable associated with reactions to objects is *appealingness* which is evaluated in terms of *attitudes*. In other words, apart from any other variables that may influence the intensity of Event-based emotions, the desirability variable necessarily influences all of them. What this means is that, other things being equal, the more desirable or undesirable the event in question seems to be, the more intense will be the emotion that is experienced. Similarly, the intensity of all Attribution emotions is influenced by the praiseworthiness variable, and the Attraction emotions are all influenced by appealingness.

Together, these three variables play a role similar to that played by the concept of appraisal in other cognitively oriented theories (e.g., Arnold, 1960; Lazarus, Kanner, & Folkman, 1980; Mandler, 1975). However, although appraisal and our three variables are all concerned with evaluation, our use of *desirability, praiseworthiness*, and *appealingness* is motivated by a desire to be more specific about the evaluation mechanism and the cognitive structures upon which it operates.

Desirability. In considering the desirability variable, we first focus on the representation of goals in the structure. Every represented goal has a value that depends primarily on where and how it is located in the goal structure. All states actually represented in the goal structure are necessarily desired states to some degree because they represent goals. Thus, the events that constitute their satisfaction must all be predominantly desirable, even though it might be possible in some cases to view a particular goal-attaining event as negative with respect to some isolated part of the goal structure, which would mean that it had some undesirable aspects. However, one would expect that on balance the achievement of a goal is more likely to facilitate than to interfere with the achievement of other goals. The degree of *desirability* associated with achieving a goal will depend primarily upon the value of the higher-level goals whose attainment the goal in question facilitates and the degree to which it facilitates them, that is, it is a measure of the degree to which the event is expected to have beneficial consequences. The degree of *undesirability* associated with achieving a goal will depend primarily upon the value of the higher-level goals whose attainment the goal in question hinders and the degree to which it hinders them, making it a measure of the degree to which the event is expected to have harmful consequences. It is important at this point to distinguish two possible senses of "desirability," because only one of them is the sense we wish to employ. The sense of "desirability" upon which we wish to focus is the sense in which an event would be desirable *if* it were to obtain. In this sense, the event is, or would be, beneficial, or of value, worth, or utility. There is, however, another, related sense of "desirability" having to do with motivation to attain some goal. This sense is probably best thought of as a product of desirability in the first sense (worth or utility) and subjective likelihood of attaining the goal. To see the difference, one might suppose that the desirability of winning a million dollars in a lottery is very high in the sense of the expected value *if* the event were to come about; however, a person might not be very motivated to try to bring it about if he or she believed that the chances of successfully doing so were very low. We always use desirability in the first sense, because the contribution of subjective likelihood is, where applicable, handled independently.

When we come to consider states that are not part of the goal structure, the same notions of desirability and undesirability can be employed, except that we can now no longer assume that the desirability of some particular goal-relevant event probably exceeds its undesirability. If the values of the facilitating relations outweigh those of the interfering relations we have a state that is perceived as being more desirable than undesirable. If the interfering relations outweigh the facilitating ones the state is perceived as being more undesirable than desirable. Thus, what we are proposing is that the formal variable that we call *desirability* has two aspects, one corresponding only to the degree to which the event in question appears to have beneficial (i.e., positively desirable) consequences, and the other corresponding to the degree to which it is perceived as having harmful (i.e., negatively desirable, or undesirable) consequences. The values of these components are generally different, largely due to the fact that the repercussions of successes and failures are different.

Consider, for example, a relatively simple plan (i.e., one with relatively little branching) to achieve some important goal such as trying to start one's car in order to drive to an appointment for a job interview. If one is successful in attaining the subgoal of starting the car, the degree of desirability will depend upon the degree to which attaining it is seen as facilitating the achievement of the high-level goal (getting the job), which is the ultimate (explicit) purpose of the activity. We assume that transitions from subgoals to high-level goals are not judged by the person to be subjectively equiprobable – for example, the person may think it more likely that he will be able to start his car than that he will be offered the job that he seeks. There are two reasons for this. First, the achievement of the lowest-level subgoal is only one of several subgoals that must be achieved in sequence. Its achievement only satisfies a precondition for the achievement of the next one. Second, in general, the subjective transition probabilities between adjacent subgoals is not likely to be the same. One might be very confident that if one starts one's car, one will be on time for the appointment, but much less confident that if one is on time for the appointment, one will be offered the job. The net effect is that the achievement of the lowest-level subgoal may make only a relatively small contribution to the achievement of the focal goal (getting the job offer) so that its weighted desirability would be relatively small – no cause for great joy. On the other hand, failure to achieve such a low-level subgoal could have significant repercussions in that it could entirely eliminate the possibility of achieving the focal goal by rendering the realization of its preconditions impossible. Thus, failure to start the car could have an undesirability value equal in magnitude to the desirability of attaining the focal goal, whereas success in starting the car will have a much smaller desirability value than the focal goal.

The notion of a *focal* goal in this context is very important. In any particular assessment of desirability a focal goal is a goal in terms of which the assessment itself is made. The assessment of desirability depends critically on the perspective from which the assessment is made. When evaluated from the perspective of some relatively close local goal such as getting to a dental appointment on time, an undesirable event such as the failure of one's car to start will be judged much more undesirable than it will relative to a more remote high-level goal such as PRESERVE GOOD HEALTH. So the perceived desirability (or undesirability) of an event depends not just on how the event is construed, and not just on the structure of goals to which it is related, but also on the particular goal in that structure in terms of which it is evaluated.

Notice that because we include I-goals, the present analysis is quite general in scope. Thus, for example, the undesirability (i.e., a negative value for the desirability variable) of the unexpected death of a friend would not necessarily be a result of failing to achieve an A-goal such as preventing the friend from dying (one might never have thought about it).

Rather, it would result from the fact that it interfered with an **I**-goal (e.g., the maintenance of the well-being of liked others). On the other hand, one might also recognize desirable aspects of such a loss. If, for example, the friend had long been suffering from a painful and incurable disease, one might view it as a "blessing in disguise" as one focused on the friend's relief from pain or the relief from anxiety and unfulfillable responsibility felt by the friend's spouse.

Thus, an event can have both desirable and undesirable aspects. The overall subjective importance or salience of the event can probably best be thought of in terms of the sum of the (unsigned) values of desirability and undesirability because these values represent the totality of the processed consequences of the event. It seems reasonable to suppose that physiological arousal is determined primarily by the subjective importance of the event so defined. However, the principal determinant of emotional intensity is whichever member of the valenced desirability/undesirability pair plays a role in the particular emotion or emotions in question. In other words, positive Event-based emotions increase in intensity as the positive component of desirability increases, while negative Event-based emotions increase in intensity with increases in the value of the negative component of the desirability variable – that is, with increases in undesirability.

An interesting implication of this view is that the intensity of a particular Event-based emotion may correlate better with a *component* of subjective importance (i.e., desirability or undesirability), and hence better with a component of arousal, than it does with arousal itself, which would be determined by the sum of the two components. It seems to us that a situation could produce a high degree of subjective importance while quite literally producing ambivalence in a person with respect to overall implications. Such a case might occur when someone who was in dire financial difficulties learns of the death of a rich relative from whom he knew he would inherit great fortune. The person might well have dearly loved the relative. In such a case the death of a loved relative could be both highly undesirable and at the same time highly desirable. Thus, in principle, it is possible to imagine the magnitude of the desirable aspects, when considered with respect to one goal, as being comparable to the magnitude of the undesirable aspects, when considered with respect to another. In such a case, the subjective importance of the event (and consequently the associated arousal) would be very high, although the person might not know whether he felt good or bad about it because of the mixed emotions he was experiencing – positive ones with respect to the desirable aspects, and negative ones with respect to the undesirable ones. However, and this is the key point, we think that it makes more sense to argue that the intensity of the

positive emotions is determined by the perceived desirability of the consequences of the event in virtue of which they arise, and so too for the
negative emotions vis à vis undesirability. Of course, there is no reason why
contextual factors might not sometimes lead to an alternating focus, first on
one aspect and then on another, as a consequence of which the person
might well experience corresponding–alternating or mixed–positive and
negative emotions.

The mechanism we have proposed for determining desirability seems
able to account for both the subjective importance of an actual or potential
state of affairs and for the evaluation of that state of affairs with respect to
both its positive and negative aspects. Furthermore, it appears possible to
specify a method of assigning a magnitude to the valenced evaluation.
Clearly, more detail is needed to work out a proper calculus for computing
desirability values (see Ravlin, 1987, for a first approach on this issue).

We have just argued that an important aspect of a model of the computation of desirability is that it be able to capture the fact that the same
event can be judged positive under one set of contextual constraints (for
example, relative to one set of expectations) and negative under another
set. Discovering that one is due for a refund of $100 from a national
taxing authority such as the IRS would presumably be judged to be positive if one had expected to pay them $300, but negative if one had
expected a refund of $500. This raises the question of what the unit of
analysis is, or should be. Is there just one event in both cases, namely, the
receipt of $100? Or are there two different events, namely the receipt of
$400 more than expected and the receipt of $400 less? The first analysis is
parsimonious with respect to the knowledge representation system, but
complex with respect to the computation of value. The second is inelegant
with respect to the knowledge representation system, but simpler from
the point of view of the computation of value. There is, of course, no
fixed answer to this question, because the reaction of a particular ex-

periencer will depend at any given moment on the salience of his expectations. Clearly in the case where the taxpayer receives only $100 of an expected $500, he will be disappointed at losing $400 when he focuses on his expectations, but pleased at receiving $100 more than he had when he focuses only on the bottom line of his bank book. Not only are both reactions possible, but in most of us, they are both quite likely to occur, perhaps even within the space of a few moments. We present a more detailed discussion of such issues in Chapter 6.

The basic idea that desirability is a computable characteristic of an event seems tenable, at least in principle. It is our view that the evaluation of events conceived of in terms of desirability (including undesirability) offers the prospect of a cognitive account of the interaction between understanding a stimulus, appraising it as good or bad to some degree, and – hence – having a valenced reaction to it. And this we consider to be an indispensable aspect of any cognitive theory of the emotions that seeks to be computationally tractable. In the context of Event-based emotions, the appraisal as good or bad is realized as an appraisal in terms of desirability. As we shall see in the next section, in the context of Attribution emotions it is realized in terms of praiseworthiness (and blameworthiness).

Praiseworthiness. When we evaluate events and their consequences with respect to goals, we construe them as being desirable or undesirable. When we evaluate the things people do (the actions of agents), we evaluate them with respect to standards. To the degree that people do things that appear to us to uphold valued standards, we find their actions praiseworthy, and to the extent that they violate them, we find them blameworthy. We shall speak of the general variable here as being that of *praiseworthiness*, treating blameworthiness as its negative counterpart.

At first sight it might seem that praiseworthiness is itself a complex construct involving many facets. For example, it might appear to depend upon effort. In the case of blame, one's intuitions are that the harder the agent tries to make something bad happen, the more blameworthy he is. This would accommodate cases in which, for example, a person invests effort in an attempt to maliciously discredit a colleague. However, blame can also arise when someone fails to invest effort that could have prevented a negative situation from arising. From that perspective, a second colleague who knows of the machinations of the first but does nothing to prevent them is also, in principle, blameworthy. He is judged more blameworthy the more easily it is judged that he could have intervened. The injured party might blame this second colleague for a "sin of omission" while blaming the first for a "sin of commission." Whereas blame can result from either of these two kinds of "sins," praise usually only results from effort invested to bring about good or prevent bad, both of which, to coin a phrase, are "virtues of commission."

Now, although factors such as effort certainly affect praiseworthiness, they do so, in our view, because they invoke other standards such as PEOPLE OUGHT TO TRY (to do good things and to avoid bad things). Thus, effort increases praiseworthiness only in those cases in which the expenditure of effort is itself judged to be praiseworthy. In other words, it behaves in exactly the same way as desirability behaves, namely, by accumulating distributed valence-compatible evaluations resulting from viewing the situation from more than one perspective.

Agency is usually considered to be under the control of the agent. Certainly, if the agent is causally involved but lacked either the intention to do what he did or the ability to prevent it, the agency would not generally be considered to be of the right kind. So, for example, a person who carries out an assassination while in a hypnotic trance could be carrying out the act without intending to, and would thus not be considered responsible in the appropriate sense. The responsible person would be the one who had induced the hypnosis with the intention of using the subject as the instrument of the assassination. Thus, responsibility needs to be viewed as a precondition for both praise and blame so that these reactions to agents' actions only arise *if* there is indeed an *attribution of responsibility*. Responsibility and intention are not identical. People can be held responsible for violations of standards without having intended to do anything reprehensible. For example, one can be held responsible for failing to fulfill a promise, when in fact one forgot to do what was required. In such a case, there was clearly no blameworthy intention, but one is held accountable nonetheless. Similarly, one can engage in intentional actions for which one is not held responsible. Children often engage in actions that they intend yet they are not necessarily held accountable because, among other things, it is assumed that young children do not fully understand the consequences of their actions. This raises complex questions about what the focus of the evaluation is. Is it the actual action the person performs, is it the import of the action – or what? These issues will not be discussed here; a more detailed discussion of the psychology of the attribution of blame can be found in Shaver (1985).

We have already noted that the agent need not necessarily be a person, or even an animate being. People, however, are certainly the best examples of agents, and thus it is arguable that when agency is attributed to something other than an individual (or to an institution, which amounts to the same thing), then the person making the attribution is anthropomorphizing the agent. So, to blame the weather, one's car, or fate for causing some mishap is to treat something that is not human as though it were, or at least to treat it as though it were an autonomous being capable of reasoning, planning, and freely choosing between what is deemed to be right, and what is deemed to be wrong.

We now need to return to the issue of what kinds of things standards are, and how they acquire their value. What we have in mind as standards are the various moral, legal, and conventional laws, rules, regulations, norms, and codes of conduct and performance. These are often standard for a culture or subculture, although some may be unique to individuals or groups of individuals. Standards differ from I-goals in that they are general and abstract, rather than practical states of affairs that one might wish to see obtain. Thus, whereas one usually does not strive to achieve an I-goal, because its content is too amorphous and one usually has too little control, one often does strive to adhere to or uphold standards to which one subscribes, at least insofar as they are relevant in a particular situation. However, this does not mean that all standards have to be explicitly represented. For example, one might evaluate a soloist's outstanding musical performance against some implicit standard. Ultimately this standard need only be considered as a particular instantiation of some more abstract standard such as PEOPLE OUGHT TO FULLY REALIZE THEIR POTENTIAL or PEOPLE OUGHT TO STRIVE FOR EXCELLENCE.

Standards acquire their value from two sources. First, some particular standard can acquire value from superordinate standards of which it is an instance. Second, as already intimated, they can acquire value through their connections to high-level I-goals. To take a specific example, a person might want to uphold a standard such as PEOPLE OUGHT TO TAKE CARE OF OTHER PEOPLE'S THINGS because he sees it as dictated by some higher standard such as PEOPLE OUGHT TO ACT IN A RESPONSIBLE MANNER or PEOPLE OUGHT TO BE CONSIDERATE OF THE NEEDS OF OTHERS. The ultimate justification for such a high-level standard might be some high-level I-goal such as MAINTAIN THE RESPECT OF OTHERS AND SELF, or even the most general standard-relevant I-goal that can be contemplated, namely, MAINTAIN THE STANDARDS TO WHICH I SUBSCRIBE. A properly worked out model of the inheritance of the value of standards would have to deal with a number of key issues. One of these would be the determination of which standards possess intrinsic value. A second, related, problem has to do with how the intrinsic value that might be associated with those (presumably rather general) standards that have it would be distributed to particular instantiations of them. Finally, the question of how to integrate intrinsic value with value accruing from whatever high-level goals might support them will have to be resolved. These are difficult, partly empirical, questions for which, as yet, we have no answers. Ultimately, however, they will have to be dealt with if one has any aspirations to develop precise, quantitative, models of the appraisal mechanism.

At this point it might be worth trying to preempt a possible criticism. It might be objected that insofar as standards are ultimately tied to goals, this causes a confounding between desirability and praiseworthiness. In fact, we do not think that there is really a problem here. If some action is evaluated only with respect to goals, any resulting emotions are Event-based emotions. If some action is evaluated only with respect to standards, any resulting emotions are Attribution emotions, even though the value of the praiseworthiness of the action may be partly determined by the desirability of the subsuming goals. This amounts to saying that actions can be evaluated with respect to standards without regard to the practical goal-relevance of the standard invoked. The associated goals may provide a justification for adherence to the standard in situations where the value or legitimacy of the standard is in question, but the standard is not itself a subgoal in the usual sense. This is not the same issue as the one that arises by noting that one can approve of somebody's action even though it may have had undesirable practical consequences – or disapprove of somebody's action even though it may not have had undesirable consequences. Actions can only be evaluated with respect to standards if they are *construed* in terms of standards (e.g., as a violation of a standard such as ONE OUGHT TO BE CONSIDERATE OF THE NEEDS OF OTHERS), and to the extent that they are, standards constitute an alternative mode of evaluation. Of course, it is quite possible, and indeed common, for the same event to be evaluated both with respect to goals and with respect to standards. This can happen, for example, in the case of reproach (an Attribution emotion) which is often coupled with frustration (an Event-based emotion). The reproach results from the fact that one blames an agent for some action, while the accompanying frustration results from being displeased at the undesirable consequences of the action. However, this is a complicated issue that will be postponed until we discuss the Attribution emotions and Attribution/Well-being compounds in Chapter 7.

Appealingness. The last central variable is *appealingness*, which is the result of people's evaluations relative to attitudes, that is, relative to their dispositions – or perhaps better, their predispositions – to like or dislike certain objects (or aspects of objects). Because appealingness is based on attitudes, and because attitudes are essentially summary *values* of the degree of (dispositional) liking or disliking, it is relatively easy to quantify the appealingness variable. Appealingness is a close relative of desirability and praiseworthiness. Just as standards are closely related to I-goals, so too are attitudes closely related to standards. Attitudes, and the associated intensity variable of appealingness, are particularly important in the context of low cognitive content emotions. Most people consider having a tooth filled to be an intrinsically unpleasant experience. However, beliefs about the long-range benefits and avoidance of harm might make this intrinsically unpleasant experience desirable. This simple example illustrates how something can be both desirable (when treated as an event) and disliked (when treated as an object). Thus, whereas the *desirability* of an event entails some sort of understanding of its significance because it involves attention to goal-relevant consequences, *appealingness* does not. This is why appealingness is particularly relevant in the context of low cognitive content emotions.

We should at this point acknowledge the danger of a certain sort of circularity in the way we handle this variable. We believe that the circularity is more apparent than real, and is a result of the fact that ordinary language does not provide us with the tools to talk coherently about the issues. The problem is that we have said that attitudes constitute the basis for evaluations of appealingness. We then go on to argue that when something is judged to be appealing, it can lead to the Attraction emotion of *liking*. However, in trying to characterize attitudes, we find ourselves forced to explain them in terms of liking and disliking. The reason that this problem is more apparent than real is that two different kinds of liking are involved. Attitudes are *dispositions* to like or dislike things, dispositions that often, although not necessarily always, are incorporated into the conceptual representations of the things themselves. As we have already explained, emotions are not dispositions but affective reactions, so that an actual liking experience constitutes little more than a realization of a liking disposition. One might argue in a similar vein that standards are dispositions to approve or disapprove. In the case of standards this seems less objectionable because one feels that standards can be independently explained. However, we think that, in reality, there is no real difference. Our ultimate defense against circularity is that the actual emotional experiences associated with standards and attitudes do not depend *only* on the standards and attitudes that are invoked. Thus, since other factors influence the emotions, the Attraction emotions and the attitudes that underlie them are theoretically distinguishable. The fact that there is no convenient way of expressing the idea that an attitude or taste can be "violated" or "attained" seems to constitute at least some evidence that part of the problem has to do with the unavailability of language to talk about, especially, tastes. It is true that one sometimes speaks of tastes being "offended," but such colloquialisms merely underscore the problem.

Summary

A person's appraisal of an emotion-inducing situation is based on three central variables in the theory: *desirability, praiseworthiness*, and *appealingness*, which apply to Event-based emotions, Agent-based emotions, and Object-based emotions, respectively. Desirability is evaluated in terms of a complex goal structure, where there is a focal goal that governs the interpretation of any event. The desirability of the event is appraised in terms of how it facilitates or interferes with this focal goal and the subgoals that support it. Similarly, the praiseworthiness of an agent's actions is evaluated with respect to a hierarchy of standards, and the appealingness of an object is evaluated with respect to a person's attitudes.

Goals are distinguished from standards in terms of what one wants vs.what one thinks ought to be. We also distinguish three kinds of goals: (1) Active-pursuit goals (**A**-goals) are goals that a person tries to obtain, such as becoming a concert pianist, (2) Interest goals (**I**-goals) are goals that are usually not pursued, because one has little control over their realization, as with preserving one's health or seeing one's friends succeed, and (3) Replenishment goals (**R**-goals) are goals that wax and wane, such as hunger and getting gas for one's car. Orthogonal to these goal types is the question of whether a goal is partially fulfillable, like making a million dollars, or fulfillable only in all-or-none terms, like winning a Nobel Prize. These distinctions all play a role in determining the intensity with which people experience different emotions.

4 Factors Affecting the Intensity of Emotions

In the last chapter, we introduced the variables of *desirability, praisewor-thiness,* and *appealingness* as central variables, each of which is uniquely associated with a class of emotions, namely, Event-based emotions, At-tribution emotions, and Attraction emotions, respectively. There are, however, a number of other factors that affect the intensity of emotions, and it is these that constitute the focus of this chapter. Some of these factors can influence the intensity of all three classes of emotions; these we refer to as "global variables." Others, that we call "local variables," have relatively local effects on emotions in particular groups. In other words, they are variables that are influential for some emotions, but not for others.

When one considers the multitude of factors that obviously can affect the intensity of emotions in one way or another, at one time or another, the total number of intensity-affecting variables that we identify might seem to be surprisingly small. In order to keep our analysis of intensity within manageable bounds, we have adopted a condition that all proposed inten-sity variables must satisfy. Specifically, for something to be a local or global intensity variable it must be capable of affecting intensity independently. The purpose of this requirement is to exclude from the class of intensity variables any factor that appears to have its effect only by virtue of the fact that it modulates the effect of another intensity variable. So, for example, the charm and physical appearance of a person almost certainly influences the intensity of any Attraction emotion that one might experience towards that person; however, we exclude the perception of charm and physical beauty as intensity variables because such factors have only *indirect* effects on the Attraction emotions through their influence on appealingness. With-out such a guiding principle, we suspect that there might be no limit on the number of identifiable factors that can influence the intensity of (at least some) emotions.

Global Variables

Some of the variables that can affect the intensity of all emotions are not ordinarily discussed in the context of emotion research. However, as we shall see, it is important to take account of them, not only because they influence the intensity of emotions, but because their effects can make the difference between there being an emotional experience and there not being one. Insofar as these global variables are not usually considered by emotion theorists, we have had to choose our own names for them. The first one that we discuss we call the *sense of reality* variable. This is concerned with the degree to which the event, agent, or object that underlies the affective reaction seems real to the person experiencing the emotion. We then discuss a related but distinct variable that we call the *proximity* variable, which is intended to reflect the psychological proximity of the emotion-inducing event, agent, or object. The third variable that we deal with, *unexpectedness*, is a more familiar one in the literature. Finally, we consider the effects of the existing level of *arousal* on the intensity of emotions. In our discussions of these variables we often speak of "emotion-inducing situations." We mean this phrase to serve as a shorthand for any state of affairs that is construed in such a way as to give rise to an emotion, regardless of whether the state of affairs (i.e., the situation) leads to a reaction with respect to an event, to the action(s) of an agent, or to an object.

Sense of reality. The first variable that has a global influence on the intensity of emotions is one that we call the "sense of reality" variable. In the detailed characterizations of individual emotions that we shall present in the next four chapters, all the emotions are specified in terms of the person who experiences them having a *valenced reaction* to an event, to the action of an agent, or to an object. But, under what conditions can such a valenced reaction arise? Ordinarily, simply bringing some event, action, or object to mind is not sufficient. For example, imagining winning a fortune in a lottery is not likely to give rise to happiness simply as a consequence of entertaining the idea. Would that it were so! In order for a person to experience an emotion in response to imagination, something else is required, even though the imagined event might be highly desirable or undesirable. In particular, the logical (or, to use a more appropriate – philosophical – term, the intentional) object of an emotion (be it an event, agent, or object) needs to be construed as being sufficiently *real* before it can have a significant effect. It is this that we mean to capture through our *sense of reality* variable (see also Frijda's 1987 discussion of what he calls the "stimulus reception process").

The sense of reality variable achieves three important theoretical goals for us. First, it helps to explain why it is that bringing to mind imaginary situations, however great their subjective importance might be, does not automatically result in an emotional experience. Second, and related to the first, it may help to explain some of the puzzles about vicarious emotions. Finally, it helps to explain why there is sometimes a time lag between the experience of some highly valenced situation and the experience of a related emotion.

Our claim is not that emotions can only result from affective reactions to "real" things, but rather, that, other things being equal, the intensity of any emotion will be increased to the degree that the object of the emotion seems real to the person experiencing the emotion. Consider the reaction an aspiring novelist might have to thinking about writing a best-seller. To the extent that the person believes this to be a real possibility he or she is likely to have a stronger reaction than if it is recognized to be sheer fantasy. This is why recollections of past emotion-inducing situations are more likely to lead to the experience of emotions than the imagination of possible ones. Recollections of past emotion-inducing situations are recollections of situations that existed, thus, they are generally endowed with a greater sense of reality than merely imagined ones. In this connection, we suspect that it is the sense of reality variable that permits people to "experience" vivid emotions in and after dreams. However bizarre dreams may be, they seem very real when they are being experienced. Thus, because of the greater sense of reality, we would expect the emotions resulting from a dreamed emotion-inducing situation (dreamed emotions, as they may be) to be more intense than those resulting from the same situation merely imagined in a normal waking state.

In much the same way as for dreams, it can be argued that the sense of reality variable plays a major role in vicarious emotions. When one reads a novel or watches a movie, one sometimes experiences emotions as an observer of the depicted situations. Our proposal is that such emotions are experienced to the degree that the stimulating fantasy succeeds in inducing a sense of reality in the reader or viewer. A discussion of the mechanisms (e.g., identification) whereby this happens are beyond the scope of this book. For our purposes, it is sufficient to note that it is a factor that contributes to the intensification of emotions and that if the potential emotion does not reach some threshold value, there will be no experience of an emotion corresponding to it.

Doonesbury   BY GARRY TRUDEAU

It is a common experience of people who unexpectedly find themselves in extremely positive or negative situations that it takes a while for the full impact of the situation to "hit" them – they become temporarily "cognitively anesthetized." This is the same syndrome that Bowlby (1980) refers to as "numbing" in the context of the loss of loved ones. In such situations people are simply unable or unwilling to believe what has happened, and they frequently say so. One explanation of this phenomenon is that the situation in question fails to produce a sufficient sense of reality for the person to accept it immediately. Once accepted, things change dramatically and the person begins to work out in more detail the full repercussions of the situation. We shall have more to say of this aspect in the last section of this chapter.

The emotional consequences of people's inability to accept situations as real, even in the face of incontrovertible evidence, has been documented in a laboratory study reported by Bridger and Mandel (1964). They found that subjects, once conditioned to respond to an electric shock following a tone, continued to exhibit physiological (GSR) evidence of apprehension in response to the tone, even after the electrodes had been removed and they had been told that no more shocks would be administered. A reasonable interpretation of this finding is that subjects were simply insufficiently confident that a threat no longer existed, in spite of protestations to the contrary by the experimenter (Dawson, 1973), or, in our terms, that the contribution of the sense of reality variable to the intensity of subjects' fear was so (inappropriately) high that it sustained their fear.

Proximity. Emotion-inducing situations tend to give rise to more intense emotions when they are close in time than when they are more remote. This factor is related to, but not the same as, the sense of reality variable. One reason we include it is that we want to acknowledge that memories of past emotion-inducing situations can give rise to emotions just as the experience of present ones can. However, as these situations recede into the past, the intensity of the corresponding emotions diminishes. The proximity variable also influences the intensity of emotions that can involve future situations, specifically, the Prospect-based emotions such as fear. The nearer in time the prospect being entertained is, the more intense the emotion. In fact, this has been documented empirically in a number of studies of fear (Breznitz, 1984) and is discussed in more detail in Chapter 6.

We have already implied that there is a close connection between the proximity variable and the sense of reality variable. One can see this by considering the fact that experiences in the remote past no longer seem as real to people as they did when they were experienced, and beliefs about the future remain subject to unanticipated changes that might result in the future events never materializing. However, this close connection does not mean that they are identical. Sometimes they work in opposite directions. Consider the case of a person who is "cognitively anesthetized" at discovering the murdered body of a loved one. In such a case, we would want to argue that the initial muteness of emotional reaction might result from the person's inability to believe that what he sees has really happened. However, the proximity is very high, even though the sense of reality may be low. Thus, there certainly can be cases in which situations that are subjectively very proximate can still be lacking with respect to the sense of reality associated with them. There can also be cases in which the sense of reality might be quite strong, even though proximity is not very high. Here we have in mind cases in which a vivid image of some possible, although temporally remote, event makes it seem very real. It may well be that various kinds of phobias – for example, fear of flying – depend for their potency on just such factors. It is for reasons such as these that we think it advisable to maintain a distinction between the two variables.

Although we have framed our discussion of the proximity variable in terms of temporal proximity, we do not wish to restrict it to that. Rather, the variable should be construed in terms of *psychological* proximity, that is, in terms of the *feeling* of closeness, be it temporal, spatial, or any other kind. So, for example, a person living in a small rural town in the American Midwest might be more likely to experience an emotional reaction with respect to the prospect of catching some deadly disease such as AIDS if others close to him were affected, than if he believed the disease to only affect people in remote urban areas such as New York and San Francisco. The reason our discussion focused on temporal proximity is that it provides the clearest case in which one can distinguish between the effects of the proximity variable and those of the sense of reality variable, but physical or

geographical proximity, as well as simply the feeling of psychological closeness, work in essentially the same way.

Unexpectedness. The notion of unexpectedness is widely recognized as being
important for emotions. It is, however, a much more complicated construct
than is generally recognized in cognitive science. In general, unexpectedness
is positively correlated with the intensity of the emotion. Other things being
equal, unexpected positive things are evaluated more positively than expected ones, and unexpected negative things, more negatively than expected
ones (e.g., Feather, 1967; Spector, 1956; Verinis, Brandsma, & Cofer,
1978). What makes unexpectedness complicated is that it can manifest itself
in many different ways. For example, as we shall discuss later in this chapter,
in the Attribution emotions unexpectedness manifests itself in terms of violations of role-based or person-based expectations.

For Event-based emotions, unexpectedness manifests itself in terms of
event types. What this means is that the intensity of Event-based emotions
is influenced by the unexpectedness of an event of the type that is encountered. It is important to distinguish this from a different but related local
variable – *likelihood* – which affects the intensity of only the Prospect-based
emotions (fear, relief, etc.) and pertains to particular events rather than to
types of events. To see the difference between unexpectedness and likelihood, imagine that two countries are at war. Somebody is lying in bed in
her darkened house during an air raid, listening to bombs exploding in the
distance. She is actively thinking about the possibility of her house being
hit, but, being brave or foolish, she confidently concludes that her house is
too far from military targets and that it will not be hit. Such a person has in
fact entertained two mutually exclusive possibilities (that she will be hit and
that she won't) and concluded that one is much more likely than the other.
Now suppose she is wrong, and her house is hit. The woman is going to be
surprised, and her surprise will be a direct result of a genuine expectation
violation – her active expectation that the house would not be hit was violated. In this case, the degree of her surprise is determined by the likelihood variable – it will be determined by how likely she thought it was that
her house would not be hit.

The sense of unexpectedness of concern to us here is, however, quite
different from the kind of active expectation failure we have just discussed.
To use an example along the same lines, imagine a situation in which some
other woman in some other country not involved in any kind of conflict is
lying in bed in her darkened house trying to go to sleep. Suddenly, without
warning, a bomb hits her house. In this case there is no violation of an
active expectation. The woman had no active expectation that her house

would not be hit by a bomb – she had no expectations about bombs, one way or the other. Yet, she would surely be very surprised, and she would be surprised because the event was (totally) unexpected, not because she had mispredicted. In this case we cannot say that her degree of surprise depends on how likely she thinks it is that her house will be hit by a bomb, because, having never thought about it, she has not attached a subjective likelihood to the event at all. Thus, unexpectedness and likelihood are not the same variable (Ortony & Partridge, 1987). Likelihood has to do with anticipated events and is forward-looking. Unexpectedness is assessed *after* an event, and is backward-looking. However, unexpectedness should not be thought of simply in terms of retrospective judgments about subjective probabilities. Kahneman and Miller (1986) offer convincing evidence that judgments about abnormality are often more potent. Events that are, for all practical purposes, subjectively equiprobable (e.g., being shot in a store one frequently visits, as opposed to being shot in a store one rarely visits), yield differential (affectively relevant) judgments (e.g., how much compensation is deserved, how much sympathy is due) as a function of the perceived normality of the situation. A detailed model of how retrospective judgments of unexpectedness and normalcy might be made can be found in Kahneman and Miller's (1986) Norm theory.

Arousal. The variables we have discussed so far are primarily cognitive in nature. The last global variable we shall discuss, physiological arousal, is not cognitive, but it certainly has important effects on a variety of cognitive processes and products. In the past, arousal has often carried a great explanatory burden in theories of emotion. We, on the other hand, have comparatively little to say about it, concentrating instead on the cognitive and computational aspects of emotion elicitation. Nevertheless, one could assume that the outcome of the cognitive appraisal processes we envision is also registered physiologically as arousal, so that changes in one's level of arousal may be roughly proportional to the subjective importance of an emotional situation. As discussed in the last chapter, this can be thought of as the sum of the absolute (unsigned) values of the perceived desirability and undesirability of an event, the praiseworthiness and blameworthiness of an action, or the appealingness and unappealingness of an object. However, other intensity variables, such as unexpectedness, probably also influence the level of arousal, so that emotional intensity could be seen as more or less the same thing as the arousal produced in the emotional situation. But arousal of the autonomic nervous system has two important properties that complicate matters. Specifically, level of arousal can be elevated by non-emotional as well as by emotional causes, and arousal has a relatively slow rate of decay, so that it can carry forward in time from its cause and be mistakenly experienced as part of one's reaction to a subsequent event. In this way, background arousal from other sources can blend with arousal from the emotional situation, leading to reactions that are more intense than the situation would otherwise induce.

Zillman and his colleagues have shown that people's ratings of the extent to which stimuli are humorous or erotic can change as a result of externally induced arousal. A prerequisite for the effect, however, is that subjects be *unaware* of the source of their arousal. For example, in one experiment Cantor, Bryant, and Zillman (1974) induced arousal through physical exercise and found that erotic pictures were rated as more erotic when assessed four minutes after the exercise (when subjects no longer realized that they were still aroused by the exercise) than when assessed either immediately after exercise (when arousal and awareness of it were greater) or ten minutes later (when exercise-induced arousal had dissipated). In this, and a number of related studies, Zillman has shown that preexisting arousal states intensify reactions to affective stimuli. Whether the arousal is incorporated into and changes the emotional experience of the event itself or whether it intensifies only the report or evaluation of the experience is not completely clear. We are inclined to share Zillman's view that such arousal states influence the emotional experiences themselves.

As an explanation of the effects of arousal (and other feelings as well) on judgment, it has been proposed (e.g., Schwarz & Clore, 1983) that feelings affect judgment because they provide information about the outcome of the experiencer's own appraisal processes. But exactly what it is that particular feelings provide information about depends on how one parses the flow of experience (Martin, 1983). To influence the intensity of an emotional state, the feelings must be experienced as part of one's reaction to the emotion-inducing situation. The arousal may or may not be a reaction to that situation; what is important is that it appear to the experiencer to be. By the same principle, arousal that has already been attributed to another source should have no effect on subsequent judgments, actions, or emotions. In other words, the role of arousal is not necessarily automatic. The existing experimental evidence is quite consistent with this hypothesis, but it may not be immediately obvious that it handles all of the everyday emotional situations that one can think of. Consider, for example, the likely reaction of a person encountering a series of problems while attempting to prepare breakfast for his family. If the person forgets to start the coffee soon enough or burns the toast or overcooks the eggs or all of these, we would not be surprised to see behavioral evidence of frustration and arousal. The person might slam cupboard doors, respond curtly to family members, or utter irrational statements about hiring a catering service to cook all the meals.

Assuming that the cook accurately sees the source of his arousal as the half-perked coffee, the burnt toast, and the overdone eggs, however, why would this arousal lead him to slam doors and speak rudely to innocent people? Are such occurrences problematic for the attribution hypothesis? Ultimately they are not, but they do require explanation. It should be noted, for example, that experiments testing the hypothesis generally involved attributions to relatively discrete, external stimuli, such as exercise (Cantor, Bryant, & Zillman, 1974), alcohol (McCarty, Diamond, & Kaye, 1982), or drugs (Zanna & Cooper, 1974). In everyday situations, by contrast, it may be rare to have available a plausible cause for one's feelings that is so isolable from the rest of one's life situation. Even in our apparently simple breakfast example, it is implausible that anyone would really attribute their feelings of frustration to the burned toast by itself. Toast gets burned because of human error. The responsibility may fall at the feet of others, including those who manufacture cheap toasters, those who expect him to cook in a disorganized kitchen, and those who are too inconsiderate to get up in time to help with breakfast. Or the cook may see the responsibility as his own. He may see the failure as implicating his inexperience at cooking breakfast, his ineptitude at cooking in general, or even his complete and utter incompetence at anything he tries to do. Indeed, to the extent that the failure in the kitchen activates scripts about personal failure and inadequacy, conflicts about family responsibilities and marital expectations, or both, there might be few targets that would fall outside the shadow of the resulting frustration and arousal. The point of all this is to show that the clear demarcation that can be made in the laboratory between reactions that should and reactions that should not be intensified are probably less easily made in everyday uncontrolled situations.

We have said that to the extent that the experiencer correctly attributes preexisting arousal to its true cause, it should have no effect on subsequent emotional reactions. But an important instance in which preexisting arousal would influence subsequent emotions even when correctly attributed to its source, is the case of sequences of emotional reactions to the same situation. A common instance of such a sequence is when one is first frustrated and then becomes angry. It is common to react with the emotion of frustration to the goal-disruption aspects of a negative event and then perhaps with reproach at the blameworthiness of the person responsible for the event. People often regret their angry outbursts when, after the initial arousal of frustration has diminished, they see that the judged blameworthiness of the agent by itself did not justify the intensity of their response. At that point they are likely to feel sheepish, embarrassed, and apologetic. The reputation of the anger emotions as particularly troublesome, irrational, and intense may owe something to this sort of process. The old admonition to count to ten before responding when angry presumably rests on a recognition that momentary arousal both heightens subsequent emotional reactions and dissipates over time.

Local Variables

We turn now to a consideration of a number of variables that have only local effects, that is, variables that can only affect the intensity of particular groups of emotions, rather than all emotions in all groups, as the global variables can. We have already discussed three of these local variables, namely, the central variables of *desirability, praiseworthiness,* and *appealingness.* As we shall see in the next four chapters, each emotion type is characterized formally by what we call a "type specification." A type specification always includes one of the three central variables as a defining variable that identifies the emotion as an Event-based emotion (if the defining variable is desirability), an Attribution emotion (if the defining variable is praiseworthiness), or an Attraction emotion (if the defining variable is appealingness). For example, the type specification for the Joy emotions involves a *desirable* event as a necessary condition, and the type specification for the Pride emotions involves a *praiseworthy* action. The desirability and praiseworthiness variables are local variables in the sense that the desirability variable affects the intensity of Event-based emotions such as joy, but not of Agent-based (Attribution) emotions such as pride, and the praiseworthiness variable affects the intensity of Agent-based emotions but not of Event-based emotions. Appealingness is similarly local to just the Object-based (Attraction) emotions. However, the intensity with which a particular emotion (for example, pride) is felt depends on the combined effects not only of the values of its defining central variable, but also on the values of other intensity variables which are not themselves part of the type specification of the particular emotion.

One of the sources of distinctiveness for the different emotion groups in our system is the particular set of local variables with which each is associated. For example, the Prospect-based emotions all involve the local variable of *likelihood* and some of them involve additional variables such as *effort.* Part of the distinctiveness of these emotions (see Chapter 6) lies in the fact that only they are influenced by unique configurations of their local variables. Similarly, in the Fortunes-of-others emotions (see Chapter 5), the degree to which the other person is perceived as *deserving* the desirable

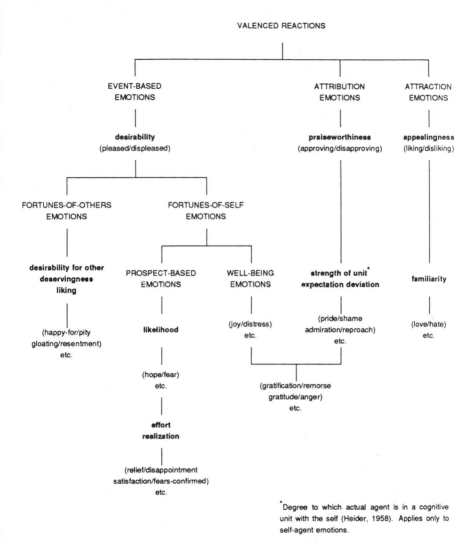

Figure 4.1. Global structure of local intensity variables.

or undesirable consequences of the event is a local variable. We shall start our discussion of local variables by taking a rather general view of their effects, examining in particular which variables are related to which groups with respect to the overall structure that we presented in Figure 2.1. This structure is replicated in Figure 4.1, but this time it depicts which variables are introduced in association with which groups of emotions.

We focus first on the Event-based emotions. As we have already indicated, all the Event-based emotions involve the desirability variable, and this is shown in the figure by having the variable *desirability* appear before the branch splits into Fortunes-of-self and Fortunes-of-others emotions. The guiding principle in interpreting Figure 4.1 is that it represents an inheritance hierarchy – every variable affects all the emotions and emotion groups below it. The variables themselves are represented in the figure in lowercase bold print. The emotion classes and individual groups are indicated in upper case, and representative emotion token words appear in parentheses as reminders to the reader of the kind of emotion types that fall into each group. As we have already explained, the Well-being emotions, which appear in Figure 4.1 on the right-hand branch under the Event-based emotions, are basically undifferentiated forms of being *pleased* and *displeased*, so that no additional (local) variables are introduced by them. We can therefore move directly to a discussion of the variables that are local to the Prospect-based emotions.

Likelihood. The general idea behind this variable was just introduced in our discussion of unexpectedness. We now consider the way in which it typically contributes to the intensity of emotions that we (loosely) call *hope* and *fear*. Suppose you are walking along a dark alley at night and you hear quickening footsteps behind you and you start to worry about being mugged. Other things being equal, the more likely you think it is that the person intends to mug you, the more intense is the fear you are likely to feel. This is the sense of *likelihood* that we intend to capture when, in the figure, we show the Prospect-based emotions as introducing it. Notice that this variable appears before hope and fear in the figure. Because hope and fear are based only on the prospect of an event (as opposed to also involving the confirmation/disconfirmation component), likelihood is the only variable that they introduce. The intensity of emotions such as hope depends in part on the person's confidence that the desired state will be achieved (although the case of hope is somewhat complicated, as is discussed in Chapter 6). Similarly, with fear, the intensity depends in part on how likely the person thinks it is that the feared situation will arise. In general, likelihood estimates are not constant over time. Sometimes they increase, sometimes they decrease. As a first approximation, one might conceive of the contribution of these likelihood estimates to emotional intensity as depending on the value of the estimate at the particular time the evaluation of the state occurs.

Simply speaking of likelihood "estimates" is somewhat misleading. First, such estimates are not necessarily conscious. Second, they are probably not "computed" very accurately, being more likely to be comparative and qualitative than absolute and quantitative. When we say that likelihood estimates need not be conscious, we mean that very often people do not even think about how likely the prospect of some event is. Rather, their behavior is compatible with their believing that it is possible that the situation will arise. Nor is it necessary to suppose that people go about the world computing values for likelihood estimates. It may be sufficient to suppose that they hold only qualitative beliefs; for example, that some particular event is very likely to occur, or that one event is more likely to occur than another. Sometimes, of course, people need to make more accurate estimates and, as has been frequently shown (see, e.g., Nisbett & Ross, 1980; Tversky & Kahneman, 1974), when they do, their subjective estimates are often not very closely tied to the objective probabilities. While this is an interesting fact, it has no impact on our claim that subjective estimates of likelihood (even crude, qualitative ones) often influence the intensity of an emotion. People perceive the world – for better or for worse, rightly or wrongly – the way that they do, and their behavior and emotions are influenced by their perceptions. The emotions are not "rational," but for most people they are not randomly related to their perceptions either. Because we seek to characterize the governing principles underlying the cognitive elicitation and intensification of emotions, we cannot ignore the explicit or implicit beliefs that people may have about such things as what will happen in the future, or how things might have turned out differently.

Returning to Figure 4.1, we can now consider the variables introduced for the remaining Prospect-based emotions, namely those emotions having to do with reactions to the confirmation or disconfirmation of the kinds of prospects that lead to hope and fear. First, however, we need to remember that the effect of the likelihood variable is inherited by the emotions represented as being below it in the Figure, although, as will become apparent in our more detailed discussion of the Event-based emotions, it is inherited through the intensity of the associated hope or fear.

Effort. If one fails to achieve something after trying very hard to achieve it, any ensuing disappointment is likely to be greater than if one fails after trying less hard. For example, the man who misses his flight after running as fast as he can through an airport to catch it will probably be more disappointed than the man who invests less effort in the attempt. This is because the *effort* invested influences the intensity of the emotion. Our notion of effort is a very general one. It is intended to include what Heider (1958) called *exertion* (i.e., physical or mental effort) as well as more materialistic kinds of investment (e.g., financial cost). Generally speaking, when effort is a factor, the greater the effort invested, the more intense the emotion. Thus, when the effort invested in trying to achieve a desirable outcome increases, disappointment is stronger if the effort is unsuccessful, and relief is stronger if it is successful. This formulation of the effect of the effort variable intentionally subsumes attempting to avoid an undesirable outcome under attempting to attain a desirable one so that, when the effort invested in trying to avoid an undesirable outcome increases, relief is stronger if the effort is successful and disappointment is stronger if it is unsuccessful. In other words, the intensity-influencing effects of the effort variable can involve either the effort that was invested in trying to attain something desirable, or the effort that was invested in trying to avoid something undesirable. We do not want to imply a linear relationship between emotional intensity and effort (or any other variable for that matter). In fact the relevant variables seem to interact in complex ways, depending in part upon their respective values, and in part upon the particular emotions involved. So, for example, it is clear that people are likely to invest more effort in order to attain goals that they deem highly desirable than they are in attempting to attain goals that they consider less desirable. In general, a person who has lost a wallet containing all his credit cards and hundreds of dollars in cash is likely to invest more effort in trying to find it than someone whose wallet contained only a one-dollar bill.

There is another important relation between effort and desirability that needs to be noted. Whereas desirability is associated with consequences of events, which ultimately means states or possible states, effort is associated with the implementation of plans. Suppose someone (being appropriately deranged) has "becoming a professor" as one of his goals. He knows that in order to achieve this goal, he has to get a Ph.D., which thus becomes a subgoal. The desirability of getting a Ph.D. in such a situation is determined by its relation to its subsuming goal(s), which thus imposes an upper bound on its desirability – if the only purpose of getting a Ph.D. is to become a professor, it cannot have greater desirability than that of becoming a professor. Thus, desirability is like (subjective) intrinsic value and is accordingly independent of the (anticipated) effort. Effort, on the other hand, depends on what one actually *does* in order to achieve one's goal(s). It relates to the implementation and execution of plans to achieve goals rather than to the goals themselves. If we assume that effort involves the utilization of a valued limited resource, then, when effort is expended in achieving (or attempting to achieve) a goal, the value of the effort expended can sometimes be added to the value of achieving the goal. At the same time, it might reduce the availability of that resource for the achievement of other goals, which itself may have negative value. In this sense, expended effort may influence the desirability of an achieved state, so that something achieved, like the Ph.D., may seem more valuable because it involved a great deal of effort and concomitant sacrifice with respect to other goals that may have been competing for it.

The empirical prediction that follows from this is that the desirability of a state that has been achieved may sometimes be greater than its desirability prior to its achievement, and possibly even greater than a not yet achieved superordinate goal whose attainment it facilitates. This claim is consistent with those made by cognitive dissonance theorists, who have found that increases in effort tend to increase the degree to which goals are positively valued (see, e.g., Aronson & Mills, 1959; Gerard & Mathewson, 1966). Note that this is not the same situation as arises when a difference in the expected value and the actual value of a state results from a person's "miscalculating" the value in the first place (e.g., a child who is disappointed when he finally gets his dream toy because it turns out not to be all that it was cracked up to be). This latter kind of discrepancy is not of great theoretical interest because it merely represents the consequences of an inaccurate (or incomplete) appraisal, whereas the case we are discussing involves no subjective errors. The possibility we are raising here is that the desirability of a goal can increase as a result of effort expended in the implementation of plans to achieve it. The determination of the truth of this conjecture, and of the conditions under which it happens (if it does happen) remains as a research question to be investigated empirically.

Effort is not always independent of likelihood – one often expends effort precisely because one believes one can change likelihood. In such cases, one can think of the effort as *instrumental*. When a student studies hard to do well in a course, the effort is invested presumably because the student thinks that the likelihood of doing well in the course will be increased. There are cases, however, in which the expenditure of effort is not instrumental. For example, a person who expects to take a vacation might expend effort in preparing for it without believing that the effort being expended will increase the likelihood of the vacation. However, noninstrumental effort, just like instrumental effort, can affect the intensity of emotions such as relief and disappointment. So, if the vacation plans fall through, the person's disappointment would be increased not only as a function of the amount of (noninstrumental) effort that was invested in preparation for it, but also as a function of the amount of (instrumental) effort invested in trying to make the vacation a reality. Thus, instrumental effort pertains to plans (actual or possible) for achieving (or avoiding) states, whereas noninstrumental effort pertains to plans (actual or possible) that are related to the state, but that are carried out on the assumption that the state will be achieved.

Realization. The last variable introduced under Prospect-based emotions involving confirmation or disconfirmation (satisfaction, relief, fears-confirmed, and disappointment) is one that we have labeled *realization* in Figure 4.1. This variable reflects the degree to which the confirmed or disconfirmed event is realized, and for this reason, it depends critically upon the kind of goal involved, specifically, whether it is a partially attainable goal or an all-or-none goal (see Chapter 3). Consider first the case of a partially realizable goal: Suppose that a man is trying to get his lawn mowed before darkness falls. He can make more or less progress, and the degree of progress he makes can influence the intensity of any resulting emotions. If he succeeds in getting a lot of it done before it gets dark, one might expect him to be less disappointed than if he gets only a little done. As a first approximation, one might propose that for partially attainable goals, if the degree of realization is high the related positive emotions will be more intense and any related negative ones less intense. Similarly, one might think that if the degree of realization is low any related positive emotions will be less intense and related negative ones more intense. In fact, however, we have to be careful here because the relation between the degree of realization and emotional intensity for partially attainable goals is not necessarily monotonic. It may be more disappointing to have some goal almost but not completely achieved than to have it only partially achieved. Here, however, we shall treat the realization variable as though its effects were monotonic. Our explanation for the possibility that, at the limit, the failure to complete a partially attainable goal might intensify an emotion such as disappointment is that, when one gets close to completion, other more general goals having to do with the desire for closure become activated. The result is that the desirability of attaining the original goal is increased because it now implicates other goals that were not previously active.

We can now compare this with the case of an all-or-none goal such as making a tight connection at an airport. Again, consider the anxious passenger running through an airport to catch a plane. He either does reach the gate in time, or he does not. In such cases, it might be thought that the realization variable really does not make much sense because there cannot be degrees of realization for all-or-none goals. However, in the case of all-or-none goals, the realization variable is intended to capture the psychological feeling of having almost achieved the goal or of it having been not even close. In this sense, the realization variable is the same as Kahneman and Tversky's (1982) notion of the ease of imagining an alternative outcome, an issue they discuss in the context of what they call "counterfactual" emotions. The effect of this variable on intensity is quite different for all-or-none goals than for partially attainable goals. For all-or-none goals, increases in the degree of realization result in decreases in the intensity of attendant positive emotions, and increases in the intensity of attendant negative ones. Given that the hurrying passenger in fact does not make his connection, the closer he gets to catching the plane the more intense will be his disappointment. Similarly, if he does make it, the closer he thinks he came to missing it, the more intense the relief.

Desirability-for-other. We turn now to the first of the three variables introduced by the Fortunes-of-others emotions. These emotions (e.g., resentment, gloating, happy-for, pity) are all concerned with reactions to events seen as being desirable or undesirable for some other person, and the degree to which the event is seen as being *desirable for the other* person is one of the factors that affects the intensity of the emotion felt by the person reacting to another's fortunes or misfortunes. In general, we have to suppose that there are two possible ways in which a person can evaluate the degree to which he supposes some event is desirable for the (other) affected person. One possibility is that he employs a model of the other person's goals and on the basis of that model, using a simplified version of the kind of mechanisms discussed in Chapter 3, he estimates how desirable the event is. Alternatively, the person can reason by analogy from knowledge of his own goals and concerns, and infer that, to the extent that the affected person is similar to him, that person will find the event desirable or undesirable to a comparable degree. In such cases, the inferences can often be invalid. For example, reasoning by analogy from how we think we would feel, it is easy to conclude that malnourished children in developing countries will find their plight extremely undesirable – we would. However, it is not at all clear that such children evaluate their situations in terms of the same set of goals and concerns that we do, and consequently, it is not clear that they in fact find their situation undesirable at all. The intensity of our emotions in response to perceptions of their situations are influenced, however, by *our* evaluations about how desirable or undesirable their situations are for them, not by *their* evaluations. The point is simply that the use of a model of their goals and aspirations, to the degree that the model is accurate, is likely to lead to a better fit between our evaluations and theirs than is an inference based on the assumption that their goals are basically the same as ours. The effect of the (presumed) desirability-for-other variable can be seen easily by considering a situation in which one feels sorry for a woman on reading that her husband was killed in a brawl. One assumes that she, like most of us, would find such an event extremely distressing. However, if further information reveals that she had been the recipient of continual physical abuse by her alcoholic husband, and that she considered the event to be desirable, we would presumably no longer feel pity for her, at least, not with respect to the event of having her husband die.

Liking. The degree of *liking* one has for the other person can also contribute to the intensity of the Fortunes-of-others emotions. For example, somebody else's good fortune is more likely to result in one feeling happy for that person if he or she is a friend whom one likes a great deal rather than merely an acquaintance for whom one has no strong feelings. Two quite different senses of "liking" need to be distinguished, one a dispositional sense, and the other a momentary sense. We discuss this distinction in more detail in Chapter 8. For the moment, we need say little more than that it is the momentary sense of liking that we view as an intensity variable. The degree to which one likes a person at the time that he or she is the object of one's emotions is clearly partly determined by one's dispositional liking for the person, and, on some occasions, there may be no difference between the two. In the case of particular people, which is the focus of the Fortunes-of-others emotions, dispositional liking means that one is disposed to experience momentary liking in the course of some direct personal, or indirect nonpersonal, interaction with them. Thus, a voter might like both of two politicians (possibly only on the basis of indirect nonpersonal interactions with them, such as reading newspaper reports, or watching them on television) while liking one better than the other. Because of this preference for one over the other, the voter could feel more pity when his preferred politician failed to be elected than when the less preferred one did.

Finally, in this connection we should point out that momentary liking or disliking can itself be an emotion if the intensity is high enough – that is what the Attraction emotions are all about. There is nothing problematic about this, however. There are no ex cathedra constraints on the kinds of things that can be intensity variables.

Deservingness. In emotions that involve reacting to the good- or ill-fortunes of others, it is clear that the reactions are greatly influenced by one's perceptions of the degree to which the event affecting the other person is fair or deserved. *Deservingness*, like all the other variables, is always from the point of view of the person experiencing the emotion. People who gloat at all (and many of us, of course, do not), gloat more if they think the unfortunate other deserves whatever misfortunes befall him or her. A tennis player might be secretly pleased that her opponent was not playing up to par, but she might not gloat if she discovered that the reason for the uncharacteristically poor performance was that her opponent's family had all been killed in an accident. Although people might disagree about what is just and what is unjust, most people believe that the world should be just, and this belief seems to be applied with respect to the fortunes and misfortunes that befall others as well as to our own fate. Deservingness can probably be operationalized in terms of some function of how much the person affected by the event is liked and how desirable (or undesirable) one takes the event to be for them. It is, however, a complicated issue worthy of a book in its own right – albeit a book that will not be written by us.

So far, we have discussed the local variables introduced by the Event-based emotions. The Attribution emotions introduce their own set of local variables. Foremost among these, of course, is *praiseworthiness* (including its negative counterpart, blameworthiness), which we have already discussed. In addition, Figure 4.1 shows two other variables as being introduced here, *strength of (cognitive) unit*, and *expectation deviation*. Both of these need considerable elaboration.

Strength of cognitive unit. Although in typical cases of emotions such as pride and shame, the person who experiences the emotion is the direct agent of a praiseworthy or blameworthy action, this is not a necessary condition for the experience of these emotions. In many cases such emotions result not directly from the contribution of the experiencing individual but indirectly as a result of the individual's association with some other person or group. For example, a person might feel proud when the institution with which he or she is affiliated is nationally recognized for its excellence, and that person would feel more proud if he or she felt a strong affiliation with the institution than if he or she felt a weaker one. The purpose of the *cognitive unit* variable is to accommodate cases in which the person experiencing the emotion is not the actual agent even though the emotion is characterized as involving the self (i.e., the person experiencing the emotion) as the formal agent. In general, the stronger the cognitive unit bond (for example, the closer one feels to the actual agent of the action) the more intense the emotion. This raises the important general question of the manner in which the notion of the self has to be construed in a theory of emotion.

According to Heider (1958), a cognitive unit gets formed when one perceives things as somehow belonging together. Such "unit formation" is a familiar notion in Gestalt accounts of perception (Koffka, 1935; Wertheimer, 1923). Unit formation is a highly context-sensitive phenomenon. Heider puts the matter like this: "If a New Yorker and a Bostonian meet in a party composed half of New Yorkers and half of Bostonians, they will very likely feel that they belong to different units. But if they meet in a party in which no one else is American, they will feel that they belong together." (Heider, 1958; p. 179). Various factors determine whether someone forms a cognitive unit with some other(s), but the most important aspect of unit formation is its context-sensitivity. In some contexts one may believe that one is in (or may be compelled to admit that one is in) a unit, as when a German might feel embarrassed about the activities of the Nazis in the 1930s and 1940s, even though he was neither a Nazi himself, nor sympathized with the Nazis. In other cases, one may exaggerate one's relation to some other person or people and see oneself in a unit that others might regard as quite tenuous. The upshot of all of this is that we define the (formal) self in the context of the agents of actions to be *the self, or some other(s) with whom one perceives oneself to be in a unit*. Thus, when we say that pride involves approving of one's own praiseworthy action, we mean that one can be proud of such an action by others with whom one considers oneself to be in a cognitive unit. This means that we have a distinction between the *formal* agent and the *actual* agent. When the actual agent is viewed as being in a unit with the person experiencing the emotion, the actual agent will be some other person although the formal agent remains the self.

The need to appeal to the notion of a cognitive unit wherein the self is viewed as some kind of extension of the actual agent of the action is applicable only to the Attribution emotions, for which – formally – the self is the agent (i.e., Pride emotions and Reproach emotions). In the context of these emotions, a sort of "converging" notion of self is employed, in which certain others can be viewed as the self. Interestingly, as we shall discuss in more detail in our discussion of the Fortunes-of-others emotions in the next chapter, we sometimes need to employ a "diverging" notion of the self, in which the person experiencing the emotion views what is happening to him as though he were another person. To take a simple example, pity is viewed as a form of distress at the misfortunes of another person. When one views one's own misfortunes as though they were those of someone else, self-pity results. The point of this observation is to emphasize the fact that if one uses a sufficiently flexible notion of the self one can explain the relationship between such things as self-focused pride and other-focused pride, self-focused pity and other-focused pity.

The dynamics of unit formation and dissolution have received surprisingly little attention from social psychologists. Such research as there is (e.g., Cialdini, Borden, Thorne, Walker, Freeman, & Sloan, 1976; Cialdini & Richardson, 1980) has tended to account for unit formation in terms of Heider's balance theory coupled with ideas about self-presentation or image management. Other factors are also likely to be relevant, at least to public claims of allegiance or association (i.e., of unit membership). Thus, insofar as a person claims to be in some kind of unit with others who might be negatively evaluated, a desire for public approbation would have to be considered as only a secondary influence. So, Mr. Jones, for example, having once announced that he was a long-time neighbor of a recently discovered war criminal, might feel obliged to hurriedly explain that he had never been particularly friendly with his neighbor. Public interest and attention would be enhanced by reporting the connection while, at the same time public disapproval would be avoided by denying too close a relationship.

Expectation-deviation. The variable we loosely call expectation-deviation has already been discussed in the context of unexpectedness. We include it here because it has a special manifestation in the Attribution emotions – namely, it is manifested in terms of deviations from expectations about what could normally be expected of this person, of such a person, or of a person in such a role. This is why, in the formal presentation of the Attribution emotions in Chapter 7, we refer to this variable as "deviations from person/role-based expectations." For example, one would probably admire a store clerk who dove into a river and saved a drowning child more than one would admire a life guard who did the same thing because such an action is much less unexpected when performed by a life guard than when performed by a sales clerk. Thus, for the Attribution emotions unexpectedness is manifested as deviations from role and person expectations, that is, as deviations from what we would expect of people in the particular role in which they are or in which we cast them, or deviations from expectations based upon what we know or believe about the individual person.

Role and person expectations are expectations that pertain to actions or *action types*, and thus are particularly relevant to the Attribution emotions. This is because role and person representations are, in fact, little more than sets of expectations about either individuals as types, individuals in certain capacities, or types of individuals in certain capacities. This is why we are not surprised at a boxer punching an opponent in the ring (which is a role-consistent action), and why we would be surprised at a priest punching a parishioner during communion (which would be a role-inconsistent action). When we construe the actions of the person who is the boxer as, for example, the actions of a father, we are no longer viewing the individual in his boxer role, but are viewing him in his father role, which, of course, carries with it a different set of expectations. One can think of roles as the social analogs of traits. Roles embody expectations about people viewed as members of classes constructed in terms of socially defined activities, whereas traits embody expectations about people viewed as individuals.

Before concluding this brief introduction to the expectation-deviation variable, a word or two needs to be said as to why it has been included. As discussed at the beginning of the chapter, the principle upon which the inclusion of intensity variables is based is that legitimate variables should be capable of having an *independent* effect on the intensity of emotions. This does not mean that they always have an independent effect, but only that they can. In the context of expectation-deviation, it might be thought that the variable always and only has its effect through the central variable of praiseworthiness, and if this were correct, then it would violate the rule for inclusion as a local variable. It is possible that this is the case, however, we are not sufficiently confident that it is to exclude it. Our reasoning for this conclusion is that in many cases the standards in terms of which praiseworthiness is assessed are viewed by people as *absolute* standards, especially if they are moral standards such as PEOPLE OUGHT NOT TO KILL ONE AN-OTHER. If this is right, then the blameworthiness of, for example, a murder would be independent of who it was who committed the murder. So – and in this context, this is an important caveat – if the only standard that is invoked in appraising a murder is PEOPLE OUGHT NOT TO KILL ONE ANOTHER, then it would be no less *blameworthy* for a serial murderer to kill someone as for a nun to do so. Furthermore, this would hold even though the *emotion* (say, contempt) that one might feel towards the nun might be more intense than it would be towards a serial murderer. According to this account, murder is wrong, and that is that.

If we assume that the degree of blameworthiness of an act such as killing someone can be independent of who it is that commits it, there remain two ways to account for any differences in intensity of emotional reaction that might result when one considers such an act performed by a nun as opposed to by a serial murderer. One of these ways has to do with the caveat that we emphasized a moment ago. It is entirely possible that in the case of the nun one *would* invoke additional standards (for example standards having to do with trust) and these would then make their own additional contribution to the value of the praiseworthiness variable. The other, and in the context of the present discussion, the more important way is that the intensity of the emotion could be increased directly, and independently, by the expectation-deviation variable (as a particular type of unexpectedness), rather than indirectly through the praiseworthiness variable. It is because we consider this to be a real possibility that we include the expectation-deviation variable as an independent local variable for the Attribution emotions.

Familiarity. Finally, the Attraction emotions are shown as introducing only one local variable – apart, of course, from appealingness – namely *familiarity*. The general idea of incorporating this variable is to reflect the fairly well-established finding that increasing the number of exposures a person has to a particular object can influence the affective response to it. A parallel finding is that the novelty of an object can affect the degree to which people report that they like it. There are many complicated issues surrounding the factors that affect Liking emotions, some of which will be briefly discussed in Chapter 8. The main issue, however, is that apart from familiarity, all the other factors that psychologists have identified as influencing the intensity of liking appear to fail our criterion for inclusion as intensity variables. That is, they all seem to be explicable in terms of their effects through appealingness, or through one of the other variables that we have identified (e.g., unexpectedness).

Variable-values, Variable-weights, and Emotion Thresholds

The final question that we need to discuss in connection with the intensity issue has to do with the way in which the variables act together to influence the intensity of emotions. In associating a set of local variables with a particular emotion type it is not our intention to assert that each variable always has an effect in all cases in which an instance of the type arises. The only variables that are necessarily operative in all cases of an emotion type are those variables that are part of the emotion specification – typically, but not exclusively, those referred to in Chapter 3 as the "central" variables: desirability, praiseworthiness, and appealingness. In the general case, the kind of intensity mechanism that we envision is something like the following: The eliciting conditions of some emotion are satisfied, resulting in the *potential* for that emotion to be experienced. We assume that there is a context-sensitive emotion-specific threshold associated with each emotion so that the emotion will only be experienced if its threshold is exceeded. We further assume that the experienced intensity of the emotion itself will be determined by the degree to which the emotion threshold is exceeded. Thus, the intensity of any particular emotion, on this account, is going to depend on the difference between the magnitude of its associated emotion potential and the current value of the emotion threshold (see Chapter 9 for a more formal discussion).

The main role of the intensity variables, therefore, is to determine the magnitude of the emotion potential. Two aspects of the variables contribute to this, the *value* of the variable, and the *weight* assigned to it. In some cases, for some local variables, the emotion-inducing stimulus might be too impoverished to enable an assignment of realistic values. For example, suppose one overhears a conversation at a party in which some person is described as having lost his entire savings by making an unsound investment. Maybe one feels a little sorry for the unfortunate individual, and maybe not, but certainly the potential for pity exists. As discussed in the previous section, two of the variables affecting emotions in the Fortunes-of-others group are *liking* (for the other) and *deservingness*. In the simple scenario we have just described, the person overhearing the conversation does not even know who the individual being described is, so we assume that the *liking* variable will retain its default value. Assuming that the variable is scaled from -1 for maximum dislike to $+1$ for maximum liking, the default value will presumably be 0, which represents neither liking nor disliking the person in question. Similarly, there is insufficient information to make an informed assessment of the value to be assigned to the deservingness variable. Perhaps the observer believes that people ought not to make foolish investments in the stock exchange, and so, for want of a better reason, he assigns a relatively high value to the deservingness variable (muttering to himself that it serves the fool right, whoever he is). It is presumably easier for the observer to assign a values to the *desirability-for-other* and *desirability* (for self) variables. As discussed above, in a case such as the one we are considering, the desirability for other might well be determined on the basis of reasoning analogically from one's own beliefs about how undesirable it would be to lose one's life savings. Finally, we would have to consider the value that might be assigned to the desirability (for self) variable. In the present example, given that the person suffering the misfortune is a total stranger, it seems unlikely that this variable will contribute very much since the only goals that are likely to be implicated are I-goals having to do with one's interests in not having people (in general) suffer. In particular, goals having to do with the welfare of friends and foes are not involved. Thus, because most of the variables that can contribute to the intensity of the emotion (of pity) do not have large values, we would not expect the emotion to be very intense, if it is experienced at all. The situation would be quite different if the other person were a close friend whom one viewed as clearly not deserving what one knew to be a devastating loss. Then one would feel pity, and, presumably, quite strongly.

Notice that in order to come to these conclusions it is not necessary to assume any great precision in the computational mechanisms. The assignment of values to individual variables can be, and doubtless often is, quite imprecise, having a strongly qualitative flavor. It seems unlikely that the internal psychophysics of value assignment is, or need be, very precise, and, in fact, even the notion of "assigning" values may be too strong. It may be preferable, and sufficient, to think of values being *available* rather than being assigned, but in the present context, this is not a very important issue. What is important is what happens to the variables and how they have their effects.

In addition to whatever values are available for the variables that are potentially operative with respect to some particular emotion, we assume that each variable also has a *weight* associated with it, and that this weight can vary from one emotion type to another within each group, and even from one emotion token to another within each type. A particularly clear example of this is presented in Chapter 6, where we discuss the difference between hope and hopeful by noting that the weight assigned to the desirability variable is much greater than that assigned to the likelihood variable in the case of hope, but that the relative size of these weights is reversed for hopefulness. What this means is that changes in the value of a variable having relatively little weight may, on occasions, result in no perceptible change in the intensity of a particular experienced emotion. The mechanism controlling the assignment of weight to different variables is not an issue that we explore in any detail, although it is probably controlled to some extent by the same kind of attentional factors that influence the elicitation of different emotion types, namely focusing on some aspects of the emotion-inducing situation rather than on others. In any event, the result of there being differential weights on intensity variables is that in some cases, a particular variable may have no effect on the intensity of an emotion with which it is associated.

Summary

Among the variables that affect the intensity of different emotions are global variables, which affect all emotions, and local variables, which affect particular groups of emotions. The global variables include: (1) the *sense of reality*, which depends on how much one believes the emotion-inducing situation is real, (2) *proximity*, which depends on how close in psychological space one feels to the situation, (3) *unexpectedness*, which depends on how surprised one is by the situation, and (4) *arousal*, which depends on how much one is aroused prior to the situation. Increases in these variables intensify the experienced emotion.

Local variables are tied to particular groups of emotions. The Event-based emotions are all affected by the *desirability* variable. In addition, the Prospect-based emotions are affected by (1) *likelihood*, which reflects the degree of belief that an anticipated event will occur, (2) *effort*, which reflects the degree to which resources were expended in obtaining or avoiding an anticipated event, and (3) *realization*, which depends on the degree to which an anticipated event actually occurs. The Fortune-of-others emotions are affected by: (1) *desirability-for-other*, which reflects how one evaluates desirability for the other person's goals, (2) *liking*, which reflects how attracted to the other person one is, and (3) *deservingness*, which depends on how much one thinks the other person deserved what happened. The Attribution emotions are affected by the central *praiseworthiness* variable, along with: (1) *strength of cognitive unit*, which reflects how much one identifies with the person or institution who is the agent of the emotion-inducing event, and (2) *expectation-deviation*, which reflects how much the agent's action deviates from expected norms. Finally, the Attraction emotions depend on *familiarity* of the object, as well as on the central variable of *appealingness*.

Some of the global or local variables may be unspecified in a given situation, in which case the variables assume neutral default values with the result that an emotion might not arise at all. However, at least one of the central variables in the theory (i.e., desirability, praiseworthiness, and appealingness) must always be specified if an emotion does arise, because every emotion involves one of these variables in its eliciting conditions.

5   Reactions to Events: I

Having now dealt with the background issues, we move to our discussion of the distinct emotion types. We start by discussing the three main groups of emotions that involve reactions to events relative to one's own goals. The emotions in one of these groups result from considering the *prospect* of certain events occurring. These Prospect-based emotions will be discussed in Chapter 6. In this chapter we shall examine the other two groups of Event-based emotions, in which people's emotional reactions to events are more or less independent of their prior expectations. One of the groups that we shall discuss pertains to the fortunes of others and the reactions that one has to them. But first, we shall discuss what we call the "Well-being" emotions, with "joy" and "distress" being representative terms that refer to them. In distinguishing Well-being emotions from Prospect-based emotions, we do not intend to suggest that the degree to which events are unexpected is irrelevant for the Well-being emotions. Unexpectedness influences the intensity of all emotions. However, the Well-being emotions result from focusing attention on the events themselves rather than on events as tempered by the *prospect* of their occurring. As suggested in Chapter 2, these emotions are essentially "pure" cases of being pleased or displeased.

The Well-being Emotions

The internal structure of the Well-being emotions is quite simple. However, associated with this group of emotions is a great variety of lexical items, as a result not of internal structure in the sense of dimensions, but rather as a result of the fact that a large number of specific words refer to changes in well-being resulting from specific kinds of events.

The Well-being emotions should not be viewed merely as affective evaluations of something as positive or negative. They are paradigmatic psychological states of feeling that arise from attending to events insofar as they

Table 5.1. *Well-being emotions*

APPRAISAL OF EVENT	
DESIRABLE	UNDESIRABLE
pleased about a desirable event (e.g., joy)	displeased about an undesirable event (e.g., distress)

are appraised as being desirable or undesirable. Sometimes the events are in the remote past (cf. nostalgia), sometimes they are in the recent past or are concurrent with the emotion (cf. grief), and sometimes they are future events, as might be the case in the joy a couple might experience on learning that they are going to have a baby. In the case of a future event such as this, care has to be taken to distinguish Well-being emotions from the Prospect-based emotions, such as hope, that might also arise.

The main factor affecting the intensity of the Well-being emotions is the degree to which the event in question is appraised as being desirable or undesirable (see Chapter 3). In general, to the extent that the person sees the object as contributing to the realization of his goals, he will tend to experience the positive emotion of the kind that we call *joy*. Similarly, to the extent that the person sees the object as interfering with the realization of his goals, he will tend to experience the negative emotion of the kind that we call *distress*. Whether or not these are exactly the right words is not important for the moment. What is important is that the Well-being emotions, whatever we call them, are the result of reacting to events that are positively or negatively evaluated in terms of their implications for a person's goals (including, as already discussed, Active-pursuit goals, Interest goals, and Replenishment goals).

In keeping with the format that we shall use to represent the different groups of emotions, the Well-being emotions are represented in Table 5.1. The table presents abbreviated structural descriptions of the emotions. Each of these abbreviated descriptions has associated with it a more formal and complete characterization that we call an "emotion specification." The structure of these specifications can best be understood by considering the cases of those for the Well-being emotions, whose relatively simple structure provides a transparent model of the way in which we characterize emotion types:

(5.1)   **JOY EMOTIONS**
TYPE SPECIFICATION: (pleased about) a desirable event
TOKENS: contented, cheerful, delighted, ecstatic, elated, euphoric,

feeling good, glad, happy, joyful, jubilant, pleasantly surprised, pleased, etc.
VARIABLES AFFECTING INTENSITY:
(1) the degree to which the event is desirable
EXAMPLE: The man was pleased when he realized he was to get a small inheritance from an unknown distant relative.

(5.2)   **DISTRESS EMOTIONS**
TYPE SPECIFICATION: (displeased about) an undesirable event
TOKENS: depressed, distressed, displeased, dissatisfied, distraught, feeling bad, feeling uncomfortable, grief, homesick, lonely, lovesick, miserable, regret, sad, shock, uneasy, unhappy, upset, etc.
VARIABLES AFFECTING INTENSITY:
(1) the degree to which the event is undesirable
EXAMPLE: The driver was upset about running out of gas on the freeway.

As these examples illustrate, each emotion specification has five major components. First is an emotion *type identification*, for example, Joy emotions. The type identification serves merely as a convenient label for the type of emotion being considered. This is followed by the *type specification*, which constitutes an approximate, if not complete, specification of the necessary conditions for the experience of emotions of that type. In the case of the Distress emotions, for example, the type specification is given as (DISPLEASED ABOUT) AN UNDESIRABLE EVENT. Notice that the type specification has two parts. The first, enclosed in parenthesis, specifies the kind of reaction (pleased/displeased, approving/disapproving, or liking/disliking). The second part, immediately following the parenthetical reaction type, which in this case is simply AN UNDESIRABLE EVENT, comprises the eliciting conditions for the emotion type. Thus, the type specification essentially identifies the location of the emotion within the overall structure proposed in Figure 2.1. The third component of an emotion specification consists of a partial list of *tokens*, that is, a list of words or phrases that constitute the family of emotions of that type and that share the same type specification as a necessary part. These tokens are presented as adjectives, adjectival forms, or nouns; occasionally as verbs. The fourth major component is a statement of the major local *variables affecting intensity*, which, for the examples above, is simply the *desirability* variable expressed in terms of desirability for the positive emotion and undesirability for the negative one. This does not mean that we shall not discuss the effects of the global variables, but only that we do not specify them in the emotion specifications. Finally, each emotion specification ends with a prototypical *example*.

We should mention immediately that we view each emotion specification, or characterization, as a *proposal* rather than as an empirically established fact. Our view is that there is indeed a distinct emotional state that can be approximately described by each of our type specifications, but that the degree to which the English language (and any other language for that matter) provides a good lexical representation of each of these emotion types varies a great deal. This means that we would be perfectly willing to acknowledge that some of the particular tokens that we associate with an emotion type might be better or equally well associated with a different type. The goodness of fit of tokens to type specifications is an empirical issue. We have done the best we can in the absence of well-established data, although in some cases we do have preliminary data that convince us that many of our assignments are reasonable. Yet, ultimately, the important questions do not have to do with whether or not we have made optimal assignments of tokens to types, but whether or not the types we specify more or less exhaust the space of human emotions, and whether they have the intensity characteristics we assign to them. Similarly, we want to emphasize that the proposed intensity variables also still only have the status of proposals. Generally, we specify these variables in a manner that suggests (but only suggests) that the intensity of the emotion is monotonically related to the level of the variable (for example, that the intensity of Distress emotions is monotonically related to increases in undesirability). However, while in many cases we suspect the relation is indeed a positive monotonic one, this is by no means always the case. We consider the determination of the functions that relate the intensity variables to emotions to be an empirical question to be investigated in future research.

As already indicated, in order to simplify the exposition, we shall often use the terms "joy" and "distress" as convenient shorthands for the reactions of being PLEASED ABOUT A DESIRABLE EVENT and DISPLEASED ABOUT AN UNDESIRABLE EVENT, respectively. The type specifications for these emotions are trivially simple. They indicate only that in the absence of any other factors, when a person reacts to a desirable event, the eliciting conditions for a Joy emotion are satisfied, and that when a person reacts to an undesirable event, the eliciting conditions for a Distress emotion are satisfied. So, for example, a person who learns that he is to receive a small but completely unexpected inheritance as a result of the death of a distant but unknown relative would feel pleased. His reaction is one of being pleased simply because he is reacting to the desirable event of increasing his wealth. In this particular example, the unexpectedness is likely to intensify the emotion through its effects as a global intensity variable. When unexpectedness is low, such emotions are correspondingly less intense. In fact, as we shall see in the next chapter, when a desirable event is *actively* expected, the dominant emotion is likely to be a Prospect-based emotion.

Our example of a Distress emotion is that of a person whose car runs out of gas on the freeway. To the extent that he thinks only about the undesirability of the event, the eliciting conditions for a Distress emotion (only) will be satisfied. His reaction will be one of being displeased simply because he is reacting to the undesirable event. The important point about Joy and Distress emotions is that they result from focusing only on the desirability or undesirability of the event. It is perfectly possible for a person to focus on other aspects of the event as well, for example that it was anticipated, or that some person was responsible for bringing it about. When this happens, more differentiated forms or different emotions arise.

The intensity of the Well-being emotions is influenced only by desirability and the global variables. In the last chapter we discussed a number of variables that always influence the intensity of emotions regardless of where these emotions lie in the overall structure. These variables include factors such as *unexpectedness* and *proximity*. Because these variables influence the intensity of all emotions, we have not specified their effects in the characterization of the Well-being emotions. In general, we do not mention these global variables in the specifications of individual emotions because to do so would be redundant and would tend to reduce the emphasis we want to place on the local variables that play a role in discriminating among emotions and emotion groups. The only exception to this rule is when a global variable manifests itself in an idiosyncratic manner for some particular group of emotions. As for desirability, clearly, if desirability is high, the intensity of the Joy emotion will be high and we might be willing to actually call the emotions "joy," "delight," or even "ecstasy." On the other hand, if desirability is low, the intensity of the Joy emotion will be low, and we might be more inclined to describe the experience as one of being "contented." If the desirability is below some threshold, there might be no emotional experience at all, even though the eliciting conditions might have been satisfied. Similarly, if the event being contemplated is highly undesirable, the intensity of the resulting Distress emotion would be high and we might prefer a term like "distraught."

One final point about the nature of the desirability variable needs to be emphasized here. *Desirability* and *undesirability* are always computed in a context. That is, there is always some (usually implicit) comparison event. In the case of the paradigm examples of joy and distress cited above (learning of an inheritance, and running out of gas) it is not easy to see this because the implicit comparison event is simply the absence of the event to which the emotion is a reaction. However, it is a simple matter to construct a situation in which this would not be the case. Compare two people living in a country ruled by a totalitarian and oppressive regime. One of these people has never had any problem with the authorities and leads what for all intents and purposes is a normal life. The second person has been held for years in a prison, branded as a "dissident." Now suppose that the dissident is released and confined to his house under "house arrest," while the other, suddenly suspected of subversive activities, is similarly confined to his house under house arrest. After the initial reactions to their new situations have subsided, each is likely to evaluate the event relative to a different comparison event so that the dissident is likely to feel happy, evaluating his house arrest in comparison to his long imprisonment, while the other is likely to feel unhappy, evaluating his house arrest in comparison to his prior freedom.

Loss Emotions and Fine-grained Analyses

In all of the emotions groups that we shall consider, there are cases in which some of the associated lexical items (i.e., "tokens") appear not to fit very well. In the present case, *grief* might be such an example because it is clearly much underspecified by the type specification for distress. There is much more to grief than being displeased about an undesirable event. As we shall repeatedly emphasize, our type specifications are not intended as definitions of the emotions appearing in the lists of tokens. Our claim is only that the type specification constitutes a necessary condition for them. The degree to which additional specification would be required to characterize particular tokens varies from almost nothing to a great deal. Thus, we think that the type specification of being DISPLEASED ABOUT AN UNDESIRABLE EVENT is both necessary and sufficient for the emotion that is commonly called "distress," but that it is only part of the story for emotions such as grief. In order to deal with such underspecified cases it is going to be necessary to undertake a more fine-grained analysis. It is beyond the scope of this book to provide such an analysis for all the apparently poorly fitting terms. However, it is important that we illustrate what it is that we have in mind here, partly to show that it is indeed possible to account for such emotions, and partly as an illustration of the principles that we think underlie such an analysis. We shall therefore consider how we would propose to handle grief in the Well-being emotions.

Our claim is that grief is a Distress emotion. That is, grief is a reaction to an undesirable event. What distinguishes grief from the more general notion of distress is that in the case of grief we are reacting to a particular kind of undesirable event, namely the irrevocable loss (i.e., death) of a loved one. In other words, what happens is that part of the type specification has been constrained to a particular value or range of values (in this case, the nature of the undesirable event is constrained to the loss of a loved one). This suggests a general strategy for undertaking more fine-grained analyses within the overall framework that we have outlined. When there appear to be several different emotions that represent the same general emotion type, except that they are differentiated from the main type by a restricted range of values on one or more of the features in the type specification, a new subtype can be created. Thus, one might propose a subtype of the Well-being emotions that could be called "Loss" emotions, for which the type specification would be DISPLEASED ABOUT THE UNDESIRABLE EVENT OF A LOSS. Such a subgroup might then accommodate tokens such as grief (irrevocable loss of a loved one), homesick (loss of the comforts of home), loneliness (loss of social contact), lovesick (loss of the object of romantic love), regret (loss of opportunity), etc. In fact, of course, this is precisely the principle that gives rise to the postulation of different groups in the main structure. So, for example, when the desirable or undesirable event has to do with prospects, we develop the Prospect-based group. The difference between those groups we have developed and those that we leave to further fine-grained analyses is that the ones we have developed are general, they are valence-independent, and, above all, they have systematic structural properties. The ones that we have not developed tend to be more specific and restricted to only one valence, that is, they apply only to one half of the superordinate emotions, as is the case with the Loss emotions, and they appear to have no systematic internal structure.

While the Loss emotions can be distilled out of the Distress emotions by restricting the range of a feature in the type specification (that is by specializing the undesirable event as a loss), more fine-grained analyses can also be undertaken by considering the effects of restricted ranges of values of intensity variables. This applies to both individual local or global variables or to their combined effects. For example, in the Distress emotions, when the value on the desirability or undesirability variable is at the high end, different words seem more appropriate to describe the resulting emotion (e.g., "euphoric," "miserable"). When the *unexpectedness* variable is in the high range, words like "shock" and "pleasant surprise" seem to better describe the emotion. The important point here is that all such terms refer to Joy or Distress emotions, but the richness of the language provides us with ways of indicating particular cases with particular characteristics in a distinct way.

Table 5.2. *Fortunes-of-others emotions*

REACTION OF SELF	PRESUMED VALUE FOR OTHER	
	DESIRABLE	UNDESIRABLE
PLEASED	pleased about an event desirable for someone else (e.g., happy-for)	pleased about an event undesirable for someone else (e.g., gloating)
DISPLEASED	displeased about an event desirable for someone else (e.g., resentment)	displeased about an event undesirable for someone else (e.g., sorry-for)

The Fortunes-of-others Emotions

We turn now to our analysis of a second group of emotions. Like all Event-based emotions, the Fortunes-of-others emotions depend on the implications of events for one's goals. In these emotions, however, the events in question always concern what happens to other people. One's affective reaction, therefore, depends in part on the presumed desirability of an event for another person and in part on the desirability from one's own perspective of the other person's experiencing that outcome. Determining the desirability for the other person requires that one have, or construct, at least a partial model of the other person's plans and goals. The desirability of the event from one's own perspective, on the other hand, is likely to be based on one of several specific factors. For example, when one is pleased for another person who experiences good fortune, the basis on which one assesses the event as desirable may simply be that one likes the other person and therefore wishes him well. Similarly, when one is pleased over the misfortune of another person, the basis may be that one dislikes the person. In other cases, a judgment of deservingness may motivate one's reaction. One might find it undesirable, for example, for someone to get an extravagant pay raise to the extent that one judges it to be undeserved. The Fortunes-of-others emotions are thus influenced both by the (presumed) desirability of the event for the other and by the desirability from one's own standpoint of the other experiencing such an outcome. The general structure of the Fortunes-of-others group is presented in Table 5.2.

Examination of the diagonals in the table reveals two subclasses of emotion types. The incongruent cells, that is those in which the desirability of the event for self is not congruent with the desirability of the event for the other, can be thought of as Ill-will emotions, whereas the congruent cells give what might be called Good-will or Empathetic emotions. When a person judges an event to be undesirable for another person and is pleased about that fact, we sometimes describe the person as "gloating" (over the misfortunes of others). This is one of the Ill-will emotions. The other arises when one is displeased about some event that one judges to be desirable for the other person. Although the English word "resentment" is somewhat ambiguous, there is one sense in which it means just this. The congruent cases consist of events that are judged to be desirable for the other also being judged desirable for the self, and events that are judged to be undesirable for the other also being judged undesirable for the self. These Good-will emotions, for which being "happy-for" and "sorry-for" (i.e., pitying) someone else are reasonable terms, are basically just cases in which what is good for others is good for us, and what is bad for others is bad for us, although the sense in which these are good and bad for us may often be simply that we wish our friends to prosper and for others to get what they deserve.

We present first the specifications for the Good-will emotions:

(5.3) **HAPPY-FOR EMOTIONS**
TYPE SPECIFICATION: (pleased about) an event presumed to be desirable for someone else
TOKENS: delighted-for, happy-for, pleased-for, etc.
VARIABLES AFFECTING INTENSITY:
(1) the degree to which the desirable event for the other is desirable for oneself
(2) the degree to which the event is presumed to be desirable for the other person
(3) the degree to which the other person deserved the event
(4) the degree to which the other person is liked
EXAMPLE: Fred was happy for his friend Mary because she won a thousand dollars.

(5.4) **SORRY-FOR EMOTIONS**
TYPE SPECIFICATION: (displeased about) an event presumed to be undesirable for someone else
TOKENS: compassion, pity, sad-for, sorry-for, sympathy, etc.
VARIABLES AFFECTING INTENSITY:
(1) the degree to which the undesirable event for the other is undesirable for oneself
(2) the degree to which the event is presumed to be undesirable for the other person
(3) the degree to which the other person did not deserve the event
(4) the degree to which the other person is liked
EXAMPLE: Fred was sorry for his friend Mary because her husband was killed in a car crash.

These two, Good-will, emotions are the *empathetic* emotions in that they depend upon the person experiencing them empathizing with the other. In our view, empathy requires a person to understand or appreciate how another person must feel, given the situation the other is in, and it requires the empathizing person to be in some related (but not necessarily identical) emotional state. Thus, empathy is not an emotion on our account, although there are empathetic emotions.

We propose four main variables as affecting the intensity of the Fortunes-of-others emotions. There is, however, no implication in the separate listing of these four intensity variables for these (or other) emotions that they necessarily always function independently of one another. The reason they are listed separately is that even though they can interact, and even though sometimes the effects of one variable are exerted through one of the other variables, it is *possible* for each variable that is listed to have an independent effect (see Chapter 4). The first variable we list as influencing the intensity of the Fortunes-of-others emotions is the same desirability variable that is involved in all of the Event-based emotions.[1] We refer to this as *desirability-for-self* to distinguish it from the second variable that also has to do with desirability, albeit with the desirability for the other person. The other two variables that we shall discuss are deservingness and liking. As with all Event-based emotions, the contribution of the desirability-for-self variable is determined with respect to the experiencer's own goals. This means that these emotions can only arise if the fortunes of the affected others are somehow relevant to one's own concerns. Beliefs about what is deserved and fair can clearly interact with this in the sense that what is desirable for a person with respect to others may be that the world "treat them fairly," that is, that they (and people in general) get what they deserve. In general, in the Fortunes-of-others emotions, the desirability of the event for oneself need not depend on active plans and goals to benefit or harm the other person. More often, it results from the impact that events are seen to have on one's interests (**I**-goals), particularly as they pertain to the well-being of others. Thus, one might be pleased for a liberal senator who is elected in another state without ever having striven for this outcome, or one might be pleased at reading newspaper stories in which virtue is rewarded, scoundrels are thwarted, and justice prevails. These involve the furtherance of one's interests and concerns in a general way and therefore represent the partial fulfillment of **I**-goals, but they probably do

---

1 We should mention that in the type specifications of the Fortunes-of-others emotions, we mean it to be understood that when the reaction is one of being pleased, the event about which one is pleased (i.e., the event presumed to be desirable for someone else) is by implication (necessarily) a desirable event for oneself. Similarly, being displeased is assumed to entail that the object of one's displeasure is undesirable for the self, regardless of its presumed desirability for the other person.

not affect one's active plans or **A**-goals. Similarly, to take the example used in our characterization of the Happy-for emotions, if Fred feels happy for Mary because she won a thousand dollars, Mary's winning is not an event for which it would make sense to say that Fred would (or even could) have an **A**-goal, but it is an event that might further his general interest in the well-being and happiness of his friends, and perhaps of Mary in particular. On the other hand, one need not even know the victims of a disaster to feel pity for them, because one has a general interest (an **I**-goal) that people should not suffer undeservedly.

Clearly, because the Fortunes-of-others emotions involve reactions to events deemed to be desirable or undesirable for someone else, the degree to which these events are judged to be desirable for the other person is going to influence the intensity of the reaction. This is represented by the *desirability-for-other* variable. Of course, the question here is not how well or badly off the target person really is, but how the experiencer perceives the other to be affected by the event. He perceives the event as being desirable or undesirable for the other, presumably in terms of his beliefs about the goals and interests of the other person. To see this, consider again the example of Fred being happy for Mary because she has won a thousand dollars. Other things being equal (especially, Fred's degree of liking for Mary), if Mary were already very wealthy, coming from a rich family that constantly showered expensive gifts on her, Fred might perceive Mary's winnings as being less desirable for her than he would have done had she been poorly paid and not from a rich family. Thus, one feels happy-for someone when something happens that one thinks is desirable for them, and the more desirable one thinks it is (although, possibly only up to a point) the more intense is the Happy-for emotion. The same pattern of effects applies to the Sorry-for emotions, as can be seen by considering the example offered in our characterization of them: If Fred learns that the husband of his friend Mary was killed in a serious accident, Fred would ordinarily feel very sorry for Mary. But suppose Fred knew that Mary's husband habitually beat her, and that she no longer had any affection for him. In this case, we might expect him to feel less sorry for her because he would presume the event to be less undesirable for her. Indeed, it is conceivable that he would (rightly or wrongly) view such an event as being a desirable event for her, in which case he might even feel happy for her (appropriately or not, as the case may be). One would expect Fred to feel a great deal of pity and sympathy if he believed that Mary had loved her husband deeply. In other words, while holding other factors constant, the assessment of the undesirability of the event for Mary, and hence the degree to which Fred might feel sorry for her, is likely to be lower in the first case than it is in the second.

The third variable affecting the intensity of the Fortunes-of-others emotions (both for the Good-will emotions and the Ill-will emotions) is *deservingness*. This variable is clearly important in that we tend to be more pleased at the good fortunes of others to the degree that we think them deserved, and we tend to have more sympathy for them in times of misfortune to the degree that we believe the ill fate is not deserved. In particular, people are inclined to have much less sympathy for others, even friends, whom they believe to have brought their ill fate upon themselves. Such beliefs are not necessarily sufficient to nullify the emotion, but they certainly temper it. Thus if a person, contrary to all the wise council of experts and friends, makes a foolish investment and loses his life savings, we are inclined to be less sympathetic than if he had been defrauded of the same amount of money.

Our account of the intensity of the Good-will emotions suggests that the more pleased one is (desirability-for-self) about a good thing that happened to another person (desirability-for-other), and the more one thinks the person deserved what he got, the more happy for the other one feels. However, as mentioned above, this does not mean that the two forms of desirability and deservingness always act independently – they can, but they need not. If the desirability of the event for the other is judged to be beyond what is deserved, one will not necessarily feel happy for the other at all, but may come to resent the other instead. For example, suppose that two players on a college basketball team recognize one another as being similarly talented and that, as friends, they wish one another well. Now suppose that one of them is drafted by a professional team and signs a million-dollar contract while the other is not drafted at all, shattering his dreams of fame and fortune. This second, unfortunate, basketball player is as likely to resent the good fortunes of his teammate as he is to feel happy for him, notwithstanding his congratulations. One reason for this is that the experiencer determines deservingness partly by reference to his or her own situation. The basketball player who is not drafted might well think that his teammate deserves to be drafted along with him, while believing that his teammate does not deserve to be drafted if he is not drafted himself. In this sense, the Fortunes-of-others emotions can be thought of as emotions based on social comparison (Suls & Miller, 1977). We shall have more to say about the social comparison aspect when we discuss the Ill-will emotions, especially resentment.

The fourth main variable affecting this group of emotions is that of *liking*. The way in which the liking variable functions in these emotions is more complicated than might appear at first sight. One reason for this is that it is possible for the empathetic emotions to be experienced even with negative values of the liking variable. During the Watergate scandal in the early 1970s many people grew to dislike Richard Nixon. Nevertheless, this dislike did not exclude the possibility that some of those people felt sorry for him as they reflected on his demise. This is why we treat liking as an intensity variable rather than as part of the eliciting condition itself. Doing so allows for the possibility that one can feel sorry for somebody one does not actively like. If liking were part of the type specification it would mean that one could not feel happy or sorry for someone unless one liked that person. In fact, it seems to us that high values of the desirability and deservingness variables can outweigh reasonably small negative values of the liking variable. At the same time, we acknowledge that paradigm examples of feeling happy and sad for others do not involve cases where the person is actively disliked. It should also be noted that expressions of sympathy for disliked others in very undesirable situations might be no more than that – mere expressions. They do not necessarily reflect *emotion* at all, although they may reflect a cognitive state in which one recognizes that some (but not all) of the requirements for an emotion have been satisfied.

Apart from the complication pertaining to the lower bound of the liking variable in the Good-will emotions, it is fairly clear that, within limits, the more one likes the other, the more intense will be the emotions. We should reiterate here that in postulating liking as affecting the intensity of Fortunes-of-others emotions, we have in mind the influence of *momentary* liking, not dispositional liking. Of course, one's momentary assessment of liking is usually consistent with, and largely determined by, one's dispositional liking for that person, but an assessment of liking or disliking may be subordinated in any given moment to other concerns, so that one may neither actively like nor dislike a dispositionally liked or disliked person in that moment. Thus, although a person who dispositionally disliked Nixon would not pity him while focusing on the dislike, he might do so while focusing on other aspects of the ex-president's situation, because he would not then be in a momentary state of dislike. By using momentary as opposed to dispositional liking as our intensity variable, we do not wish to deny that dispositional liking can have important influences on the Fortunes-of-others emotions. One of these influences, as we have just seen, is through the control that dispositional liking exerts over momentary liking. Another influence is through the desirability-for-self variable. Clearly, the more one likes a person, the more important are the fortunes of that person going to be with respect to one's own goals.

The Fortunes-of-others emotions are uniquely social emotions, to which

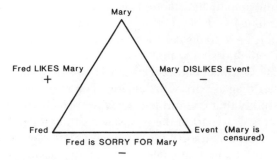

Figure 5.1. Example of how the balance principle can constrain emotional response.

a variant of a uniquely social principle can be applied, namely, Heider's (1958) balance principle. Although the balance principle is not generally applied to emotions as such, Heider and a generation of social psychologists influenced by his work discussed how affective relationships tend toward a balanced state. A balanced state is one in which the product of the valences of the three sides of a triangle representing affective relationships is positive. If one attempts to apply this principle in the context of emotions, then, to the degree that one likes or dislikes the other person, one might expect the valence (and intensity) of one's reaction to their good or ill fortune to be partially constrained. If, for example, Fred likes Mary (+) and she is honored by her co-workers (+), a balanced state will prevail if Fred responds with a positive emotion by, for example, being happy for her (+). If Fred likes Mary (+) but she is censured by her co-workers (−) then, as shown in Figure 5.1, Fred is likely to react negatively, perhaps by feeling pity for her (−); and if Fred dislikes Mary (−) and she is censured by her co-workers (−), a balanced state would exist if Fred were to gloat (+). Unlike the traditional balance triangle in which the three vertices all represent individuals, in order to apply the concept to emotions, we have assumed that only two of the vertices are individuals and that the third is an event, as illustrated in Figure 5.1. Thus, in this example, we have one vertex representing Fred and one representing Mary. The side that joins them represents Fred's liking for Mary. The third vertex is the event that affects Mary–her being censured by her co-workers. The side relating Mary to this event is negatively valenced by virtue of the assumed undesirability of the event for Mary. The third side represents Fred's affective reaction (i.e., the emotion) to this event happening to Mary, the valence of which, we are proposing, can be thought of as being constrained by the balance principle. Thus, in this particular example, if Fred has a negative emotion, the product of the valence of the sides of the triangle will be positive and a balanced state will result.

There is an important qualification on the applicability of the balance principle. Social psychologists (e.g., Wegner & Vallacher, 1981) have observed that balance applies only to *nonexclusive* relationships, that is, to relationships that are not characterized by being mutually exclusive. Suppose John and Philip represent two of the vertices of the balance triangle, and John likes Philip, which gives one positive side. Suppose, further, that the third vertex is the event of Philip receiving the love and affection of Mary, and that the side of the triangle relating Philip to this event is positive, representing the fact that it is desirable for Philip. If John has no romantic ambitions vis à vis Mary, the balance principle leads to the conclusion that John could be happy for Philip. However, if, in competition with Philip, John also loves Mary, viewing Philip's receipt of Mary's affection as excluding his receiving it, the exclusivity constraint will prevent the balance principle from operating, thus blocking the conclusion that John feels happy for Philip, even though the product of the signs of the three elements would be positive if the balance principle were to apply. We therefore do not expect liking to intensify the Happy-for emotions when the desirable event for a friend directly frustrates goals of the experiencer. Under these conditions, the desirability-for-self variable would be negative (perhaps along with the perceived deservingness variable), which would greatly decrease the intensity of any Happy-for emotion, or, more probably, would create the conditions for jealousy and resentment instead.

We move now to our specifications of the Ill-will emotions.

(5.5)   **RESENTMENT EMOTIONS**
TYPE SPECIFICATION: (displeased about) an event presumed to be desirable for someone else
TOKENS: envy, jealousy, resentment, etc.
VARIABLES AFFECTING INTENSITY:
(1) the degree to which the desirable event for the other person is undesirable for oneself
(2) the degree to which the event is presumed to be desirable for the other person
(3) the degree to which the other person did not deserve the event
(4) the degree to which the other person is not liked

EXAMPLE: The executive resented the large pay raise awarded to a colleague whom he considered incompetent.

(5.6)   **GLOATING EMOTIONS**
TYPE SPECIFICATION: (pleased about) an event presumed to be
undesirable for someone else
TOKENS: gloating, Schadenfreude, etc.
VARIABLES AFFECTING INTENSITY:
(1) the degree to which the undesirable event for the other person is
desirable for oneself
(2) the degree to which the event is presumed to be undesirable for the
other person
(3) the degree to which the other person deserved the event
(4) the degree to which the other person is not liked
EXAMPLE: Political opponents of Richard Nixon gloated over his
ignominious departure from office.

At least in Western cultures, the Ill-will emotions are among the most
distasteful – people don't like to acknowledge that they experience them,
but most people experience them nonetheless, at least occasionally. Pleasant or not, they cannot be ignored in any attempt at a comprehensive
treatment of emotions.

The contribution of the desirability variables (both desirability-for-self,
and desirability-for-other) is analogous to that in the empathetic, Good-
will, emotions. In the example that we present in the specification of the
Resentment emotions, an executive resents the fact that an incompetent
colleague received a large pay raise. In this example, the assessment of the
desirability of the colleague's raise is that it is undeserved, although it is
assumed to be desirable for the incompetent employee. For this situation to
give rise to a Resentment emotion, it has to be construed by the executive
as being in some way undesirable for himself, although quite possibly only
insofar as the event thwarts his **I**-goal of seeing justice prevail. Thus, Resentment emotions do not *require* (as part of their specifications) that the
good fortunes of others be wanted and unavailable for the self. It is possible
to resent the good fortunes of others, even when one has no directly related
aspirations oneself. In such cases there may appear to be no real disadvantage to the resentful person. For example, an academically gifted student
might resent the fact that an academically inferior student was awarded an
athletic scholarship to a prestigious school. The gifted student might have
no aspirations for going to that institution. Nevertheless, he may resent the
athlete's good fortune because he considers a scholarship for study on the
basis of ability in sports to be undeserved. To the extent that he considers
this unfair, his resentment will be intensified. Similarly, the executive can
be resentful that his colleague received a large pay raise, even if he (the
executive) received a larger one.

Resentment is certainly intensified when it is focused on a resource of some kind for which there is competition, that is, a resource that cannot be shared and which the resentful person actually desires. This is accommodated by the fact the other's gain is one's own loss, so that the other's desirable situation becomes much more undesirable for the self. In such cases, the fact that the other possesses something excludes the possibility that the resentful person can possess it, with the consequence that it directly thwarts one of the resentful person's goals and, in particular, can directly thwart an A-goal. Cases of this kind are usually referred to as "envy," which we take to refer to resentment that some other has something one would find desirable oneself. In fact, we think that additional factors may make envy a more specific example of resentment. In particular, envy seems to require that the envying person focus on the fact that he or she (also) wants the object, whereas in the case of resentment, the resentful person may focus more on the undeservingness of the other person enjoying the benefit.

A related special case of a Resentment emotion is that of *jealousy*, which seems to add to envy an additional condition, namely, that the possession by the other excludes or diminishes one's own possession especially, but not exclusively, in the context of the attention and affection of others. Insofar as envy and jealousy involve resentment over the possession by others of things one wants for oneself, they are likely to be more intense because the undesirability for self will be higher. In simple cases of resentment, the undesirability may only be based on the implications of the event relative to I-goals. So, a secretary in some huge multinational corporation may resent the fact that the chairman of the corporation gets a $200,000 pay raise. She may feel resentment on the basis of general I-goals about fairness and social values. Were she to focus on the money and her desire for it, rather than on the injustice of the chairman's receiving it, she might experience envy, and if, in addition, she were to believe that the chairman's getting such a large raise reduced or excluded the possibility of her getting a large raise, she could experience jealousy.

This last point again shows the relation between desirability and deservingness. The big raise may be resented less if it is judged to be deserved. Sometimes deservingness seems to influence desirability directly. Part of the executive's problem with his colleague's pay raise is that he believes his colleague to be incompetent. He considers it unfair for undeserving people to be rewarded, because it violates some sort of "just deserts" principle. Notice, however, that liking plays an important role here too. If the colleague were a close friend, the executive might feel happy for him rather than resentful, because an I-goal having to do with the prosperity of friends would be facilitated. It is also entirely possible for a person to take both perspectives and to have "mixed feelings" about such an event – partly happy for the good fortune of a friend and partly resentful of the perceived injustice.

In the sociological and social psychological literature, resentment is often discussed in the context of feelings of *relative deprivation* (e.g., Crosby, 1976; Davis, 1959; Merton & Rossi, 1957; Runciman, 1966) and inequity (e.g., Adams, 1965; Homans, 1974; Walster, Walster & Berscheid, 1978). The concept of relative deprivation came from a study of American soldiers in which it was found that airmen were more dissatisfied with the Army's promotion system than were military policemen, even though the former enjoyed more rapid promotion than did the latter (Stouffer, Suchman, DeVinney, Star & Williams, 1949). The reason apparently was that policemen were comparing themselves to a reference group consisting of other enlisted men, while airmen were comparing themselves with men who had already been made officers. The concepts of reference group and relative deprivation appear to have considerable explanatory value. The reference group concept is particularly important for understanding the role of social comparison processes in the Resentment emotions. One is much less likely to experience resentment over the riches of princes than over the pay raises of co-workers, because for most of us princes are not part of our reference group.

Accounts of relative deprivation are close to our own analysis of resentment. Davis (1959), for example, concludes that feelings of relative deprivation occur when an individual who lacks something he desires compares himself with someone within his own social group who has it. We have not included in the specification of Resentment emotions the requirement that one must either lack or desire the outcome enjoyed by the other, because some examples of BEING DISPLEASED ABOUT AN EVENT PRESUMED TO BE DESIRABLE FOR SOMEONE ELSE (i.e., resentment) involve neither. Nevertheless, these factors are probably more often present than absent when resentment occurs, and they clearly intensify the emotion. Indeed, as our discussion of envy and jealousy suggests, they may be necessary components of those particular forms of resentment. Nor have we listed relative deprivation or reference group membership as intensity variables for Resentment emotions, although it is clear that sometimes these are important influences. We have not listed them because we suspect the work they do is mediated by one of two other variables. Specifically, these factors may achieve their effects through the desirability-for-self variable or through the deservingness variable. Certainly one's sense that the other does not deserve his good fortune is likely to be much keener to the extent that it is fueled by one's own sense of privation and by a perception that the other is comparable to oneself.

There is an important issue lurking in the background here. We have suggested that resentment results from being displeased at an event presumed to be desirable for another person, and that this can arise when one views the desirable event for the other to be undeserved. Clearly, the judgment that something is or is not deserved is a judgment that can only be made by invoking standards. However, it does not follow from this that we have incorrectly located the emotion of being DISPLEASED ABOUT AN EVENT PRESUMED TO BE DESIRABLE FOR SOMEONE ELSE, and that it ought to have been located in the Attribution emotions because of its dependence on standards, rather than in the Event-based emotions, which are rooted in goals. The reason this emotion is an Event-based emotion is that the *central* variable upon which it depends and which is featured in the emotion specification is that of desirability. There is nothing in the system that we propose that prohibits other local variables from inheriting their value from sources different from those of the central variables. Indeed, the fourth listed intensity variable in the Fortunes-of-others emotions, namely the *liking* variable ultimately inherits its value from attitudes.

Now, there is no doubt that people who resent some fact (such as that an incompetent colleague gets an inordinately large pay raise) can *also* feel contempt or anger towards those responsible for what they consider to be a blameworthy act. Notice, however, that in the case of anger, let us say toward the colleague's boss, for making such a recommendation, the anger is focused on the action of the boss rather than on the recipient of the pay raise precisely to the degree that the boss is held responsible. The executive might feel contempt for the boss but not for his colleague, but he would resent *the fact that* his colleague received too large a raise, that is, he would be focusing on the event rather than on agency. It is clear that these two aspects of an event (the outcome and the agency) can sometimes be very closely intertwined. This is perhaps the reason why some emotion words, at least in English, seem applicable to both. Thus, there is a sense of "resentment" that *does* focus on agency, as when one resents someone meddling in one's affairs, even if no harm results. This second sense of "resentment" in fact belongs in the Attribution emotions (it is a Reproach emotion). It might be profitable to distinguish these two forms of resentment as "Event-focused" and "Agent-focused" resentment. Before leaving this topic, we should note that the ambiguity of words such as "resentment" constitutes another example of why it is that we think our general approach of characterizing emotions in terms of *type* specifications and then assimilating emotion word *tokens* to them is superior to attempting to *define* emotions by examining emotion word tokens.

We turn now to gloating, which we take to be the closest word in English to represent the emotion of delighting in the misfortune of others (the German word "Schadenfreude" means precisely this). The same variables are at work here. Within limits, the greater the misfortune, the greater the satisfaction that the malicious "gloater" derives. However, there *are* limits. At some point, increases in the presumed undesirability of the event for the other may start to lead to pity. Just as in the case of being happy for someone, we noted that it is possible for there to be an upper limit on the degree to which the event is presumed to be desirable for the other, so too, for the same reason, there can be an upper limit on how undesirable the event is in the case of gloating. Consider how Nixon's political opponents might have gloated over his departure from office. We are supposing that this is because they thought he "got what he deserved." However, even the most staunch opponent would probably agree that public physical torture would have been entirely inappropriate – it would have been worse than he deserved. If the event affecting the other person is so undesirable that it is worse than is deserved, gloating might turn to pity. The punishment must (appear to) fit the crime.

There is another interesting connection between gloating and pity. We have just seen how gloating can change to pity if the undesirability for the other person moves out of the range required to render it desirable for the experiencer. This fact is perfectly consistent with the corresponding type specifications. It is also the case that liking behaves in essentially the same way for both. In the case of the Sorry-for emotions we noted that it was not necessary to actively like the other person in order to feel sorry for him, although increases in liking would certainly intensify the emotion. So too in the case of the Gloating emotions, it is not necessary to actively dislike other people in order to gloat over their misfortune, although the less one likes them, the more intense is the emotion likely to be. To see the truth of this, one has to remember that the misfortunes of the other people only need to be *relatively* undesirable for them – all that is required is that they be at a relative disadvantage. So, for example, when, during the course of a casual game of chess between friends, one player makes an ill-considered and foolish move, the other player may gloat over his relative advantage without in any way disliking his opponent. At the same time, we have suggested, if the game is not so friendly, and the opponent is in fact disliked, the gloating may be more intense, even though, quite possibly, and perhaps atypically, the gloating person may be less likely to *express* his emotion.

In discussing resentment, we raised the question of the relation between the desirability of the event for the other person and for oneself. As we have just seen in the example about the chess game, in the case of Gloating emotions, it is even more clear that one needs a rather liberal interpretation of the mismatch between desirability for the self and for the other. Specifically, the eliciting conditions of being (PLEASED ABOUT) AN EVENT PRESUMED TO BE UNDESIRABLE FOR SOMEONE ELSE will be satisfied if either of two discriminable events occurs. First, the victim of the misfortune may directly experience something undesirable that is only desirable for the gloating person in that it furthers his I-goals; it does not facilitate the achievement of any of the gloating person's Active-pursuit goals. An example of this would be the kind of Gloating emotion that a committed Democratic voter not otherwise actively engaged in politics might have experienced in response to Nixon's resignation. No A-goal of the gloating person need be facilitated, although an A-goal, and in this particular example, probably, a Preservation goal, of the unfortunate *other* is certainly thwarted. Alternatively, it might be the gloating person who is the direct beneficiary of an event that he thinks places him at some sort of advantage relative to the other person, so that the gloating person is essentially responding to the relative deprivation of the other person. In this case, the gloating person will be responding to the facilitation of one of his A-goals that might only be relevant to the I-goals of the victim of his malice. An example of this kind might be the reaction that one person in a company could have to the fact that she receives a larger pay raise than one of her co-workers. The upshot of all this is, again, the observation that the question of desirability and deservingness in the context of the Fortunes-of-others emotions involves social comparisons (Suls & Miller, 1977). What is at issue can best be described as *relative* advantages and disadvantages enjoyed by the self vis à vis the other, as we saw in the example of the basketball player whose friend is drafted while he is not. Since people cannot help but evaluate the fortunes of others at least in part with reference to their own situations, this is a perfectly reasonable conclusion.

Perhaps gloating is a particularly objectionable emotion because in many cases there can be no benefit to the gloater resulting from the misfortunes of some other, however disliked that other may be. There are, of course, particular cases in which this is not true, cases that might be construed as the converse of envy, but in general, the gloating sentiment is pure ill will. It is obviously intensified by lack of liking for the suffering person and by the gloater's beliefs about how the suffering other deserves his or her misfortunes. Because gloating can result from the misfortunes of another construed in terms of the gloater possessing something that the other lacks, gloating can be somewhat close to pride, at least in the case of pride in which the experiencer focuses on the fact that "generic" others lack his good fortunes. We shall have more to say about pride in Chapter 7.

Self-pity and Related States

The Fortunes-of-others emotions all involve the experiencer being pleased or displeased about the effects of some event on another person. There are many occasions, however, in which one can feel "sorry for oneself." How can this be explained? Our approach to dealing with this question is to argue that people sometimes detach themselves from their own situations and view themselves as though they were someone else. This transformation of the self into a detached other is more transparently applicable to the negative cases of the Fortunes-of-others emotions (resentment and pity) than to the positive ones (happy-for and gloating). The case corresponding to resentment we characterize as being DISPLEASED ABOUT AN EVENT PRESUMED TO BE DESIRABLE FOR ONESELF (VIEWED AS ANOTHER). Such an emotion might be elicited if, for example, a person were to receive a prestigious prize that he knew he did not in fact deserve. In such a case, it seems possible that the person would describe himself as feeling undeserving or guilty. One might wonder why in such a case it is necessary to think that the person must view himself as another. Our answer to this question is that a certain degree of detachment of this kind is necessary for people to perceive themselves as not deserving what they have. The easiest case in which to see the kind of self-distancing we have in mind here is provided by being DISPLEASED ABOUT AN EVENT PRESUMED TO BE UNDESIRABLE FOR ONESELF (VIEWED AS ANOTHER). This seems to be precisely what happens when people experience self-pity – they view themselves as though they were someone else, they view their misfortune as undeserved, and they complain "Why me? What have I done to deserve this?"

The analogues of the positive Fortunes-of-others emotions in which the self is viewed as another are proposed with much more caution. In the case of the analogue for the Happy-for emotions, part of the difficulty lies in the fact that if one is PLEASED ABOUT AN EVENT PRESUMED TO BE DESIRABLE FOR ONESELF (VIEWED AS ANOTHER), one will have necessarily satisfied the eliciting conditions for one of the self-focused Event-based emotions (e.g., satisfaction) which may be more salient in experience. However, there are words in English, such as "vindicated," that come close to characterizing what we have in mind here. Vindication seems to carry with it a suggestion of being deservedly right about something. What it lacks is a strong focus on the being pleased component so that it may strike one as a poor example of an emotion. There is a similar difficulty with an analogue for the Gloating emotions, which would have to be characterized as PLEASED ABOUT AN EVENT PRESUMED TO BE UNDESIRABLE FOR ONESELF (VIEWED AS ANOTHER). Particularly difficult in this case is the idea that one might be pleased at an undesirable event, which, in terms of our system, appears to be a contradiction. The nearest word that seems to capture what this concept might be is "contrition." The state we are trying to characterize is one in which a person has some sort of positive reaction to the misfortunes he or she is suffering. These proposals must be regarded as very tentative – much more so even than the negative cases corresponding to resentment and pity.

We have presented this brief excursion into some states that are systematically related to the Fortunes-of-others emotions primarily because it constitutes another example of the kind of further fine-grained analysis that we think can be undertaken with the system we are proposing. Just as we were able to propose the Loss group as a subgroup of Distress emotions resulting from constraining the value of the undesirable event to some kind of loss, so too in the Fortunes-of-others emotions it is possible to identify a subgroup by constraining the identity of the target person to a "transformed-self-into-other." We consider this principle of constraining features in type specifications to be an important one – much more important, in fact, than the question of whether the particular constraints that we propose are reasonable.

Summary

The two Well-being emotions are characterized simply as being PLEASED ABOUT A DESIRABLE EVENT (e.g., joy) and being DISPLEASED ABOUT AN UNDESIRABLE EVENT (e.g., distress). The only variable, other than global variables, that affects the intensity of these emotions is the desirability of the event. There are a large number of lexical items associated with the Well-being emotions, reflecting reactions to different types of events. For example, we have included in the Distress emotions different types of Loss emotions such as grief (loss of a loved one) and homesickness (loss of the comforts of home). Such emotions could be distinguished in a finer grained analysis, but they do not form a system with characteristic eliciting conditions and intensity variables beyond the level of analysis presented.

The second group of four emotions discussed in the chapter are the Fortunes-of-others emotions. Their eliciting conditions are characterized by two variables: one's own reaction to the event, and the presumed value of the event for the other person. Two of these emotions, PLEASED ABOUT AN EVENT PRESUMED TO BE DESIRABLE FOR SOMEONE ELSE (e.g., happy-for) and DISPLEASED ABOUT AN EVENT PRESUMED TO BE UNDESIRABLE FOR SOMEONE ELSE (e.g., pity) can be thought of as Good-will emotions. The other two emotions, PLEASED

ABOUT AN EVENT PRESUMED TO BE UNDESIRABLE FOR SOMEONE ELSE (e.g., gloating) and DISPLEASED ABOUT AN EVENT PRESUMED TO BE DESIRABLE FOR SOMEONE ELSE (e.g., resentment), are Ill-will emotions. There are four variables that affect the intensity of the Fortunes-of-others emotions: (1) the desirability of the event for oneself, (2) the desirability of the event for the other person, (3) the deservingness of the other person, and (4) one's liking for the other person. While these variables often interact (e.g., one's evaluation of a person's deservingness sometimes depends on how much one likes that person at the moment), each of the four variables can vary independently in some situations. It is also possible to view oneself sometimes as through the eyes of another, which leads to a set of self-referenced Fortunes-of-others emotions that might be thought of as self-pity (= sorry-for), feeling undeserving (= resentment), vindicated (= happy-for), and contrition (= gloating). These proposals for self-referenced Fortunes-of-others emotions must be regarded as very tentative.

6   Reactions to Events: II

We often experience emotions in response to expected or suspected events (e.g., fear), and in response to the confirmation or disconfirmation of such events (e.g., relief). Emotions resulting from the consideration of such *prospects* and their confirmation or disconfirmation comprise the group that we call the "Prospect-based" emotions. In many cases the prospect of an event involves a conscious expectation that it will occur in the future, although, as we shall see shortly, the fact that it appears to be possible for there to be experiences of what might be called "retrospective" fear and relief suggests that this need not always be so. In this chapter we discuss these emotions and a number of related issues.

The Prospect-based Emotions

The Prospect-based emotions are all characterized as reactions to (i.e., being pleased or displeased about) the prospect of an event, or to the confirmation or disconfirmation of the prospect of an event. In those cases involving the confirmation or disconfirmation of the prospect of an event, the most typical cases are ones in which the event has already occurred (or failed to occur) but in which the prospect of the event had earlier been entertained. However, a person can also react to the prospect of an event counterfactually, by thinking about or imagining what it would have been like had the contemplated event transpired. Thus, although the experience of fear is usually a reaction to an anticipated *future* undesirable event, it is possible to retrospectively contemplate events in the sense that one can "think back" about what one's cognitions were, or might have been, prior to some event, or entertain how things would have been had they turned out differently. In such cases, fear can be experienced *after* one knows that the event in question has transpired. For example, following the initial shock of having almost been killed in a car accident, one might well be frightened upon considering how close the prospective event (of being

109

Table 6.1 *Prospect-based emotions*

| | APPRAISAL OF PROSPECTIVE EVENT | |
STATUS OF EVENT	DESIRABLE	UNDESIRABLE
UNCONFIRMED	pleased about the prospect of a desirable event (e.g., hope)	displeased about the prospect of an undesirable event (e.g., fear)
CONFIRMED	pleased about the confirmation of the prospect of a desirable event (e.g., satisfaction)	displeased about the confirmation of the prospect of an undesirable event (e.g., fears-confirmed)
DISCONFIRMED	displeased about the disconfirmation of the prospect of a desirable event (e.g., disappointment)	pleased about the disconfirmation of the prospect of an undesirable event (e.g., relief)

killed) was to being realized. In such cases it seems reasonable to say that the fear is a reaction to the *prospect* of the event of being killed in a car crash, rather than a reaction to a future event. Perhaps more compelling is the fact that one can experience relief without there having been any prior consideration or expectation of the event. A person who discovers that the plane he missed crashed, killing all the passengers, is likely to experience relief (as well, quite possibly, as retrospective fear). Such phenomena are accommodated in our system by characterizing the Prospect-based emotions in terms of *prospects* of events, rather in terms of future or expected events.

The six Prospect-based emotions are represented in Table 6.1 which shows the various relations between possible appraisals of prospective events and the current situation (i.e., the status of the event). In the table, the columns represent the appraisal of the prospective event as desirable or undesirable, and the rows represent the status of the event. As always, the emotions depend not on the actual state of affairs in the real world, but on the experiencing person's beliefs, so that the status of the event depends not upon the actual occurrence or nonoccurrence of the prospective events, but on the experiencing person's beliefs about such occurrences. We distinguish three levels of the status of the event. First, the experiencer may not (yet) know whether or not the event has transpired – or at least, views it in that light. This is labeled the "unconfirmed" status. Second, the person may believe that the event has occurred (labeled "confirmed"), and third, the person may believe that the event failed to occur (labeled "disconfirmed"). Thus, the three rows correspond to three subclasses of the Prospect-based emotions. The first class of Prospect-based emotions is made up of the *Prospect emotions*, of which fear is a good example. These are the emotions that result from reacting to the prospect of a desirable or undesirable event without reference to whether or not the event has transpired. So, for example, a person might react with hope at the prospect of being offered a job that she had applied for, or with fear at the prospect of not being offered it. The second class of Prospect-based emotions contains the *Confirmation emotions*, of which satisfaction is an example. These result from reacting to the (believed) confirmation of an event that did produce (or could have produced) a Prospect emotion. Confirmation emotions can only arise *after* the event is believed to have occurred. Thus, if the woman in the example just given were to be offered the job, she might feel satisfied with respect to her earlier hope. If she feared she would not get the job, and her application turned out to be unsuccessful, she might feel that her fears had been confirmed. Finally, the third class consists of the *Disconfirmation emotions*, such as relief. These too can only arise *after* the event is believed to have occurred, except, of course, that the event associated with the related Prospect emotion is believed to have been disconfirmed. So, for example, if the woman were offered the job that she had feared she would not get, the ensuing relief would be a disconfirmation emotion, as would be the disappointment she would feel on discovering she was not to be offered the job.

As with all the other emotion types that we identify, each cell in the table is best regarded as a family of emotional states. The most salient dimension along which members of each family differ is intensity. As the intensity changes, so does the appropriateness of any particular emotion word within the family. If, say, DISPLEASED ABOUT THE PROSPECT OF AN UNDESIRABLE EVENT is of relatively low intensity, the specific emotion seems better expressed by a word like "apprehension." If it is moderately strong, "fear" or "fright" may be appropriate, and if very strong, "dread" or "terror" might be the most appropriate labels. If the intensity is too low, there may be no emotional experience at all. In such cases we might have a cognitive state such as concern, rather than an emotional state (see Ortony & Clore, 1981).

In addition to intensity, members of cell families sometimes differ in other respects. For example, one of the ways in which individual tokens of Fear emotions (DISPLEASED ABOUT THE PROSPECT OF AN UNDESIRABLE EVENT) differ from one another is that some forms relate to a specific object (e.g., being scared) and others to more diffuse causes (e.g., being anxious). Another dimension along which they vary is the subjective proximity of the event being considered. We tend to use words like "fear" and "fright" to refer to relatively imminent situations, particularly when they might threaten bodily harm, whereas we use terms like "worry" and "apprehension" with respect to more remote and possibly less serious threats. In addition, the language provides lexical items that seem to refer to different referential components (see Ortony, Clore, & Foss, 1987) of the same emotion type. For example, in the context of fear, there are words such as "worry" that highlight *cognitive* aspects of fear, words like "jittery" that seem to focus on *physical* aspects, and words like "cowering" that emphasize *behavioral* factors. Further evidence of this sort of linguistic richness is noted in the section on suspense and related states toward the end of this chapter.

We now present the emotion specifications of the families of emotions that constitute the Prospect-based emotions. First, we shall discuss the Prospect emotions themselves, that is, the emotions that are reactions to the prospect of events. As discussed in Chapter 2, these reactions are always some form of the reactions of being *pleased* or *displeased*.

(6.1) **HOPE EMOTIONS**
       TYPE SPECIFICATION: (pleased about) the prospect of a desirable event
       TOKENS: anticipation, anticipatory excitement, excitement, expectancy, hope, hopeful, looking forward to, etc.
       VARIABLES AFFECTING INTENSITY:
       (1) the degree to which the event is desirable
       (2) the likelihood of the event
       EXAMPLE: As she thought about the possibility of being asked to the dance, the girl was filled with hope.

(6.2) **FEAR EMOTIONS**
       TYPE SPECIFICATION: (displeased about) the prospect of an undesirable event
       TOKENS: apprehensive, anxious, cowering, dread, fear, fright, nervous, petrified, scared, terrified, timid, worried, etc.
       VARIABLES AFFECTING INTENSITY:
       (1) the degree to which the event is undesirable
       (2) the likelihood of the event
       EXAMPLE: The employee, suspecting he was no longer needed, feared that he would be fired.

The most convenient type identifications for the two Prospect emotions are "Hope" and "Fear," although, as we shall see shortly, the ordinary language terms "hope" and "fear" do not behave like perfect antonyms. For both of these emotions we indicate *desirability* and *likelihood* as influencing intensity. The effects of desirability are clear. The girl who thinks about being asked to the dance will experience hope with greater intensity the more desirable it is for her that the boy ask her out. Similarly the employee who fears being fired will experience a more intense emotion if he sees the prospect of being fired as disastrous and therefore as highly undesirable than he will if he is unhappy in his present job and thinking about moving anyway.

In general, the desirability or undesirability of the event has to be above some threshold for an emotion to be experienced at all. In cases where it is not, there are two possibilities. First, there may be no particular mental state that arises over and above the cognitive states associated with entertaining the prospect of the event. So, if a person thinks he may have lost a quarter, the prospect of the loss, while slightly undesirable, normally does not give rise to any corresponding emotional state. In fact, it probably would be accurate to say that the person was *indifferent* to the prospect of the loss. It would be odd, however, to suggest that the prospect of the loss could *cause* indifference, because that would suggest some additional resulting mental state that might well not exist. Indifference is best construed as the *absence* of any valenced reaction, and in our view all emotions are *valenced* reactions. Second, if the desirability or undesirability of the event is greater, but still below threshold, there might be an attendant affective state, but one which is still of insufficient intensity for it to be experienced as an emotion. For most nondestitute adults in most contexts, the prospect of having lost five dollars would not give rise to the emotional state of being DISPLEASED ABOUT THE PROSPECT OF AN UNDESIRABLE EVENT, although it might lead to a corresponding *cognitive* state that one might think of as (mild) concern. Fear emotions are only experienced when the undesirability of the prospective event exceeds some threshold value. Thus, for example, people might well experience a Fear emotion if they believe that they may have lost their savings in an uninsured, collapsed, savings and loan institution.

There remains a further issue that needs to be discussed in connection with the desirability variable and the Prospect emotions. In fact, the issue is a quite general one concerning the relation between desirable events and the absence of undesirable ones, and between undesirable events and the absence of desirable ones. Often there is no difference; however, subtle differences may arise in the experience of emotions resulting from these slightly different sources. Consider a young man who, having finally plucked up the courage to ask out a woman to whom he is much attracted, is waiting for her arrival at the agreed upon place. As the time of her expected arrival approaches, we assume that he is PLEASED ABOUT THE PROSPECT OF A DESIRABLE EVENT; that is, he is filled with hope or, perhaps better, with anticipatory excitement. As time passes, any doubts he may have had about whether or not she would indeed show up begin to loom larger. Slowly, his anticipatory excitement starts to turn to concern or worry that she will not appear, and eventually to resignation, hopelessness, and disappointment. However, notice that the undesirable event that constitutes the object of this concern is that the earlier anticipated desirable event might not materialize, that is, it is of the *complement* of an earlier anticipated event. In other words, initially he reacts to the prospect of her arriving, but later, he reacts to the prospect of her *not* arriving.[1] In fact, the situation is quite symmetrical. If one experiences a Fear emotion with respect to some prospective event that is undesirable to some degree, then the absence of that event will be desirable to the same degree. If one fears something that is extremely undesirable, one will consider it extremely desirable that the feared event not happen, and, of course, if one reacts to this latter prospect, the eliciting conditions for a Hope emotion are satisfied. Thus, insofar as hope and fear have complementary objects (an event occurring and not occurring) the contribution of desirability to the intensity of the two emotions will also be the same, so that one might expect the intensity of fear and of hope to sum to a constant for the occurrence and nonoccurrence of any prospective event.

The other local variable that affects the intensity of the Prospect emotions is the likelihood variable, which is manifested in these emotions as the subjective likelihood of the prospective event occurring. In the case of the Fear emotions, it seems fairly clear that intensity will increase as the subjective likelihood of the prospective undesirable event increases. An interesting aspect of the likelihood variable in fear has to do with what happens when the subjective likelihood of the prospective event reaches such a high value that the person views it as inevitable. At this point, "fear" becomes an inappropriate label for the emotion; "dread" is much better. Perhaps this is because whereas "fear" focuses on the *possibility* that the feared event will occur, "dread" seems to *presuppose* that it will. This seems to be reflected in ordinary language. It is much more natural to say "I have to undergo root canal treatment tomorrow. I am dreading it," than to say "I might have to undergo root canal treatment. I am dreading it." In the former case, it is presupposed that the undesirable event will take place, so that the reaction of dread is to the prospect of something assumed to be

1 Notice, incidentally, that whereas the emotion that characterizes this latter reaction (however strong) can reasonably be thought of as a Fear emotion in the sense that it is a case of being displeased about the prospect of an undesirable event, English does not seem to have an entirely appropriate word for the particular quality of this emotion. Certainly "fear" does not adequately capture it, although one might come close to expressing it if one described him as being "anxious about her not arriving."

inevitable. In the second case, the treatment (i.e., the prospective event) remains merely a possibility, so that there seems to be something odd about dreading it, given that it might not happen. The upshot of this is that dread appears to be a limiting case of a Fear emotion, characterized by the difference between reacting to the prospect of an event assumed to be probable to some degree, and the prospect of an event that is assumed to be inevitable.

In general, we do not attempt to arbitrate between different intensity variables with respect to the relative degrees to which they contribute to the intensity of the emotions they affect. Our reason for this is that the issue is an empirical one for which, in most cases, relevant data do not yet exist. However, in the case of the Fear and Hope emotions the issue warrants some discussion. There is no reason to suppose that in the case of Fear emotions the contributions of undesirability and likelihood are comparable. Ordinarily, these emotions only occur when people think the prospective event is at least moderately probable and moderately undesirable. And, in fact, we are inclined to make the same general statement about the Hope emotions conceived of as being PLEASED ABOUT THE PROSPECT OF A DESIRABLE EVENT. However, the situation is somewhat different for the emotion that is ordinarily called "hope." Like fear, hope involves a component having to do with desirability and a component having to do with likelihood but, unlike fear, ordinary language marks two distinguishable states, one of which focuses on one of these components, and one on the other. We refer here to the two terms "hope" and "hopefulness." The two are different. Hope focuses on desirability, whereas hopefulness focuses on likelihood. Most people who buy state lottery tickets very much *hope* (i.e., desire) to win, but those who are even slightly realistic are rarely very *hopeful* (i.e., they do not think it very likely) that they will. The two variables, desirability and likelihood, operate not in concert, as they seem to do in Fear emotions, but substantially independently, one on each of the two distinguishable states. The intensity of hope is influenced almost exclusively by desirability. One hopes more for highly desirable events than for less desirable ones, but the degree of subjective likelihood contributes relatively little. Conversely, hopefulness is influenced primarily by likelihood. One is more hopeful about events one deems more likely to occur than one is about events one views as less likely, but the desirability of the event contributes little provided that it is above some minimum value. In fact, it might be argued that hopefulness (as opposed to hope) is not an emotion at all. This is because it focuses on likelihood (which is unvalenced) rather than on desirability (which is), and so, because its intensity is not affected by desirability, it cannot be a differentiated form of being pleased. For this reason we have proposed elsewhere (Ortony, Clore, & Foss, 1987) that "hopefulness" refers to a cognitive state reflecting degree of confidence rather than to an emotional state. A high degree of hopefulness can be construed as being the positive analogue of some negative state such as resignation, although the latter carries with it the additional implication of an acceptance of the inevitability of an undesirable event.

The common wisdom is that hope and fear are direct opposites, but as can be seen from the above analysis this is not quite accurate because likelihood does not significantly influence the intensity of hope whereas it does have a significant influence on the intensity of fear. Again, as we consider the fact that some emotion words in English focus on some components of an emotion specification at the expense of others, we see the virtues of characterizing the emotion types in general terms such as being PLEASED ABOUT THE PROSPECT OF A DESIRABLE EVENT. This state is clearly not quite the same as those usually referred to as "hope" or "hopefulness," which we take to be special subcases of it. The state we characterize as the emotion type of Hope emotions represents a sort of union of the two states referred to in English as "hope" and "hopefulness." Probably the expression that maps onto it most accurately is that of "anticipatory excitement," the intensity of which is a function of both desirability and likelihood. However, because our goal is not to define English emotion words, but to give the cognitive structural descriptions of a set of distinct emotion types, the fact that the quality of mapping of emotion words onto emotion types varies does not constitute a special problem.

Because the global variables affect the intensity of all emotions, we do not routinely discuss them in presenting our discussions of particular emotions and groups of emotions. However, in the case of the Prospect-based emotions, some of the global variables behave in interesting ways. One example of such a global variable is *proximity*. At first sight it might be thought that proximity is the same as likelihood. However, this is not so. As discussed in Chapter 4, proximity is intended to refer not only to the approach in time of some prospective event, but more generally to its psychological proximity. This might sometimes be realized in terms of spatial proximity. For example, one might suppose that people living close to the site of a nuclear power plant accident would be more afraid, other things being equal, than those living further away from it. However, spatial proximity and temporal proximity are usually highly correlated. If proximity is construed in this general way, that is, as subjective closeness, one would not expect it to have an effect in cases where the prospective event was a future one for which the timing was unknown. So, if a confidently expected future event is expected to arise at some unspecified future time, the subjective proximity need not change appreciably even though the passage of time logically necessitates an increase in *objective* proximity. For example, if a woman knows that a decision regarding her job application is going to be made at a particular meeting on a particular day, the intensity with which she may experience a Fear emotion because she thinks that her application will not be successful, or the intensity with which she may experience a Hope emotion that it will, is likely to increase as the day in question approaches. If, in contrast, she only knows that the decision will be made some time in the future, subjective proximity might not increase from day to day because she is, as it were, shooting at a moving target. That the proximity variable is impotent in such cases has been demonstrated in a number of empirical studies (e.g., Elliott, 1969; Mansueto & Desiderato, 1971; and Petry & Desiderato, 1978), all of which found that when the exact time of an anticipated negative event is not known, the intensity-of-fear curve shows a gradual relaxation after the threat, with no concomitant increase as time goes on.

When proximity does affect the intensity of the Prospect emotions, it does so in a fairly straightforward manner. Given that one is hoping for or fearing something, the intensity of the emotion increases as one's subjective proximity to the situation increases, provided that the event is expected to materialize at some particular known future time. Imagine a man who suffers from fear of flying and who knows on some particular day that the following day he will have to take a flight. He knows that there is no alternative for him, and that his taking the flight is certain, and unavoidable. As the time at which he has to take the flight draws closer, the objective likelihood of the feared situation stays constant and we assume that the subjective likelihood stays constant too.[2] Nevertheless, the intensity of Fear emotions will increase as the time draws closer even though the subjective likelihood remains constant. Breznitz's (1984) extensive studies on the time course of fear after warnings confirms this analysis. His data, and those of other investigators, reveal a U-shaped function of the intensity of fear reactions over time (as measured by, for example, heart rate and skin conductance). The first peak occurs at the time of the warning when,

2 Technically, it might be argued that in the general case this may not be quite accurate. At least in the case of desirable events, there is some evidence (e.g., Pyszczynski, 1982) that subjects lower their likelihood estimates, presumably as a strategy to avoid disappointment in the event that the attractive outcome fails to materialize. However, such reassessments of likelihood (and in fact of the desirability of the event) already presuppose a level of subjective likelihood with respect to which the estimate is lowered, and are as likely to represent the effects of superstition and personality as they are genuine beliefs about changes in likelihood of events beyond the subjects' control.

for the first time, subjects realize that they are going to be subjected to an unpleasant experience (an electric shock). This initial intense reaction, which is presumably at least in part a result of the contrast between the prior relaxed state and the sudden realization of an impending aversive stimulus, quickly falls off. It is followed by a gradual increase in intensity as the time of the unpleasant stimulus approaches. Whether one wants to argue that these results pertain to the intensity of fear or to the intensity first of shock, then of fear, and finally of dread is not the issue here. Rather, the point is the indisputable effect of proximity to the prospective event, as distinct from the effects of subjective likelihood.

Our analysis of the intensity of Fear emotions in terms of desirability, likelihood, and global variables like proximity permits a coherent account of the nature of "irrational" fears, or phobias. We characterize a phobia as a case in which a person experiences fear partly because the subjective likelihood of the feared event is much greater than it is for nonphobics. That is, somebody who, for example, has an irrational fear of flying may have a higher subjective likelihood of a disaster on particular flights than would normal fellow passengers. This could be true, even though the phobic might agree that the likelihood of airplane crashes in general, and thus the objective likelihood of his being on a flight that does crash, is in fact quite low. One of the ways in which such increases in subjective likelihood arises in phobics may be through vividly imagining the particular feared event (i.e., this plane crashing with me on it). Research on Tversky and Kahneman's (1973) "availability heuristic" has shown that vividly imagining the occurrence of a particular (future) event results in increases in people's estimates of the likelihood that the event will in fact occur (Carroll, 1978). As mentioned in Chapter 3, in terms of our own theory, one might characterize this process as one in which vividly imagining some future situation increases the contribution to the intensity of fear made by the global sense of reality variable. Thus it may well be that increases in subjective likelihood in phobics are due at least in part to increases in the sense of reality associated with a certain class of prospective events.

We move now to a discussion of that subset of the Prospect-based emotions that we call the "Confirmation" emotions, namely reactions that result from believing that an event that can give rise to a Prospect emotion has in fact occurred.

(6.3)   **SATISFACTION EMOTIONS**
TYPE SPECIFICATION: (pleased about) the confirmation of the prospect of a desirable event
TOKENS: gratification, hopes-realized, satisfaction, etc.

VARIABLES AFFECTING INTENSITY:
(1) the intensity of the attendant hope emotion
(2) the effort expended in trying to attain the event
(3) the degree to which the event is realized
EXAMPLE: When she realized that she was indeed being asked to go
to the dance by the boy of her dreams, the girl was gratified.

(6.4)   **FEARS-CONFIRMED EMOTIONS**

TYPE SPECIFICATION: (displeased about) the confirmation of the
prospect of an undesirable event
TOKENS: fears-confirmed, worst fears realized
VARIABLES AFFECTING INTENSITY:
(1) the intensity of the attendant fear emotion
(2) the effort expended in trying to prevent the event
(3) the degree to which the event is realized
EXAMPLE: The employee's fears were confirmed when he learned
that he was indeed going to be fired.

The two Confirmation emotions specified above are interesting in that
they are not associated with many lexical items in English. "Satisfaction"
and "fears-confirmed" seem to be the best way we have to express them.
Nevertheless, they do seem to be phenomenally distinct emotions, although, as we shall discuss shortly, they may not be experientially very
salient because they are often masked by other emotions.

Three factors are proposed as influencing the intensity of these particular emotions. The first is the intensity of the attendant Prospect emotion
(hope or fear). In addition, two other variables play a role, namely effort
and degree of realization. The intensity of the attendant Prospect emotion
carries the effects of those variables that influenced it (specifically, desirability, likelihood, and whatever global variables were operative). This
means that variables such as desirability and proximity have their effect
on Confirmation emotions *through* their effect on the attendant Prospect
emotion. For example, in the case of the girl who is asked to the dance by
the boy of her dreams, we are proposing that the intensity of the Confirmation emotion (e.g., satisfaction) she experiences when he does will
depend in part on the intensity of the Prospect emotion (e.g., hope) that
is related to it. The more she hoped for it, the greater will be the subsequent satisfaction when he does. The same holds for the man who feared
he would be fired. The more fear he had, the stronger will be his sense of
fears-confirmed. If he had anticipated it, but had had no attendant fear,
then there would be no Confirmation emotion. This is not surprising if
one considers that the eliciting conditions for hope and fear (THE PROS-
PECT OF A DESIRABLE EVENT, and THE PROSPECT OF AN UNDESIR-

ABLE EVENT) are actually contained in the type specifications of the Confirmation (and indeed, of the Disconfirmation) emotions.

The Confirmation emotions are the first ones we discuss that involve the *effort* variable. In the case of the girl, we assume that, apart from the contribution made by her degree of prior hope, the intensity of her being PLEASED ABOUT THE CONFIRMATION OF THE PROSPECT OF A DESIRABLE EVENT will depend on the amount of effort she invested in trying to bring about the invitation. The more she tried, the more satisfaction will she feel as a result of her successful efforts. Similarly, the more the man who fears being fired tries to avoid it, the stronger will be his feeling of being DISPLEASED ABOUT THE CONFIRMATION OF THE PROSPECT OF AN UNDESIRABLE EVENT when he is fired. Thus, as discussed in Chapter 4, the investment of effort increases the intensity of these emotions.

The Confirmation emotions presuppose a high degree of similarity between the prospective event and the realized one. However, these events need not be identical. A person may anticipate some rather general undesirable situation but the realized event, because it is an actual event, cannot be comparably vague and nonspecific. For example, a person might fear that he will get a minimal pay raise because of poor performance for the year. In such a case, there could be a whole range of actual events (getting no raise, getting a 1% raise, a 1.5% raise, a 2% raise, and so on) that are to some degree compatible with the prospective event. However, although the prospective event of getting only a small raise is not identical to the realized event of, for example, getting no raise at all, both can be readily assimilated to a superordinate description of getting no significant raise that would render them equivalent. At least in this sense, the construals of the prospective and realized events must be identical. This means that in general, prospective events can be realized to a greater or lesser extent, so that the degree to which they are realized becomes a factor that influences intensity. We shall discuss this issue in more detail in the section on the interrelationships among the different Prospect-based emotions.

In Chapter 4 we argued that one of the variables that affects the intensity of all emotions is unexpectedness. However, a moment's thought will reveal that in the case of the Confirmation emotions, there are strong constraints on how unexpected the event of interest can be. If the unexpectedness is too high then the eliciting conditions cannot be satisfied. For the prospect of some event to be confirmed, there must *be* some prospect of it and this means that the event cannot be unexpected. The Confirmation emotions are thus limited in their intensity as a result of the restricted range over which unexpectedness can apply, making these emotions atypical not only with respect to the other Prospect-based emotions, but with respect to emotions in general. It may well be that the self-limiting nature of the intensity range of these emotions is one of the reasons why there are rather few lexical items in the language that refer to them, and why they seem to be somewhat unsatisfactory and pale as emotions.

There is, however, another, related reason to suppose that these emotions are not experientially very salient. This second reason has to do with an issue we have not yet discussed – namely, competition between potentially cooccurring emotions. In this discussion, we shall focus on satisfaction, although the same principles hold with respect to fears-confirmed. When one has correctly anticipated some event (be it desirable or undesirable) it is necessarily the case that if a Confirmation emotion ensues then the eliciting conditions for other emotions are also satisfied. For example, because satisfaction results from the confirmation of a desirable event, the eliciting conditions for Joy emotions will be satisfied by virtue of that desirable event. Thus, these two emotions, satisfaction and joy, are *both* elicited by the same event. Our proposal is that in most cases, when two emotions cooccur that are compatible in this way (i.e., the elicitation of one entails the elicitation of the other) the more intense emotion presents itself to conscious awareness more insistently than the less intense one. Because satisfaction is limited in intensity, both by the limited role that unexpectedness can play, and by the intensity of associated hope, any other attendant positive emotion such as joy is likely to be more intense. Such other emotions, being more insistent and cognitively salient, may to some degree subordinate the experience of the Satisfaction emotion. Thus, in general, satisfaction and fears-confirmed are more likely to be available in consciousness when the desirability of the event in question is not very high.

We turn now to the emotions arising from the disconfirmation of the prospect of events.

(6.5) **RELIEF EMOTIONS**
TYPE SPECIFICATION: (pleased about) the disconfirmation of the prospect of an undesirable event
TOKENS: relief
VARIABLES AFFECTING INTENSITY:
(1) the intensity of the attendant fear emotion
(2) the effort expended in trying to prevent the event
(3) the degree to which the event is realized
EXAMPLE: The employee was relieved to learn that he was not going to be fired.

(6.6)   **DISAPPOINTMENT EMOTIONS**
TYPE SPECIFICATION: (displeased about) the disconfirmation of the
prospect of a desirable event
TOKENS: dashed-hopes, despair, disappointment, frustration,
heartbroken, etc.
VARIABLES AFFECTING INTENSITY:
(1) the intensity of the attendant hope emotion
(2) the effort expended in trying to attain the event
(3) the degree to which the event is realized
EXAMPLE: The girl was disappointed when she realized that she
would not be asked to the dance after all.

The Disconfirmation emotions are a subset of a category of emotions
that Kahneman and Tversky (1982) refer to as "counterfactual emotions."
For Kahneman and Tversky, the intensity of such emotions is determined
by "the ease of imagining" (p. 203) alternative outcomes. Whereas we
consider it reasonable to suppose that the ease of imagining alternative
outcomes is related to intensity, we do not find it very helpful as an *explanation* of emotional intensity. We think that the ease of imagining alternatives
is a complex construct comprising the combined effects of variables such as
the degree of realization and likelihood, and that ultimately it will have to
be explained in terms of variables such as these. Our own view is that the
three factors that influence the intensity of the Confirmation emotions
(satisfaction and fears-confirmed) also affect the intensity of the Disconfirmation emotions, namely, the intensity of the attendant Prospect emotion, the effort expended in trying to attain or prevent the prospective
event, and the degree to which the event is realized. For example, in the
case of being PLEASED ABOUT THE DISCONFIRMATION OF THE PROS-
PECT OF AN UNDESIRABLE EVENT (relief), the intensity depends in
part on the intensity of the attendant Prospect emotion (fear). The man
who had feared being fired would be more relieved if the attendant fear
had been intense than if it had been relatively weak.

At first sight, it might appear that because the realized event might not
be identical to the prospective event, the desirability of the realized event
should also be considered as contributing to the intensity of Disconfirmation emotions. In the examples just presented, the (realized) event is
simply that the man is *not* fired. And, as we discussed in the context of fear,
the desirability of the absence of some feared negative event is assumed to
be zero, which means that the desirability of the realized event neither
enhances nor detracts from the intensity of the experienced relief. Many
cases of relief are of this kind, namely, cases in which the alternative to the
undesirable outcome is simply that the undesirable outcome does not arise.
However, many are not. Sometimes, as well as the prospective event being

undesirable, the realized event is too, in which case one might want to argue that less relief would be experienced. Thus, if an agent of a taxing authority such as the Internal Revenue Service (IRS) determines in an audit that a person owes only $900 instead of an expected $1000 in unpaid taxes, the realized event is still quite undesirable, and to the extent that it is, it could be viewed as reducing the intensity of the relief that might otherwise have been felt (as when, for example, the IRS agent determines that the man owes nothing).

However, an alternative analysis would suggest that relief might not be diminished when the event that is realized is undesirable. For example, consider a person who suspects that her loved one has been fatally injured in an accident and learns that in fact he has only broken his ribs. It seems likely that her experience of relief might be as intense under these circumstances as it would be had he escaped unscathed. That is, the intensity of relief would be governed primarily by the intensity of the underlying fear. The undesirability of the realized event, however, could give rise independently to a negative emotion such as distress. Which of these two models applies probably depends on how the individual parses the situation. If, for example, the concern had not been specifically about the death of the loved one but about the seriousness of injury, then perhaps the disconfirmation of serious injury and the occurrence of a relatively minor injury would be seen as one event that would occasion a single (muted) reaction of relief. Similarly, if the anticipated and the realized events differ greatly in value (as in death vs broken ribs) they might be more likely to be seen as separate events than if they are similar in value (paying $900 vs $1000 in back taxes).

Before leaving this topic, there is one other issue that should be mentioned. In general, we have discussed variations in emotional intensity as variations in the magnitude of an emotional experience at a given moment in time. But the intensity of an emotional reaction might also be seen to implicate the *duration* of the experience. Viewed from this perspective, the intensity of relief could also be reduced by the occurrence of undesirable outcomes even if the person does see the anticipated and the realized outcomes as separate events leading to different emotions (e.g., relief and distress). Thus, the relief on learning that one's loved one was alive might be decreased by learning that he was nevertheless injured simply because the state of relief would terminate prematurely as one's focus of attention was drawn to the injury, a shift that would also occasion distress.

The other variable that affects the intensity of the Disconfirmation emotions is effort. Other things being equal, relief will be more intense if the person invested a great deal of effort in trying to prevent or avoid the prospective event, and disappointment more intense if the person invested a great deal of effort in trying to attain it. In fact, the effort variable can have an effect in the absence of invested effort too. Consider the example offered in the characterization of the Disappointment emotions in which a girl is disappointed at not being asked to a dance. Suppose that she is told that the boy whom she had wanted to take her had decided to take someone else and that it is this revelation that is the occasion for her disappointment. Now suppose that she also learns that with a minimum of effort on her part, he would have asked her rather than the girl he did ask. It seems reasonable to suppose that under these conditions her disappointment could be intensified because the undesirable outcome could have been so easily avoided. Similarly it seems reasonable to suppose that a Relief emotion will be intensified if the person believes that a great deal of effort would have been required to avert the undesirable outcome, even though it was in fact averted without the expenditure of effort at all. Thus, hypothetical effort can also influence the intensity of these emotions, although it might be argued that such influences are mediated by the degree of realization variable.

In considering Disappointment emotions, it may be instructive to see again how the same event can simultaneously satisfy the eliciting conditions for two distinct emotions. Consider two cases of a person who fails to receive an anticipated promotion. In the first case the reason is that the company has been told by its parent corporation that it has to impose a freeze on pay raises and promotions. In the second it is because the person forgot to submit a crucial progress report. Both examples satisfy the eliciting conditions for disappointment and distress, but they differ in one important respect. In the first example, we are assuming that the person believes that the freeze on pay raises and promotions has been imposed on the company so he is not inclined to blame the company because he considers the company to have had no choice. In this case he would experience primarily disappointment and distress. However, in the second example, not only are the eliciting conditions for disappointment and distress satisfied, but, as we shall see in Chapter 7, so too are the conditions for self-anger because the person blames himself for the realized event. Thus in this situation he can experience a mixture of disappointment, distress, and self-anger. Similarly, in the first example, if the person does find himself blaming someone, then he is likely to be angry in that situation too (although, of course, his anger will be directed towards the person he blames rather than towards himself).

Finally, as mentioned earlier in this chapter, Relief emotions and Disappointment emotions have the interesting property that they can arise in the absence of prior fears and hopes. This raises the question of what is meant in the emotion specifications by indicating that their intensity is affected by the intensity of the "attendant" Fear emotion or Hope emotion. Our answer to this question is to again take refuge in our claim that the Prospect-based emotions have to do not with *expectations* of events, but with *prospects* of events. We have already indicated that we believe that it makes perfectly good sense to think in terms of retrospective fear and hope. To see how this helps, let us consider a prototypical case of relief and disappointment in the absence of prior fear and hope. We have already mentioned such a case for relief, namely, the situation in which a man discovers that the plane he missed crashed and killed all the passengers. A typical example for disappointment would be a case in which one discovered that one had missed a golden opportunity to achieve some desired goal. For example, a woman might discover that had she only known in time, all she would have had to do to win a free car was to have mailed in some competition application by a certain date. Instead, not giving the matter a moment's thought, she allowed the application form bearing the winning number to become buried under other documents on her desk. In the first case, the eliciting conditions for fear are satisfied because the man can react to the prospect of being killed in a plane crash. The prospective event is (presumably) extremely undesirable, and in taking the retrospective perspective on the event, we can say that the subjective likelihood of being killed was extremely high. In this sense, fear can result from a retroactive construction of what might have happened, and its intensity will influence the intensity of the relief. The same analysis applies to the case of disappointment in the absence of prior hopes. The desirability of the event is high, and the retrospective subjective likelihood is judged as certain. In both cases, it is possible to argue that the intensity might be slightly lower than had there been corresponding hopes and fears because global variables such as proximity and sense of reality might have been more influential had the man actually been on the plane and been the sole survivor, or had the woman been told she would win the car, only to discover subsequently that she was ineligible because of some technicality.

Shock and Pleasant Surprise

At first sight, it might be supposed that hope and fear are systematically related to surprise and shock in that the former focus on anticipated desirable and undesirable events whereas the latter focus on unanticipated desirable and undesirable events. However, since we characterize the Prospect-based emotions in terms of prospects rather than in terms of expectations, they leave no room for shock and surprise. Rather than viewing this omission as a shortcoming, we in fact view it as a virtue. This is because we can provide a more parsimonious account of shock and surprise. The account that we propose takes advantage of the fact that we include unexpectedness as a global intensity variable. This means that insofar as they are emotions, shock and surprise can be considered merely as unexpected undesirable and desirable events, without reference to prospects.

The nature of unexpectedness in shock and surprise is an issue that warrants some attention. We shall briefly discuss some aspects of this issue in the context of shock, although the general principles also apply to pleasant surprise. Whereas one ordinarily thinks of shock as involving an unexpected event, the event need not in fact be totally unexpected. Imagine that a person hears that her son has been involved in a traffic accident, and that he has cuts and bruises for which he is being treated at the local hospital. Presumably she is likely to experience initial shock in response to this news. Now suppose that upon arriving at the hospital she discovers that her son was severely injured and that he has multiple fractures. She may now experience a second shock as she realizes that the injuries are much more serious than she has initially thought. Certainly it is possible that the intensity of the second shock would be lower than that of the first, because in the second she would already have been facing the prospect of an undesirable event so that the closely matching event that she encounters would no longer be totally unexpected. However, what we have in this imaginary situation is a case in which there is shock even though the shock-inducing situation is not now totally unexpected.

A second kind of case in which shock can arise without the shock-inducing event being totally unexpected occurs when one contemplates the prospect of some event but rules it out on the grounds of its extreme improbability. For example, a man may know that a number of people in the company for which he works will lose their jobs but may conclude, for whatever reason, that he cannot possibly be vulnerable. When he is subsequently informed that his services are no longer needed, he might well experience shock even though, again, the event was not totally unexpected – certainly, not as unexpected as it would have been had he never considered the possibility that he might be dismissed at all.

What these examples suggest is that the key to shock is not so much that the event be unexpected, but that it not be (actively) expected. In spite of their surface similarity, these are cognitively quite different (Ortony & Partridge, 1987). These examples also suggest an interesting relationship between shock and fear. To the extent that an undesirable event is anticipated, fear increases, and to the extent that it had not been anticipated, shock increases when the event is realized. A similar relationship would then also exist between hopefulness and surprise: As a desirable event is anticipated, hopefulness increases, and to the extent that it was not anticipated, surprise increases when the event is subsequently realized.

We have, in this discussion, referred to the positive counterpart of shock as "pleasant surprise." We think it preferable to refer to the emotion commonly called "surprise" as "pleasant surprise" because, as we have already indicated, we do not consider unvalenced surprise to be an emotion at all – unvalenced surprise is pure unexpectedness, and if something is to be an emotion it must either be a positive or negative reaction. While the term "shock" usually (although not always) implies an unpleasant surprise, the English word "surprise" is much less constrained in implying positive valence. In the absence of a valence-supplying context, it simply refers to something unexpected and is neutral with respect to valence. It is easy to find examples to substantiate the claim that surprise need not be valenced at all. For example, a person might well have no valenced reaction to the surprising fact that the winner of the 1985 Wimbledon men's tennis tournament was an unseeded player. Such a surprise might be neither pleasant nor unpleasant, in which case it would not constitute either shock or pleasant surprise. On the other hand, when a child returns from a day at school to discover a brand new bicycle waiting for him, one might well expect the eliciting conditions for a Joy emotion to be satisfied. Furthermore, his happiness or joy is likely to be intensified as a result of the unexpectedness of the desirable event. Our main point is that we do not consider the *surprisingness* of the desired event for the child to be an emotion that is distinct from the happiness that it produces. When surprise, conceived of as an awareness of unexpectedness, is accompanied by a Joy emotion, we have an unexpected desirable event and the reaction might well be appropriately called "surprise" or "pleasant surprise." When it is accompanied by a Distress emotion, we have an unexpected undesirable event, and "shock" or "unpleasant surprise" are appropriate labels. But when surprise is not accompanied by either a positive or negative emotion, we have no emotional reaction at all, we just have an awareness of unexpectedness, and that, according to our analysis, is not itself an emotion at all. We say all this in sharp contrast to the many psychologists who have included surprise as one of a small set of basic emotions (see Chapter 2), but we say it with the benefit of some empirical data that subjects judge surprise to be a relatively poor example of an emotion compared to, say, anger or fear (Clore, Ortony, & Foss, 1987; Ortony, 1987).

Some Interrelationships Among Prospect-based Emotions

A number of interesting relationships exist among some of the Prospect-based emotions, and between them and the Well-being emotions. In this section we shall discuss some of these, not only because the relationships are interesting in their own right, but also because the discussion may provide an illustration of exactly how some of the pieces of the system we are proposing fit together, and, in particular, what some of the consequences of differing degrees of realization of a prospective event can be.

The particular relationships to be examined are those between the Well-being emotions, which, for convenience, we shall continue to refer to as "joy" and "distress," and the Confirmation and Disconfirmation emotions. Again, to simplify the exposition, we shall refer to these as "satisfaction" and "fears-confirmed," and "relief" and "disappointment." As our examples, we will consider two classes of cases, one of which corresponds to hope, and one of which corresponds to fear. In both cases we shall use as our example somebody who has been informed that he is to be audited by the Internal Revenue Service. We shall assume that the person, on receiving the notification, goes back to his records and recomputes what he takes to be his tax liability. In the PROSPECT OF AN UNDESIRABLE EVENT case we shall assume that as a result of these efforts the person reluctantly concludes that he will be assessed an additional $1000. In the PROSPECT OF A DESIRABLE EVENT case we assume that the person now confidently believes that he is in fact due a refund of about $1000, because he failed to take some major deductions to which he now believes he is entitled.

The first set of cases, in which the person anticipates that he will have to pay an additional $1000, is shown in the upper block in Table 6.2 (labeled −$1000). The second set of cases, in which the person anticipates that he will receive $1000, is shown in the lower block (labeled +$1000). For each prospective event, five different realized outcomes are shown in the column labeled OUTCOME. First, we shall consider the cases in which the person faces the prospect of an undesirable event – he expects that he will have to pay $1000. The first case shown in the OUTCOME column is the one in which he is assessed *more* than he expected (i.e., he is assessed $1400). Our analysis of this situation is that in addition to fears-confirmed, which arises because the prospect of the undesirable event of being assessed $1000 was confirmed, there is additional unexpected distress resulting from the extra $400 he must pay. This additional distress is likely to be quite intense because it is modulated by a high degree of unexpectedness, whereas the distress resulting from the fears-confirmed is more expected (expected, in fact, to the degree to which the original prospect of the undesirable event was considered *likely*). The influence of this expectedness is reflected in the intensity of the fear associated with the fears-confirmed. The second case is quite simple. The man expects to have to pay $1000 and he does. He feels fears-confirmed. In the third case, he is required to pay significantly *less* than he had expected ($400 instead of

Table 6.2. *Some relationships between Prospect-based and Well-being emotions*

PROSPECT	OUTCOME	EMOTIONS
	−$1400	fears-confirmed ($1000) unexpected distress ($400)
	−$1000	fears-confirmed ($1000)
−$1000	−$400	relief ($600) fears-confirmed ($400)
	$0	relief ($1000)
	+$400	relief ($1000) unexpected joy ($400)
	+$1400	satisfaction ($1000) unexpected joy ($400)
	+$1000	satisfaction ($1000)
+$1000	+$400	disappointment ($600) satisfaction ($400)
	$0	disappointment ($1000)
	−$400	disappointment ($1000) unexpected distress ($400)

$1000). Here, he might experience relief with respect to the $600 that he didn't have to pay, but there is a residual fears-confirmed with respect to the $400 assessment. The next case is also simple. Here, the man discovers that he has to pay nothing and experiences relief as a result of not having to pay the expected $1000. Finally, things can be better still for the anxious tax payer. He may find not only that he doesn't have to pay the $1000, but that the audit reveals that he is in fact due a refund of $400. In this case, we have the same degree of relief as in the previous case, but there is additional unexpected joy or pleasant surprise resulting from the $400 gain.

We hope that this characterization of the interrelations between the Well-being emotions and the Prospect-based ones serves to illustrate how the intensity of the Confirmation and Disconfirmation emotions are related to those of the attendant Prospect emotions (in this case, fear). It should be pointed out that we are not claiming that the intensity of the experienced emotions in the examples just discussed must be proportional to the amount of money gained or lost. It is particularly clear in the case of the unexpected joy and distress that this need not be so. On the other hand, they are not unrelated. In fact, problems having to do with the calibration of intensity of different emotions make it difficult to be precise about the overall outcomes in terms of intensity of some of the situations we are describing. However, it is clearly possible to propose models for how the different emotional reactions associated with the entries in the table combine into a single affective reaction of a particular intensity. As a first approximation one might treat unexpectedness as a weighting factor applied to the value of the outcome with the resulting intensity being represented in terms of the sum of these weighted values.

When the person faces the prospect of the desirable event of getting a $1000 refund, the different cases give results exactly analogous to those we have just discussed. If the person gets a refund in excess of his expectations, he will experience satisfaction for the expected part and additional unexpected joy for the extra. If he gets what he expects he will experience satisfaction; if he gets something ($400), but less than he expects, he will experience disappointment about having to pay $600, along with some residual satisfaction that he got some ($400) of what he expected. If he gets nothing he will feel disappointment, and if he discovers that rather than a refund, he actually must pay $400, unexpected distress will be added to the disappointment.

Before leaving this example, a word needs to be said about the relation between the Prospect-based emotions and the Well-being emotions. We have shown these emotions as being distinct. For example, in the first case, in which, expecting to be assessed for $1000, the man is in fact assessed for $1400, we have indicated fears-confirmed in response to the confirmation of the prospect of a $1000 loss, and unexpected distress in response to the additional $400. However, there is another way of looking at this, namely, one in which there is simply expected distress at "losing" $1000 along with unexpected distress at losing the additional $400. Our claim is that this is indeed a reasonable alternative analysis, and that it is predicted by our account because of the fact that there is a degree of hierarchical structure in the emotional system. Recall that we have said that the Well-being emotions really are undifferentiated forms of being pleased and displeased, and that the Prospect-based emotions are differentiated forms of those reactions. This is clear from the emotion specifications in which, for example, Joy emotions are characterized as being PLEASED ABOUT A DESIRABLE EVENT, whereas Relief emotions, for example, are characterized as being PLEASED ABOUT THE DISCONFIRMATION OF THE PROSPECT OF AN UNDESIRABLE EVENT. Because the disconfirmation of the prospect of an undesirable event is itself a desirable event (the event about which the experiencer is pleased), it is clear that the specification of Relief emotions has embedded within it the eliciting conditions for Joy emotions, with the consequence that Relief emotions are a particular differentiated form of

Joy emotions. Whether, in any particular situation, a Relief emotion or a Joy emotion will be experienced depends upon whether the experiencing person focuses on the disconfirmation of the prospect of an undesirable event, or whether he or she merely focuses on the desirability of the outcome.

Suspense, Resignation, Hopelessness, and Other Related States

There are a number of emotions and emotionlike affective states that bear interesting relationships to the Prospect-based emotions. In this section we shall briefly discuss some of these states and examine their connections to the emotions we have already discussed. We consider first, *suspense*. We view suspense as involving a Hope emotion and a Fear emotion coupled with the cognitive state of uncertainty. Clearly, uncertainty alone is not enough. Uncertainty is not always suspenseful – a person might be uncertain about whether it is going to rain, but, except in unusual circumstances, is not likely to be in suspense waiting to find out. In this sense, uncertainty is like surprise; when it is emotional, it is because of the contribution of other factors. Specifically, the event about which the person is uncertain must have sufficiently desirable or undesirable consequences, and, because it pertains to outcomes not already known, it will inevitably implicate one or both of the Prospect emotions.

One characteristic of emotional experiences, especially vicarious ones, is that in many cases they seem to thrive on some associated suspense. The mental preparation for or forecasting of alternative possible events produces a kind of tension between alternative constructions that when resolved produces a more powerful effect than would have been the case without the suspense-inducing material. Research by Brewer and Lichtenstein (1981, 1982) has shown that some sort of suspense or suspenselike reaction by readers of stories is an essential ingredient that differentiates genuine stories from storylike narratives that are not in fact considered stories at all. Thus, if a text describes the slowly rising tide about a rock exposed in the ocean, the text is considered a story when there is mention of a person on the rock (whose life is potentially endangered by the rising tide), but the same text without the threatened person on the rock is not considered such.

Whereas it seems reasonable to think of suspense as having emotion constituents, it is less clear that a case can be made for *resignation*. Our view is that resignation is a particular kind of cognitive state, namely a belief state that has as its object the inevitability of some undesirable event. Thus, the focus of resignation is not on the event in question (which is captured by emotions such as fear), but on beliefs about likelihood and on a corresponding reluctant acceptance of the event's inevitability. Resignation is very close to *hopelessness*, although the two are certainly not identical. Hopelessness focuses on the belief that the undesirable event is irreversible, that is, on the belief that there is nothing that can be *done* to prevent it. Interestingly, while it is *people* who become resigned to the inevitability of expected undesirable events, it is *situations* that are held to be hopeless.[3] This suggests that a person who views a situation as hopeless views it as not being susceptible to significant improvement. Thus, the mental state of a "feeling of hopelessness" refers primarily to a belief that some situation has this characteristic. However, it also seems to have a component that refers to the distress associated with such a realization, distress that may well result from the person's anticipated inability to cope with the expected outcome. Thus, we consider hopelessness to be a slightly better example of an emotion than resignation. Hopelessness, like despair, focuses on the prospect of a specific undesirable situation, namely that of a person's presumed ineffectiveness to undo, offset, or cope with an anticipated negative event. We see here how rich the language is in isolating certain components of feelings so as to focus sometimes on the raw affective aspects (e.g., fear), sometimes on the cognitive aspects (e.g., resignation), and sometimes on the person's control (or lack of it) over the expected course of events (e.g., hopelessness). Resignation and hopelessness both have positive counterparts in confidence and optimism, although the meaning of these terms is not as well differentiated as in the negative cases.

Summary

There are six Prospect-based emotions: Two center around the *prospect* of an event (Hope emotions and Fear emotions), two center around the *confirmation* of a prospect (Satisfaction emotions and Fears-confirmed emotions), and two center around the *disconfirmation* of a prospect (Relief emotions and Disappointment emotions). The eliciting conditions for the two Prospect emotions are (PLEASED ABOUT) THE PROSPECT OF A DESIRABLE EVENT (e.g., hope) and (DISPLEASED ABOUT) THE PROSPECT OF AN UNDESIRABLE EVENT (e.g., fear). The variables that affect the intensity of the Prospect emotions are: the desirability of the event, and the likelihood of the event. The word "hope" seems to focus much more on desirability than on likelihood, whereas "hopeful" has the reverse empha-

3 There is, of course, another reading of the word "hopeless," which is applied to people and implies utter incompetence, but this sense of the word has nothing to do with the issue at hand.

sis; "anticipatory excitement" perhaps better characterizes the emotional state that depends on both variables.

The eliciting conditions for the Confirmation emotions are (PLEASED ABOUT) THE CONFIRMATION OF THE PROSPECT OF A DESIRABLE EVENT (e.g., satisfaction) and (DISPLEASED ABOUT) THE CONFIRMA-TION OF THE PROSPECT OF AN UNDESIRABLE EVENT (e.g., fears-confirmed). Similarly, the eliciting conditions for the Disconfirmation emotions are (PLEASED ABOUT) THE DISCONFIRMATION OF THE PROSPECT OF AN UNDESIRABLE EVENT (e.g., relief) and (DIS-PLEASED ABOUT) THE DISCONFIRMATION OF THE PROSPECT OF A DESIRABLE EVENT (e.g., disappointment). The three variables that affect the intensity of these emotions are: (1) the intensity of the attendant hope or fear, (2) the effort expended in trying to attain or prevent the event, and (3) the degree to which the event is realized. The Confirmation and Disconfirmation emotions always cooccur with the Well-being emotions (Joy emotions and Distress emotions) because the confirmation and disconfirmation of undesirable and desirable prospects, respectively, themselves constitute desirable events, and the confirmation and discon-firmation of desirable and undesirable prospects, respectively, constitute undesirable events, so that the eliciting conditions of the Well-being emotions are necessarily satisfied. It is possible to analyze how different degrees of realization of the prospective event lead to different combinations of the Well-being and the Confirmation or Disconfirmation Emotions.

7   Reactions to Agents

The last two chapters dealt with emotions that result from reactions to desirable or undesirable events. However, there are also important qualitative differences among emotions that depend on *how* we believe salient events to have come about. When we consider this question, we focus on an *agent* whom we take to have been instrumental in the event, rather than on the event itself, although, as we shall see in the section on Compound emotions in this chapter, sometimes emotions result from focusing on both simultaneously. Just as the central variable for the Event-based emotions is the desirability of the event computed in terms of its goal relevance, so in the case of the Attribution emotions the central variable is praiseworthiness (which, in its technical sense, we take as including blameworthiness) computed in terms of the *standards* that are invoked in evaluating the agent's action. From an adaptive standpoint, focusing on an agent's actions may be important because, particularly in the case of undesirable events, it raises the possibility of controlling and being prepared for similar events in the future.

The Attribution Emotions

The situations in which people find themselves or in which they find others are frequently viewed as resulting from actions of one sort or another. Responsibility for these actions is often attributed to an agent. Thus, the Agent-based emotions are Attribution-of-responsibility or, simply, the Attribution emotions. When the agent is judged to have done something *praiseworthy,* the person experiencing the emotion is inclined to *approve* of the agent's action, and when the agent is held to have done something *blameworthy,* the experiencer is inclined to *disapprove* of the agent's action. This means that the *praiseworthiness* variable (which includes blameworthiness) serves the same function in the Attribution emotions as does the desirability variable in the Event-based emotions, and, concomitantly,

the affective reactions of approving or disapproving serve the same function that being pleased and displeased serve in the Event-based emotions.
As with other emotions, the issue is not whether or not the blamed or
praised person is *in fact* wholly or partially responsible for the situation, but
whether or not the experiencer believes the agent to be responsible, and
hence subject to praise or blame for his or her action. For example, a
subway vigilante who kills a teenager in the New York subway will not
experience shame unless he believes that what he did was blameworthy. In
other words, he has to believe that his action violated some standard or
principle in which he believes. If in fact he views his action as upholding
some principle (regardless of the opinions of others) he is more likely to
feel pride than shame. On the other hand, we as observers can quite
consistently view his action as blameworthy by our standards, in which case
we would have satisfied the eliciting conditions for an Attribution emotion
such as contempt.

Just as the entire group of Attribution emotions introduces praiseworthiness as an intensity variable, so too, when the agent is the self, the *cognitive
unit* variable is introduced (see Chapter 4). The notion of unit formation
allows the use of an extended notion of self as being self or other with
whom one forms a (sufficiently) strong cognitive unit. This, in turn, enables
us to explain how it is that pride, for example, can result from the praiseworthy actions of certain others. However, as Heider (1958) pointed out,
unit formation is highly context sensitive. This context sensitivity is particularly interesting in the case of emotions because it permits unit formation to
occur when the going is good, while permitting it to disintegrate when the
going gets rough. A person is more likely to form a unit with an individual
whom he views as being of great worth, and more likely to distance himself
or to try to disassociate himself from an individual whom he judges to have
done something thoroughly reprehensible. Thus, situations of praise are
more likely to be accompanied by a tendency to increase unit strength,
thereby rendering pride in the achievement of others more likely, while
under conditions of blame there is likely to be a tendency to try to decrease
unit strength, with the result that it will be more difficult and more unusual
to experience an emotion like shame in response to the actions of others.
People's behavior often provides evidence of attempted dissociation. For
example, a woman who sees her brother convicted of some terrible crime
may tend to "disown" him, perhaps protesting that they were never very
close. Nevertheless, in many cases the prior unit strength is so great (for
example, between members of the same family) that its total disintegration
may be impossible, with the result that people do feel ashamed (and embarrassed) at the misdemeanors of those to whom they are close. In contrast,

Table 7.1. *Attribution emotions*

IDENTITY OF AGENT	APPRAISAL OF AGENT'S ACTION	
	PRAISEWORTHY	BLAMEWORTHY
SELF	approving of one's own praiseworthy action (e.g., pride)	disapproving of one's own blameworthy action (e.g., shame)
OTHER	approving of someone else's praiseworthy action (e.g., admiration)	disapproving of someone else's blameworthy action (e.g., reproach)

the tendency to publicly proclaim one's association with a successful other is well documented. For example, in a series of studies Cialdini et al. (1976) found that after a victory of their college football team, students were more likely to wear school colors, and were more likely to use the first person pronoun, "we," than the third person pronoun, "they," in referring to the football team. In all such cases – that is, in cases where the person experiencing the emotion considers himself to be in a cognitive unit with the actual agent, regardless of whether they involve actions judged to be praiseworthy or blameworthy – we allow some other or others to be the actual agent while still identifying the formal agent as the self.

A second important point having to do with the identity of the agent arises in cases in which the agent is not a person. Even though in the Attribution emotions the agent is prototypically a person, peripheral cases arise in which the agent is an animal or even an inanimate entity such as the weather. People are quite willing, perhaps through the use of some analogical principles, to "blame" the rain for ruining the parade, although when they do so, it is usually with some awareness of the technical peculiarity of the implied attribution. Nevertheless, a consequence of this tendency is that the notion of an agent has to be sufficiently flexible to accommodate nonhuman, and possibly even inanimate, agents, so that attributions of responsibility can be made to assumed causes that cannot properly be considered to be willful agents.

Table 7.1 presents the structure of the emotion types that result from the reactions of approving or disapproving of the actions of agents. We start by presenting the specifications of the two cells in the first row. These cells represent the emotions that result from approving or disapproving of the self as agent, where the self is broadly conceived, as discussed above. The resulting emotions are typically those that in English we refer to as "pride" and "shame," although, again, it should be emphasized that these are good examples of convenient English terms for these emotion specifications, not renamings of them. Nevertheless, we shall frequently talk about these emotions in terms of pride and shame for convenience. It is perhaps worth pointing out that, in English, the verb forms of these words typically take three arguments, so one can say, in general terms, that "*A* is proud/ ashamed of *B* for (doing) *C*." In other words, the structure is PROUD (*A, B, C*) and ASHAMED (*A, B, C*). The same is true for the verbs "to approve" and "to disapprove," as one would expect if our claim that the Attribution emotions are differentiated cases of approving and disapproving is correct. The point about the three arguments is that it is part of the structure of these verbs, and of the corresponding concepts, that there be a subject (designated as *A*), an agent to whom responsibility is attributed and towards whom the sentiment is directed (designated as *B*, although, of course, there is no reason why *B* cannot be the same as *A*), *and* something (*C*, typically, an action or achievement) in which *B*'s involvement is judged by *A* to be praiseworthy or blameworthy. This means that these concepts really do involve an appraisal of an *agent's actions*, as opposed merely to an appraisal of the agent alone (which would result in the attribution of a trait such as *skillful* or *honest*), or of the action alone (which would have more of the characteristics of an event). In the Attribution emotions the attentional emphasis is on the agent, and his or her causal role, rather than on the outcome. As is discussed in the next section, when the value of the event itself is factored in, compound emotions result.

(7.1)   **PRIDE EMOTIONS**
TYPE SPECIFICATION: (approving of) one's own praiseworthy action
TOKENS: pride
VARIABLES AFFECTING INTENSITY:
(1) the degree of judged praiseworthiness
(2) the strength of the cognitive unit with the actual agent
(3) deviations of the agent's action from person/role-based expectations (i.e., unexpectedness)
EXAMPLE: The woman was proud of saving the life of a drowning child.

(7.2)   **SELF-REPROACH EMOTIONS**
TYPE SPECIFICATION: (disapproving of) one's own blameworthy action
TOKENS: embarrassment, feeling guilty, mortified, self-blame, self-condemnation, self-reproach, shame, (psychologically) uncomfortable, uneasy, etc.
VARIABLES AFFECTING INTENSITY:
(1) the degree of judged blameworthiness
(2) the strength of the cognitive unit with the actual agent
(3) deviations of the agent's action from person/role-based expectations (i.e., unexpectedness)
EXAMPLE: The spy was ashamed of having betrayed his country.

As already indicated, the emotions we have here are often those referred to in English as "pride" and "shame." Consider, first, the example of pride. In the paradigm example, a woman, call her "Mary," is proud of having saved the life of a drowning child. For Mary to be proud, she must view her action as being praiseworthy, the more praiseworthy, the more intense the pride. This is the way in which the praiseworthiness variable has its effect. Because the standards that are invoked in evaluating the praiseworthiness of saving the life of a child are of greater value than those invoked in evaluating the saving of the life of, say, a squirrel, we assume that the praiseworthiness in the first case would that in the second so that the experienced pride would be correspondingly more intense.

It might be thought that the degree of effort invested by the agent should be a separate intensity variable affecting the intensity of these emotions. After all, it seems intuitively reasonable to suppose that Mary's pride would be more intense if she had overcome difficult obstacles in order to save the child's life. However, in the context of the Attribution emotions, we incorporate effort directly into the judged praiseworthiness. As discussed in Chapter 4, effort has to be construed not simply in terms of how much effort was invested, but more generally as *cost*. We use the term "effort" to refer to the utilization of resources, and that includes both the effort of trying and the cost. This has the nice feature that one can be judged praiseworthy for trying to help, even if the results of one's efforts are not altogether successful. So, the intuition that effort intensifies Pride emotions is accommodated by proposing that the expenditure of effort to bring about certain kinds of (personally and socially) desirable outcomes is positively appraised as a result of invoking another standard. At the same time, it is interesting to note that if a person invests a disproportionate amount of effort in attaining some goal, he may feel foolish or embarrassed rather than proud. If Mary were to go to unreasonable lengths to try to save the life of a squirrel, it would strike many people as odd, if not obsessive. This suggests that actions that are judged irrational or inappropriate to the situation might not be judged as praiseworthy even if they have beneficial results.

Praiseworthiness is often assessed in terms of the social value of the agent's action, even when the formal agent is the self, as in cases of pride and shame. If Mary thinks that the social standard in terms of which she evaluates her saving of the child renders the act of great value, it will also have great value to her. If she thinks that such a social criterion renders the saving of a squirrel's life of much less value, it is likely to have less value for her. At the same time, of course, there is absolutely no reason why the actual attainment of the goal should not also give rise to an Event-based emotion such as joy or satisfaction (especially, for example, if the child were her own). When, in such cases, a person focuses on *both* the praise-worthiness of the action and the goal relevance of the outcome, something qualitatively different from pride is experienced, as discussed in the section on compound emotions.

One consequence of our analysis is that somebody could feel proud of an action that was not socially valued if he or she were mistaken about its social value. Such cases typically arise when a person moves into a completely different culture but continues to evaluate actions against the standards of the old culture, even though they no longer apply. For example, in some developing countries chickens are left to run wild in villages, darting to and fro across roads and dirt tracks. When a Western visitor to such a country first drives a vehicle along one of these roads and runs down one of these errant hens, he may well feel ashamed at having carelessly killed someone's chicken. By Western standards one can appropriately be concerned that it is wrong to harm the livestock of others, so a Self-reproach emotion might result. However, such a reaction would not be understood by the locals. The societal norms are that no blame is attached to the accidental killing of chickens under routine circumstances of this kind. There is a different societal norm that is invoked in such situations, namely that the driver does not move or remove the dead or injured bird. It belongs as much to its owner dead as it does alive – it was probably destined to be killed for food anyway. So, in general, failure to coordinate one's *beliefs* about societal standards with the *actual* standards can lead to the emotions of pride and shame (and other Attribution emotions) in situations where they are not judged appropriate, and it can lead to the absence of such emotions in situations in which the cultural standards would warrant them.

In considering the contribution that the praiseworthiness variable makes to the intensity of the Attribution emotions, the role of responsibility needs to be reviewed. While we do not list responsibility as an intensity variable, it certainly is a precondition for attributing praise and blame. If, having saved the life of a drowning child, Mary is to view her action as praisewor-thy, she has to attribute to herself responsibility for it, which means that she has to believe that she undertook her heroic act out of her own free will; if so, she would be appropriately proud of her actions. But suppose that she had been forced at gun point to save the child's life. This would eliminate her praiseworthiness. Notice too that if she knew she had saved the life under these circumstances, she would probably feel no pride and would probably not consider herself praiseworthy, even though other people, ignorant of such facts, might view her as a heroine. How much credit people receive and how much they deserve are not always the same. Much the same is true for intention. Did Mary *mean* to save the child's life, or was it some accidental by-product of a completely unrelated action? Clearly, lack of intention also can eliminate praiseworthiness. Thus, responsibility and intention could be viewed as preconditions for making the attribution in the first place, rather than as variables affecting intensity. However, there is an interesting asymmetry vis à vis positive and negative emotions with respect to the role of intention. While praiseworthy acts clearly have to be considered to have been intended, blameworthy acts do not. Failing to do what is expected of one can be blameworthy even if the failure was unintentional. Negligence, far from being acceptable as an excuse, is itself blameworthy, albeit, less so than malice (see Rule, Dyck, & Nesdale 1978; Turner, 1987). All this means is that intention is not a precondition for the attribution of blame. To the extent that somebody does something blame-worthy, and does so intentionally, any resulting emotion (usually, of course, other-directed) will have increased blameworthiness because another standard such as ONE OUGHT NOT TO INTENTIONALLY HARM OTHERS is invoked.

The second variable that influences the intensity of pride and shame is cognitive *unit strength*. In order to see the point here, we have to modify our examples slightly. For example, Mary might be proud of her daughter for saving someone's life, and some other person might be ashamed of, say, a colleague for being a spy. In both cases, pride and shame result from actions that are in fact carried out by *others*. However, in order for Pride emotions and Self-reproach emotions to result, the actual agent has to be somehow connected to the self as part of a cognitive unit. The stronger the unit bond, the more intense the emotions. Thus, the *actual* agent is seen as a kind of extension of the self, which is why we classify such cases as ones involving the self as the *formal* agent. As we have indicated before, one has to employ an extended notion of the self to accommodate such cases.

Apart from praiseworthiness and cognitive unit strength, there is one other key variable that affects the intensity of Attribution emotions. This variable can be thought of as a particular form of the global variable, *unexpectedness*, which manifests itself as deviations from person or role-based expectations. Whereas we do not usually include global variables in our emotion specifications, we do include unexpectedness in the case of the Attribution emotions because of the special way in which it is realized in these emotions. Consider again the example of Mary saving the drowning child. If Mary were elderly and infirm, as opposed to young, strong, and energetic, both she and others would be likely to consider her saving the child with even greater approval. This is because one would view her feat as a greater deviation from stereotyped expectations – rightly or wrongly, one considers little old ladies to be less likely to be able to do such things than youthful lifeguards.

The issue of deviation from person and role-based expectations is a complex one. Suppose someone, call her Jane, has embarked on a career as a novelist and she sees her first novel prominently displayed in the bookstore on the day that it is first published. Assuming that Jane feels proud on seeing her book in the bookstore, in what sense does what she has done deviate from expectations based on her model of herself as a person, or on her beliefs about her role? Notice first, that such deviations are not part of the type specifications for the Attribution emotions, so they are not *necessary* for their generation – they merely intensify them when they arise. Continuing with the example, since we are considering Jane's *first* novel, she is not likely to have stereotyped herself as someone who habitually writes novels. Rather, she must view herself as someone who has never had a novel published before, and, this being the case, having a novel published does constitute a substantial deviation from her representation of herself. By the time she has published half a dozen novels this is no longer likely to be true, in which case we would predict that she would experience less pride because having a novel published will now be more consistent with her stereotyped representation of herself. In fact, after writing several novels she probably would see herself in the role of a novelist, in which case writing novels is exactly what she would expect of herself. Of course, this does not exclude the possibility that the *object* of her pride (and hence the action she evaluates for praiseworthiness) may change from writing *a* novel to, for example, writing *so many*, but if the object changes, one cannot compare the effects of an intensity variable in any meaningful way.

Because pride and shame are emotions that often invoke social standards, it is hardly surprising that public awareness of the actions that underlie them can influence their intensity. The woman's pride in saving the child and the spy's shame at his misdeeds will be intensified and perpetuated to the degree that the woman and the spy believe that others are aware of their deeds and view them with approval or disapproval. We might expect Mary to be proud of her actions being the topic of newspaper and television stories. She may want to inform others. The spy, on the other hand, is likely to prefer not to. The last thing he wants is for his violations of social standards and trust to become a topic of public debate and censure. Notice that if he is in fact indifferent to the broadcasting of his actions, it is probably because he feels no shame in the first place. To the extent that he does, however, the shame will be intensified if his misdemeanors are publicized. Again, this intensification results not from the contribution of a new variable, but from the fact that other standards, such as ones having to do with social appearances, are invoked.

Now although we have been talking about the emotion type of DISAPPROVING OF ONE'S OWN BLAMEWORTHY ACTION in terms of shame, it should be noted that the emotion identification we use for this family of emotions is "Self-reproach" rather than "Shame." Our reason for this is that the moral overtones of "shame" render it too limiting as an appropriate identification. The Self-reproach emotions accommodate a wider range of emotions than does shame. For example, embarrassment often has no moral overtones, but it too is a Self-reproach emotion. In fact, embarrassment and shame frequently cooccur. Suppose a rich elegant society lady is caught stealing clothes from an exclusive boutique. She might well experience a Self-reproach emotion resulting from her disapproving of her own actions. In other words, it is quite possible that she would be ashamed of what she had done. In violating a moral principle, she violated a standard that she took to be important. However, she might easily feel embarrassment as well. In our opinion, embarrassment is a special case of Self-reproach that depends on the violation of a particular standard having to do with what the person judges to be appropriate social conduct, particularly as it pertains to being able to do the socially appropriate thing. The closeness of shame and embarrassment results from the fact that most people who disapprove of their own blameworthy actions because they have violated a moral standard don't know what to *do* when confronted by others so that the social standard having to do with appropriate conduct is also violated. Thus, shame is linked to embarrassment because the fact that one has cause to be ashamed is likely to constitute an occasion for being unable to conduct oneself appropriately, which in turn is likely to cause the embarrassed person to believe that others may lower their esteem for him.

Another emotion that we have assimilated into the Self-reproach emotions is *feeling guilty* (as distinct from *guilt*, which, as discussed in Ortony, 1987, we do not take to be an emotion at all). The experience of feeling guilty seems to us (and to others, for example, see Wicker, Payne, & Morgan, 1983) to be rather different from shame. In order to feel shame, one must have violated a standard one takes to be *important*, as moral standards are. Such violations are held to be inexcusable. This is not

"There's so much talk these days about this kind of guilt and that kind of guilt. Isn't anybody just plain ashamed anymore?"

necessary for a person who is feeling guilty. One can feel guilty as a result of an action one thought was harmless and innocent but which subsequently turns out not to have been. Often, when one describes oneself as "feeling guilty" one merely means that one believes oneself to be to some degree responsible for something, although this responsibility is frequently only "technical." In fact, we do not think that there is a distinct emotion of feeling guilty. Rather, we view feelings of guilt as mixtures of distinct emotions such as shame and regret, perhaps accompanied by certain cognitive states, such as the belief that one was, at least technically, responsible.

Typically, feelings of guilt are less intense than are feelings of shame because the standards that are invoked are of less value than those involved in cases of shame. For example, consider the case of shame we have just discussed, in which the society lady is caught shoplifting. Her shame is due to her realization that she has violated a standard such as PEOPLE OUGHT TO BE HONEST and that the violation was inexcusable. This, we assume, is a relatively important moral standard. Had she only *thought* about stealing the clothes – a "technical" transgression – but decided that because it was wrong she could not do it, she might describe herself as "feeling guilty." For most people, thinking bad thoughts is less of a transgression than doing (the corresponding) bad deeds. It would be a mistake to suppose that the standards involved in Self-reproach emotions must necessarily be *moral* in nature. A supposed expert on some topic could feel ashamed at not knowing some important fact in his field, although, admittedly, it might be difficult to distinguish his emotion from embarrassment. What would make it a case of shame would be that the violation was of a standard he held to be subjectively important such as ONE OUGHT TO BE WELL-INFORMED ABOUT WORK IN ONE'S FIELD, and that he believed the violation to be in some sense inexcusable.

Before leaving the topic of shame and feelings of guilt, one other observation about frequent cooccurrences of emotions is worth mentioning. When a person has violated some standard and feels guilty or ashamed as a result, it seems plausible to suppose that just as he or she might be embarrassed upon realizing that others know about the transgression, so too might that person *fear* the possibility of such knowledge by others. In this connection, it is interesting to note that the Australian Aboriginal language Gidjingali appears to subsume what we would consider to be shame and fear under one lexical item (see Hiatt, 1978). This suggests that in this culture fear might involve conceptual differentiations into fear of physical events and fear of psychological events, such as the discovery of moral or other transgressions, both of which might be seen in terms of the associated action tendency of wanting to get away from the situation. Perhaps the language does not mark the distinction because it is too fine-grained. We shall discuss the relationship between emotions, language, and culture in more detail in Chapter 9, but for the moment this cross-cultural fact underscores our claims in Chapter 1 that linguistic evidence has to be used cautiously. This is particularly true if one seeks to use ordinary language to make claims about emotions as opposed to claims about the folk theory of emotions that is embedded within the culture and the language.

Ultimately, a comprehensive treatment of the Pride and Self-reproach emotions, that is, a treatment that identifies the particular values of the features in the type specification in terms of which emotions such as feeling guilty, shame, and embarrassment can be distinguished, will require the same kind of fine-grained analysis that we discussed in the context of some of the Event-based emotions. It may be that such an analysis will reveal not just that different standards are implicated in these different emotions, but also that the associated blameworthiness and praiseworthiness flows from different kinds of violations. For example, it might be that it will turn out that feelings of guilt arise in response to *violations* of standards, whereas feelings of shame arise from failures to *reach* standards (Piers & Singer, 1953). The resolution of such issues is beyond the scope of the present book.

We turn now to the Attribution emotions that focus on the agency of others.

(7.3) **APPRECIATION EMOTIONS**
TYPE SPECIFICATION: (approving of) someone else's praiseworthy action
TOKENS: admiration, appreciation, awe, esteem, respect, etc.
VARIABLES AFFECTING INTENSITY:
(1) the degree of judged praiseworthiness
(2) deviations of the agent's action from person/role-based expectations (i.e., unexpectedness)
EXAMPLE: The physicist's colleagues admired him for his Nobel-prize-winning work.

(7.4) **REPROACH EMOTIONS**
TYPE SPECIFICATION: (disapproving of) someone else's blameworthy action
TOKENS: appalled, contempt, despise, disdain, indignation, reproach, etc.
VARIABLES AFFECTING INTENSITY:
(1) the degree of judged blameworthiness
(2) deviations of the agent's action from person/role-based expectations (i.e., unexpectedness)
EXAMPLE: Many people despised the spy for having betrayed his country.

The other-focused Attribution emotions are somewhat less complicated than the self-focused ones. In the case of the Appreciation emotions, of which *admiration* is perhaps the most representative example, the emotion is a reaction of approval for some praiseworthy action, the more praiseworthy, the more intense. So, in the paradigm example, the physicist's colleagues can have a great deal of admiration for his prize-winning work – much more so than for his having a routine article accepted. Similarly, in the case of the Reproach emotions, of which *contempt* is a good example, the reaction is one of disapproval, so that in the example of the spy, people are likely to have contempt for him to the degree that they consider being a spy to be reprehensible. Presumably they would have less contempt for the spy if they knew he was a double agent on "our side," and they would have less contempt for some person who engaged in activities that they considered immoral or illegal but which they viewed as being less important. For example, they might have less contempt for a person who drove his car without a valid license, or smoked marijuana. The more heinous the crime, the more intense the contempt.

Of course, not all Reproach emotions are well characterized by the word "contempt," which is why we call them "Reproach" emotions rather than "Contempt" emotions. If, for example, a young child persists in disobeying his or her parents, "contempt" is not likely to capture the feeling of censure that the parents probably experience. "Reproach" seems closer. Fortunately, it is not incumbent on us, given our goals, to specify what the most appropriate word is to describe this, or any other particular case. For our purposes it is sufficient to establish that the emotion type that we have identified characterizes the emotion, and we think that the emotion type of DISAPPROVING OF SOMEONE ELSE'S BLAMEWORTHY ACTION is a fair characterization *both* of cases of contempt, and of cases such as that of the disobedient child.

The effect of the unexpectedness variable (deviation from person or role-based expectations) can be seen by considering how much more admiration one might feel in the case of admiration for the physicist if he were a graduate student as opposed to an already established, eminent scientist. And in the case of contempt for the spy, the Reproach emotion is likely to be more intense if the spy were, say, a minister as compared to a disgruntled sailor, because the former case would represent a greater deviation from role-based expectations than might the latter.

Since the effects of expectation-deviation and of praiseworthiness and blameworthiness are exactly the same as for the self-focused emotions in the Attribution emotions there is little point in elaborating upon them further. What does require discussion is the relation between the Attribution emotions and emotions like gratitude and anger. It is to this topic that we now turn.

Gratitude, Anger, and Some Other Compound Emotions

We noted in Chapter 2 that we utilized a notion of compound emotions to account for emotions such as gratitude and anger. These compound emotions are characterized by the fact that they result from the conjunction of the eliciting conditions of two emotions from different classes and by the fact that their intensity can be affected by all of the variables affecting the intensity of their constituent emotions. The emotions that we place in this group all result from such a compounding of Attribution emotions with Well-being emotions. This yields four compound emotions, namely those that result from the conjunction of the eliciting conditions of a positive Event-based emotion (such as joy) with the two positive Attribution emotions, and of a negative Event-based emotion (such as distress) with the two negative Attribution emotions. The result is the following set of equivalences:

approving of someone else's praiseworthy action (admiration)	+	pleased about a desirable event (joy)	→	gratitude
disapproving of someone else's blameworthy action (reproach)	+	displeased about an undesirable event (distress)	→	anger
approving of one's own praiseworthy action (pride)	+	pleased about a desirable event (joy)	→	gratification
disapproving of one's own blameworthy action (shame)	+	displeased about an undesirable event (distress)	→	remorse

What this indicates is that gratitude is the compound emotion that results from the conjunction of the eliciting conditions of admiration and joy so that one feels more gratitude the more praiseworthy an action is *and* the more desirable the outcome is. An analogous interpretation applies to anger as well as to gratification and remorse. We should make clear immediately that we are not proposing these equivalences as *temporal* relations, nor as the simple cooccurrence of the constituent emotions. The idea is not that one first feels, for example, reproach and distress, and then, as a result, feels anger. Nor are we proposing that anger is merely a mixture of reproach and distress. Rather, the claim is that if one focuses on *both* the blameworthiness of the agent's action *and* on the undesirable event (related to it), then the eliciting conditions for anger are satisfied. Whether, on any particular occasion, a person focuses also on one or another of the constituent eliciting conditions individually is a separate issue. If a person does focus on the constituents individually, then the associated emotions are likely to be experienced along with the anger. Notice that because the compound emotions implicate intensity variables from two sources, they are likely to be more intense than their constituent emotions. This may explain why it is that in any given situation in which both could be experienced (with respect to the same situation, that is) gratitude feels like a stronger emotion than admiration, and anger a stronger emotion than reproach. As discussed in Chapter 6, when emotions compete, it is probably the case that the more intense emotions present themselves to consciousness with greater insistence.

It is, of course, possible to provide emotion specifications for these compound emotions:

(7.5)   **GRATITUDE EMOTIONS**

TYPE SPECIFICATION: (approving of) someone else's praiseworthy
action and (being pleased about) the related desirable event
TOKENS: appreciation, gratitude, feeling indebted, thankful, etc.
VARIABLES AFFECTING INTENSITY:
(1) the degree of judged praiseworthiness
(2) deviations of the agent's action from person/role-based expectations
(3) the degree to which the event is desirable
EXAMPLE: The woman was grateful to the stranger for saving the life
of her child.

(7.6)   **ANGER EMOTIONS**

TYPE SPECIFICATION: (disapproving of) someone else's
blameworthy action and (being displeased about) the related
undesirable event
TOKENS: anger, annoyance, exasperation, fury, incensed, indignation,
irritation, livid, offended, outrage, rage, etc.
VARIABLES AFFECTING INTENSITY:
(1) the degree of judged blameworthiness
(2) deviations of the agent's action from person/role-based expectations
(3) the degree to which the event is undesirable
EXAMPLE: The woman was angry with her husband for forgetting to
buy the groceries.

(7.7)   **GRATIFICATION EMOTIONS**

TYPE SPECIFICATION: (approving of) one's own praiseworthy
action and (being pleased about) the related desirable event
TOKENS: gratification, pleased-with-oneself, self-satisfaction, smug,
etc.
VARIABLES AFFECTING INTENSITY:
(1) the degree of judged praiseworthiness
(2) the strength of the cognitive unit with the agent
(3) deviations of the agent's action from person/role-based expectations
(4) the degree to which the event is undesirable
EXAMPLE: The man was gratified by his daughter's achievements.

(7.8)   **REMORSE EMOTIONS**

TYPE SPECIFICATION: (disapproving of) one's own blameworthy
action and (being displeased about) the related undesirable event
TOKENS: penitent, remorse, self-anger, etc.
VARIABLES AFFECTING INTENSITY:
(1) the degree of judged blameworthiness
(2) the strength of the cognitive unit with the agent
(3) deviations of the agent's action from person/role-based expectations
(4) the degree to which the event is undesirable
EXAMPLE: The spy felt remorse at the damage he had done in
betraying his country.

The proposal that these four emotions are *compound* emotions means
that they result from focusing on both the desirability and the praiseworthi-

ness of some situation in its entirety *at the same time*. Certainly, insofar as anger is viewed as a compound emotion in this way, the proposal is radically different from most current views of emotions. As Table 2.1 showed, almost every modern theorist who entertains the notion of a set of "basic" emotions includes anger in that set. For us, anger is a compound emotion that has two components, and when a person focuses on only one of them, the nature of the experience changes and a different emotion arises.

Whereas the emotion specifications for the compound emotions appear to be categorically different from those of their constituents, experientially they seem to merge into one another. However, in terms of the analysis that we have proposed, this is not altogether surprising. To see how this is so, we can consider the case of gratitude in which we reduce the effect of the desirability variable while holding the other variables (as) constant (as possible). For a given level of praiseworthiness, the similarity of the actual eliciting conditions to those for admiration will increase, because, although one is focusing on the praiseworthiness of the action and the desirability of the related event *at the same time*, the salience of the desirability component will be lowered, making the overall situation much more similar to that for simple admiration.

The first compound emotion we shall discuss is that of the Gratitude emotions, partly because of the obvious connection between them and Appreciation emotions, such as admiration. The special character of gratitude is that the person who experiences it usually considers himself to be the intended, and sometimes is the actual, beneficiary of an agent's action. Apart from being influenced by the variables that affect the intensity of Appreciation emotions, the intensity of gratitude is influenced by the *desirability* of the actual or potential consequences of the agent's action. So, for example, other things being equal, a woman is likely to feel more gratitude to someone who saved the life of her child than to someone who saved the life of her guinea pig, or the life of somebody else's child.

Now although the desirability of the actual or potential consequences of the agent's action *typically* affects the intensity of gratitude, it does not follow that it *necessarily* does so. It seems that we need to be able to establish this, for otherwise our proposed analysis of gratitude as involving an Attribution emotion *and* a Well-being emotion will be in jeopardy. This means that we need to establish that it is not possible for a person to feel grateful toward someone who performs a praiseworthy action that has no desirable consequences for the person. Certainly, gratitude cannot result merely from good intentions. Even though one might express gratitude, one does not *feel* grateful to someone who, while intending to help, in fact fails to do so, perhaps even making matters worse. Yet, it does seem that one can be grateful to somebody who tries to help, even if they fail, and if we are to say that gratitude necessarily involves some related desirable event for the grateful person, we have to be able to say where this desirability comes from. Suppose, for example, that one's young daughter disappears and a friend searches unsuccessfully for her. One now has an Active-pursuit goal to find one's daughter and the friend's efforts are seen as attempting to facilitate this goal. Thus, it is easy to construe one's friend's efforts, even if unsuccessful, as facilitating certain high-level Interest goals. For example, it furthers one's interests in having other people attempt to do good things for one. In this way, the *potential* desirability of the event that the friend tries to bring about (i.e., the event of finding one's daughter) can indirectly influence the intensity of the gratitude. Furthermore, the fact that other people uphold or surpass one's standards (the source of the praiseworthiness of the action) can itself constitute another source of desirability insofar as it facilitates I-goals such as MAINTAIN THE STANDARDS TO WHICH I SUBSCRIBE. Thus, we conclude that in situations that elicit gratitude there is always some personally desirable aspect of the agent's action, even though it is not necessarily an aspect that results from the actual achievement of an A-goal. The net effect of all of this is that some sort of desirable event is, after all, necessary rather than merely typical for gratitude.

One can ask the parallel question about whether or not praiseworthiness is necessary for gratitude. Can people genuinely experience gratitude towards someone who only accidentally effects a desirable outcome for them – that is, in cases in which the preconditions for praiseworthiness are not satisfied? Our response to this is that they can not, and that the only conceivable reason for believing otherwise is that people sometimes *talk* that way. The fact that conventions of politeness might require us to thank those who inadvertently are the agents of beneficial outcomes is for us a fact about the linguistic conventions surrounding politeness, not a fact about emotion.[1] If the agent's action is not viewed as praiseworthy, people do not experience admiration or gratitude.

Whereas we have just tried to establish that both desirability (which is the primary variable associated with the Well-being emotions) and praiseworthiness (which is the primary variable associated with the Attribution emotions) are necessary for gratitude, the realization of this goal is not really essential. As we have said before, when we provide an emotion

---

1 A compelling illustration of the dissociation between socially mandated expressions of emotions and experienced emotions can be seen in the reactions of losing contestants towards the winner of a beauty pageant. The losers, while stifling their tears of disappointment and distress, can often be seen forcing smiles of praise and admiration and expressing Happy-for emotions with an attempted enthusiasm that has to be seen to be believed!

specification we are not providing definitions of emotion words. Thus, even if our arguments over the role of desirability and praiseworthiness in Gratitude emotions turned out to be defective, we could still consistently maintain that there is an emotion that is characterizable as approving of someone else's praiseworthy action and being pleased about the related desirable event, and that, as a matter of fact, many cases of gratitude (even if not all) have exactly this character.

The analysis of gratitude that we have just proposed can be applied in exactly the same way to its negative counterpart, which, perhaps surprisingly, turns out to be anger. We say "surprisingly" because one does not ordinarily think of gratitude and anger as being "opposites." Nevertheless, if we are right that anger involves both reproach and an undesirable outcome, then it really is opposed in this way to gratitude. When, for example, somebody drives out of his driveway into *your* car, damaging it beyond repair, anger is certainly one of the first reactions. You are displeased about an undesirable event (distress) *and* you disapprove of the blameworthy action of another person (reproach). Typical reactions to such events include accusations of irresponsibility, carelessness, and assertions, subvocal or otherwise, such as "You're not fit to drive a car, you shouldn't be allowed on the roads, you should be locked up . . . ." These reactions of outrage and indignation are reflections of *moral* or *quasi-moral* evaluations, as though part of the anger had to do with one's beliefs that the agent was *morally* reprehensible. The injured party appears to be influenced by beliefs such as that only someone with no consideration for others could do such a thing. And, lacking consideration for others is, if not a moral shortcoming, at least a flagrant violation of a social standard. Thus we see that a typical case of anger is one that involves *both* an undesirable outcome and the attribution of responsibility in the form of blame for the outcome to an agent.

However, the same question arises as in the case of gratitude. The fact that a typical case of anger involves both reproach and an undesirable event does not establish that these two components are necessary. In order to have some confidence in such a conclusion, we need to consider whether we are justified in eliminating cases in which it might be claimed that one or another component is absent. How can we explain anger in the absence of any obvious direct harm to the angry person? In 1986, many ordinary Americans reacted strongly to the revelation that members of the White House staff had been secretly arranging for arms to be sold to Iran and diverting the profits to the Contras in Nicaragua. Many of these people felt contempt toward the administration because they thought the whole affair deceitful and wrong. It violated what for them were standards of appropriate behavior for a civilized Western power. But some of these people also felt angry. Why? As in the parallel case of gratitude, our answer is that *if* they felt anger (as opposed to only a Reproach emotion such as contempt), and if no *direct* harm was done (e.g., in the form of thwarting Active-pursuit goals), then they must have perceived *indirect* harm by viewing the violation of the particular standards they invoked as threatening one or more of their Interest goals. Here it is easier than in the case of gratitude to see what such goals might be. Angry Americans presumably construed helping the Iranians, whom they viewed as the source of insults and humiliation, and financing the Contras through the use of illegal and clandestine operations, as interfering with their interests in a variety of ways. They might have construed such activities as interfering with I-goals having to do with the maintenance of standards of honesty, the maintenance of a leadership role for their country, the maintenance of their dignity (as Americans), and so on. Furthermore, the undesirable aspects may have come even closer to home for those who viewed such activities as involving the expenditure of tax dollars, including, indirectly, their own. Of course, it is only necessary to view the affair in this sort of way if one is trying to explain why somebody might have felt angry about it. To explain the reproach that might have been felt toward the perpetrators of such deeds requires only that the actions were judged in terms of their blameworthiness, without regard to any actual or potential undesirable consequences.

In general, one can be angry over otherwise harmless violations of standards because the values of standards are ultimately related to one's interests. Standards are not just standards that everyone else has. Individuals subscribe to them too, and individuals have an interest in their being upheld. One may focus only on the violation of the standard, and thus experience a pure Reproach emotion, or one may also focus on the undesirability of the action, in which case an Anger emotion can result.

We still need to consider how a Distress emotion arising from simple goal-blockage in the absence of a blameworthy agent can lead to anger. Why can one be angry when, for no apparent reason, one's car will not start? In our view, this only happens if, in fact, one does attribute causal agency (quite possibly, wrongly, and knowingly so) to something (the weather, the car, the garage mechanic, the person who last drove it, etc.). One might call these "desperation" attributions because they represent a desperate attempt to attribute responsibility, even when there is no culpable agent available. In any event, they are a very natural response to such situations. Indeed, sometimes it seems as though the desire to identify some possible cause, however bizarre and unreasonable the candidate selected in the heat of the moment may be, results from an unconscious understanding that one's anger presupposes that there exists such a cause.

Interestingly, failure to find some at least temporarily satisfactory agent (scapegoat), can sometimes constitute its own source of frustration, thereby exacerbating the original problem and intensifying the felt anger.

Among the tokens that we have associated with the Anger emotions is "offended." This warrants some discussion. The elicitation of Anger emotions implicates both the violation of standards and the thwarting of goals. If someone is insulting or abusive one can feel offended, presumably because of the violation of standards such as PEOPLE OUGHT TO BE CONSIDERATE OF THE FEELINGS OF OTHERS. The reason we include "offended" as a token under Anger emotions is that it is an appropriate label for a particular differentiated form of the emotion type. This form is one in which the negative impact is of a particular kind, namely, the belief that the agent did not take appropriate account of the experiencer's psychological needs. In general, this means that a particular I-goal is implicated – specifically, a Preservation goal such as MAINTAIN THE RESPECT OF OTHERS. The perceived threat to this goal involves the respect that other particular individuals, rather than of people in general, have for one.

As far as the other two compound emotions, the Gratification emotions and the Remorse emotions are concerned, there is really little that can be added to what we have already said. The chief difference between them and anger and gratitude is that they involve the self as the formal agent. Like the self-focused Attribution emotions (pride and self-reproach) these emotions can also be quite intense when the actual agent is some other person with whom the experiencing person considers himself to be in a cognitive unit. A father can be proud that his daughter graduates with distinction from Harvard, and to the degree that it was an aspiration of his that his daughter would do this, he can be gratified too. Both his pride and his gratification will be influenced by the degree to which he thinks his daughter's achievement is praiseworthy, and the closer he feels to her, the more intense will both emotions be. Furthermore, to the degree that he views his daughter as having done much better than the typical Harvard student, the more proud and the more gratified will he be, because her achievement will deviate more from that role-based norm. Notice here that if his daughter has always distinguished herself relative to her peers, and if the father evaluates her Harvard success relative to these person-based expectations, the emotions of pride and gratification could be less intense. So, how intense they are depends on the norm that he recruits in evaluating his daughter's achievements (Kahneman & Miller, 1986). What distinguishes gratification from pride, by our account, is that the intensity of gratification is also influenced by the desirability variable.

To illustrate this point, we shall use the example from the Remorse emotions. The example is that of a spy who feels remorse at the damage he has done in betraying his country. Notice, first, that remorse is not the same as regret. Regret has to do with wishing that what was done had not been done and is perhaps best considered as a Loss emotion (see Chapter 5) because it seems to implicate a lost opportunity to have acted differently. Regret in no way requires an acknowledgement of standards violation, whereas remorse clearly does. The contribution of the undesirable event to Remorse emotions is captured by the requirement in the type specification that the agent be displeased about the "related" event. But how should the event be related to the action? There are right ways and wrong ways. For example, if the spy is sentenced to life in prison, this is clearly an event related to his espionage activities, but not in the right way. The related event must be a relatively immediate consequence of the blameworthy action – in this case, harming his country. This may be easier to see if one considers a simple case of self-anger.

Suppose an absent-minded professor shuts and locks his car, only to realize that he has locked his keys inside his car. In such a situation, the unfortunate professor might well feel angry with himself. If so, he would, by our account, both disapprove of his blameworthy action (presumably finding it blameworthy in terms of some standard such as that he ought to think about what he is doing) and he would be displeased about the related undesirable event of locking himself out of his car – undesirable, we presume, because of its undesirable consequences. Now, suppose the professor, for all his practical incompetence, knows himself well enough to always keep a spare set of car keys with him. He might well still feel self-reproach at his incompetence. He might say to himself something like, "There I go again. I really ought to think about what I'm doing." Our claim, however, is that he will not be angry with himself because his action has no further harmful consequences, unless, of course, he forgets that he has a spare set of keys with him (which, in our experience of absent-minded professors is entirely possible). Self-anger requires that one also focus on the relatively immediate undesirable consequences of one's blameworthy act, which, if considered alone, is sufficient only to give rise to self-blame or reproach.

Summary

The Attribution emotions focus on the actions of agents rather than on events themselves. The two Attribution emotions that center on the self (or extended self) as agent have the eliciting conditions (APPROVING OF) ONE'S OWN PRAISEWORTHY ACTION (e.g., pride) and (DISAPPROVING OF) ONE'S OWN BLAMEWORTHY ACTION (e.g., shame).

The variables that affect the intensity of these two Attribution emotions are: (1) the degree of praiseworthiness or blameworthiness of the agent (which include variables like effort, responsibility, and intention), (2) the strength of the cognitive unit, where the agent is not oneself but a person or institution with whom one identifies, and (3) deviations from the person- or role-based expectations of the agent.

Two other Attribution emotions focus on the agency of others. Their eliciting conditions are (APPROVING OF) SOMEONE ELSE'S PRAISEWORTHY ACTION (e.g., admiration) and (DISAPPROVING OF) SOMEONE ELSE'S BLAMEWORTHY ACTION (e.g., reproach). The variables that affect the intensity of these two emotions are: (1) the degree of praiseworthiness or blameworthiness of the agent, and (2) deviations from person- or role-based expectations of the agent.

Four other emotions appear to be compound emotions in that they focus on both the agent of the event and the desirability of the outcome. These emotions are: (1) gratitude, which combines the approval of an agent's action with pleasure at the desirable outcome, (2) anger, which combines disapproval of an agent's action with displeasure at the undesirable outcome, (3) gratification, which combines approval of one's own action with pleasure at the desirable outcome, and (4) remorse, which combines disapproval of one's own action with disapproval of the outcome. The intensity of these emotions is affected both by the variables that affect the related Well-being emotions and by those that affect the related Attribution emotions.

8   Reactions to Objects

Having offered a fairly detailed analysis of the different emotions that arise when people react to events and to the actions of agents, we are left with the final major group of emotions, those resulting from reacting to objects or aspects of objects. While the structure of this group is quite simple – there being only one positive and one negative emotion type – in reality, these emotions are among the most complex of human reactions. The Attraction emotions are rooted in evaluations of appealingness, which in turn are based on attitudes. In this context, the notion of an attitude has to be treated sufficiently broadly to include tastes as well.

The Attraction Emotions

The Attraction emotions are momentary reactions of liking and disliking, and as such, they are among the most salient experiences we have. At the same time, they appear to be more immediate, more spontaneous, and less affected by accessible cognitive processes than almost all of the other emotions. The foundations upon which they are built – attitudes – do not all readily lend themselves to detailed analysis, although it is possible to identify some factors that affect them. The other emotions we have discussed are cognitively differentiated forms of more basic and undifferentiated affective reactions. They achieve their distinctiveness by virtue of these cognitive constraints. Thus, the Prospect-based emotions are reactions to the prospect of events, the Fortunes-of-others emotions are concerned with people's reactions to events as they affect other people, and so on. By contrast, the Attraction emotions seem to be directly experienced as relatively undifferentiated affective reactions. There are only two distinct Attraction emotions. One corresponds to liking or attraction and is occasioned by reacting positively toward some appealing object, and the other, corresponding to aversion or dislike, is occasioned by reacting negatively

Table 8.1. *Attraction emotions*

APPRAISAL OF OBJECT	
APPEALING	UNAPPEALING
liking an appealing object (e.g., love)	disliking an unappealing object (e.g., hate)

towards some unappealing object.[1] The structure of the Attraction emotions is shown in Table 8.1.

The characterizations of the Attraction emotions are deceptively simple. Their eliciting conditions are quite straightforward, and we have indicated only two intensity variables for them.

(8.1) **LIKING EMOTIONS**
TYPE SPECIFICATION: (liking) an appealing object
TOKENS: adore, affection, attracted-to, like, love, etc.
VARIABLES AFFECTING INTENSITY:
(1) the degree to which the object is appealing
(2) the degree of familiarity with the object
EXAMPLE: Mary was filled with affection as she gazed at her newborn infant.

(8.2) **DISLIKING EMOTIONS**
TYPE SPECIFICATION: (disliking) an unappealing object
TOKENS: aversion, detest, disgust, dislike, hate, loathe, repelled-by, revulsion, etc.
VARIABLES AFFECTING INTENSITY:
(1) the degree to which the object is unappealing
(2) the degree of familiarity with the object
EXAMPLE: John disliked the concert so much that he left in the middle.

The central variable that affects the intensity of the Attraction emotions is the perceived *appealingness* of the object. As discussed in Chapter 3, we view the appealingness of objects to be ultimately rooted in attitudes. Although we consider attitudes, along with standards and goals, to constitute *sources* of value in the appraisal mechanism that underlies emotions, we think it important not to confuse attitudes with the ordinary sense of values. The potential for confusion arises because there is a familiar sense

1 Note that we use the term "unappealing" in the sense of the contrary of appealing, in which something is unpleasant rather than in the sense in which it is the contradictory and simply lacks appeal.

of the word "values" in which it refers to the elements of a *value system*, and these elements seem to correspond more closely to the standards that we have described as constituting the basis of the Attribution emotions than they do to attitudes. Second, insofar as one does think of values as being part of a value system, attitudes – and especially that subset of them that we call "tastes" – are different in that there does not appear to be any comparable systematicity that underlies them. The problem is particularly acute with respect to tastes. It is difficult to analyze or explain one's tastes; they are not the kinds of things for which justifications are usually sought, or offered. One does not get very far when one asks why somebody likes strawberries or dislikes anchovies. At best one might learn that he or she likes the (sweet) taste of one and dislikes the (salty) taste of the other, which amounts to little more than a restatement of the original preference. The same is true in domains other than gustatory taste, although in more complex domains there sometimes exists the possibility of making slight progress on such questions. A person might offer as an "explanation" of why she liked the music of Rossini the fact that she found appealing its vibrant, excited, and optimistic quality. However, even were one to accept this as a genuine "explanation," continued questioning as to why *those* qualities appealed would not be likely to reveal much more.

In order to understand how appealingness affects the intensity of the Attraction emotions we shall first raise some issues having to do with how the dispositional likes and dislikes that we call "attitudes" arise and how they might be represented. The analysis we propose is based on distinguishing between mental representations, or schemas, on the one hand, and experienced instances of the things represented on the other. What we have in mind here is the difference between one's schema for caviar or one's mother-in-law or the sport of basketball and some particular experience of caviar or one's mother-in-law or a basketball game. This distinction corresponds to the difference between *dispositional* liking or disliking, which determines appealingness (in our technical sense of the term), and the affective reactions of *momentary* liking or disliking, which constitute the Attraction emotions. Dispositional liking has to do with schema-derived liking or disliking wherein values are determined by a value component incorporated in stored representations, or schemas. Thus, a dislike of snakes or of rock music is a predisposition to dislike all instances of snakes or rock music, and a dislike of one's mother-in-law is a predisposition to dislike her on all occasions. Similarly, a liking for vodka or the paintings of Monet is a predisposition to like all instances of vodka or all paintings of Monet, and a liking for one's daughter is a predisposition to like her on all occasions.

Tastes derive both from innate sources (e.g., a liking for sweet substances and a dislike of bitter substances) and from cultural and personal
influences (Mandler, 1982, 1984). Some tastes appear to be universal (e.g.,
the dislike of feces and mucus; Angyal, 1941), but cultural and personal
influences also create individual and societal differences in taste. For example, many people in the world would think the rotted meat Eskimos enjoy
is offensive, but Eskimos apparently feel the same way about the rotted
milk that most of the rest of the world calls cheese (Cherfas, 1986). Particularly important in this connection is the fact that cultural and personal
influences can, with the passage of time, override innate preferences. For
example, an innate dislike of bitter substances can be suppressed so that
the English have come to like bitter beer, and the French and Italians have
come to like Campari. One suspects that if one gave some Campari to an
infant for the first time and it cried, it would not be crying for more. This is,
of course, characteristic of "acquired" tastes – initially they are disliked, or
at the very least, not liked. In this regard, cultural and personal influences
are very strong. Not only can they *add* valence to initially value-free stimuli, but they can *change* the valence from negative to positive or vice versa.
The personal influences on dispositional liking consist largely of acquired
attitudes resulting from a history of experiences with the object or objects
of the same kind, which is why we think of attitudes as being part of stored
representations.

The effects of one's history of experience with an object on one's
dispositional liking for it are relatively easy to see in cases where the
appealing object is a person or some other complex object having many
aspects and about which a variety of valenced beliefs can be held. Indeed,
the primary source of our mental representation of an individual is the
incorporation of positive or negative information in the form of valenced
beliefs into one's schema of that individual. Such schemas are routinely
created and updated through the process of trait attribution (see, e.g.,
Jones & Davis, 1965; Kelley, 1967).

When one's representation of a person is altered through trait attribution
as a result of an affectively significant event, it is likely that subsequent
Attraction emotions toward that person will be consistent with it. To see
how an attitude toward an object can influence momentary liking, we shall
consider first how dispositions to like whole categories of objects influence
the Attraction emotions. People are more likely to experience a (momentary) Liking emotion toward some particular object if they have a dispositional liking for the category of which they consider it to be a member. To
the degree that an instance is perceived to fit the schema, prototype, or
best example of a larger category of persons or objects, it may trigger affect

linked to that category (Fiske, 1982). People who find dogs in general appealing are more likely to like some particular dog than are people who consider dogs in general to be unappealing. For the typical dog lover, however, a Mexican hairless or a Pekinese may elicit only moderate liking if they are viewed as poorer examples of the category than, say, an Old English sheep dog. To test this hypothesis with respect to social categories, Fiske (1982) obtained affective reactions to a variety of stimulus persons. She found that to the extent that subjects applied to a person their stereotype of either a *politician* or a *nurd,* the person inherited the negative affect that is part of those schemas, whereas if subjects applied their stereotype of an *old flame,* then the person triggered the positive affect inherent in that schema. Partial matches in which the schema was evoked but the match was poor triggered less consistent affective reactions (see also Fiske & Pavelchak, 1986).

This same process also explains how dispositional or schema-based liking of a particular object may influence an emotion of momentary liking for that object. If, for example, Mary harbors a dispositional dislike of John on the basis of a schema of him as a pedantic person, she is likely to experience momentary dislike when he is being pedantic to the extent that his behavior fits her schema. That is, insofar as Mary's momentary dislike of John is mediated by her dispositional dislike, it will depend on his behavior firing the John-the-pedant schema rather than, say, the more favorable schema that she might also have of him as John-the-scholar. In either case, the Attraction emotion that Mary experiences toward him will depend on the dispositional liking for him (i.e., appealingness) that is incorporated in the representation that Mary invokes. Similar effects of evaluation by association and categorization have been found for the Disliking emotion of disgust (Rozin & Fallon, 1987). Presumably, the mother's affection for her newborn infant is based on such associative and categorization mechanisms.

From time to time in the preceding chapters, we have alluded to the effects of context on the nature and intensity of emotions. Usually (e.g., Chapter 6), the contextual factors we have considered have had to do with prior expectations. Contextual factors, especially the specific existing affective state of the experiencer at the time he or she is focusing on the object, render the appealingness variable particularly volatile (e.g., Kearney, 1966; Konečni & Sargent-Pollock, 1976; Steck & Machotka, 1975). For example, a person who dispositionally dislikes sweetbreads might, under conditions of near starvation, or in a context in which the only alternatives were even less to his taste, have a momentary liking for sweetbreads, or at least, a contextually-determined diminution of his dislike. Similarly, one might dislike rock music, but find some particular song quite appealing after a forced diet of Stockhausen!

To the extent that the appealingness of an experience, and hence how much it is liked, is dependent on the context in which it is encountered and evaluated, liking can be a quite ephemeral experience. Adaptation level theory (Helson, 1964) suggests that we tend to adapt to our current level of stimulation, so that, for example, when one eats more than usual for a period of time, the level of food intake needed to keep one from feeling hungry also rises. Applied to the level of pleasantness one experiences, Brickman and Campbell (1971) suggest that such adaptation processes condemn us to a kind of hedonic treadmill in which the more pleasant our current situation is, the less pleasant our future can be (see also Parducci, 1968). Brickman and Campbell argue that how much we like our life situation depends on a variety of kinds of comparative judgments, including *social comparisons*, in which we compare our outcomes with those of comparable others, *temporal comparisons*, in which we compare our current outcomes with those enjoyed in the past, and *spatial comparisons*, in which we compare the outcomes in one aspect of our lives with those afforded by other aspects (e.g., income level versus educational level). Some of the complexities of these judgments have already been alluded to in our discussion of social comparison processes in Chapter 5, where, with respect to the concept of a reference group, it was pointed out that in order to know whether individuals will be pleased or displeased with their life situations, we need to know with whom they see themselves as comparable.

There are two schools of thought regarding the nature of context effects in judgment. The adaptation level view implies that one's actual experience of a stimulus depends on the context in which it is encountered, as for example when a light appears brighter after one's eyes have adapted to the dark. Others suggest that context has its effect primarily on people's judgments about their experience rather than on the experiences themselves. According to this view, context effects essentially concern changes in the apparent appropriateness of particular responses for judging one's experience rather than changes in the experience per se (Parducci, 1965; Upshaw, 1969).

These two positions would seem to have rather different implications, but even if one takes the view that context merely influences judgments about experiences rather than experiences themselves, it is clear that the resulting effects have important implications in that they are a major source of attitudes. This can be seen from the results of a study in which subjects were asked to judge the importance of recycling in the context of either very important or very unimportant issues (Sherman, Ahlm, Berman, & Lynn, 1978). As would be expected, the ratings showed contrast effects–

recycling seemed more important when considered in the context of other issues deemed relatively unimportant, and less important in the context of very important issues. But the most interesting results concern what happened later, outside the context of the experiment, when subjects were approached by a confederate and asked to help out on an actual recycling project. Those who had considered recycling in the context of unimportant issues volunteered more help than those who had rated it in the context of important issues. Even though the elevated importance judgments may have resulted from a momentary context-produced bias in how subjects expressed themselves, the context nevertheless had lasting effects. When deciding whether to volunteer, the recycling concept would have been activated in memory and the prior judgment of recycling as "very important" would have been retrieved also. In this way, the momentary effects of context, once they become part of one's schema of a stimulus, can have lasting effects by creating or changing attitudes.

The context-effects that we have just discussed essentially show how, under different conditions, different representations will be accessed leading to different evaluative results. Another kind of effect pertains to the affective state of the emotion-experiencing person at the time the stimulus is encountered. There is a wealth of recent research showing that momentary liking is influenced by the affective state or mood of the experiencer when focusing on the object of evaluation (e.g., Bower, 1981; Clark, 1982; Griffitt & Veitch, 1971; Forgas & Moylan, 1987; Isen, 1984; Schwarz & Clore, 1983). These studies typically find that when elated or sad, momentary liking for almost anything is affected as long as the true cause of the feelings is not salient. This effect occurs because, ordinarily, affective feelings are the result of having appraised some stimulus as significant, so that if some stimulus is made salient at the time the feeling is being experienced, there is a tendency for the two to seem causally related. For example, if a child has an unpleasant feeling of revulsion when he sees broccoli on his plate, he is likely to attribute it to his distaste for broccoli. However, if this feeling of revulsion at the sight of broccoli arises just after he has gorged himself on a snack of cookies and pickles, he may still attribute his disgust to his distaste for broccoli, even though, unknown to him, it is in fact due to the ill-effects resulting from his snack. Various explanations have been given for such effects, including not only a misattribution explanation (Schwarz & Clore, 1983), but also explanations based on association (Clore & Byrne, 1974) and on the selective activation of emotion-congruent cognitive categories (Bower, 1981; Isen, Shalker, Clark, & Karp, 1978). Regardless of which of these is correct, they all share the feature of predicting that a preexisting affective state can influence evaluations made in that state.

While the example of the broccoli and the cited research show how irrelevant affect can bias liking, these effects presumably occur only because affective reactions ordinarily provide accurate and useful feedback from one's appraisal processes (Clore, 1985). That is, the feelings encountered when focusing on a particular stimulus are usually genuine reactions to that stimulus, and they are reactions that, under normal conditions, provide important information for subsequent judgment and decision making. For example, if John were critical of Mary in public, the intensity of her negative feelings while focusing on the event would probably accurately reflect the undesirability of the event for her. Similar feelings while focusing on John's behavior (or on John himself) would usually reflect accurately how blameworthy she found his behavior (or how much she momentarily disliked him). These considerations suggest that one can like others on the basis of momentary feelings that are (accurately or inaccurately) linked to them without ever having altered one's schema of them. Of course, this is not to deny that experiences with others that change our momentary liking for them often change our beliefs about them as well (Fishbein & Ajzen, 1975). Indeed, such belief-changes are the primary source of changes in dispositional liking.

This rather sketchy discussion of attitudes and tastes has been necessary for two reasons. First, it is intended to show that our account of the Attraction emotions is not circular – the Attraction emotions are reactions of *momentary* liking or disliking, but the appealingness variable that drives them is based on *dispositional* liking or disliking, and the two, while interacting in important ways, are clearly different. Second, it seems helpful to chart enough of the terrain to permit a sense of its complexity to emerge. This was the point of our earlier remark, that although the Attraction emotions are superficially simple, what underlies them is not. To summarize: Attitudes are encoded in representations of objects or categories. On any particular occasion upon which an object is encountered, the encoded evaluations found in the representation of it, and/or of the category of which it is seen as being a member, will be accessible. It is these schema-based evaluations that constitute the locus of the attitudes that control appealingness.

We move now to a discussion of the second variable that we propose as influencing the intensity of the Attraction emotions – *familiarity*. Various structural considerations such as the kind of schema-fitting effects discussed by Mandler can influence the intensity of momentary liking. These include factors such as well-formedness and closure that were central to the concerns of the Gestalt psychologists, as well as what Berlyne (1960) called the "collative variables," the most important of which are novelty (the inverse of familiarity), surprisingness, and complexity. According to Berlyne, factors such as these are central to an understanding of aesthetic appreciation. They represent aspects of stimuli that cannot be properly thought of as properties of the stimuli, but that can only be understood if compared against (collated with) information from some other source. One feature of structural factors is that they make it possible to have differential reactions to different members of the same category. We do not like to the same degree *all* the paintings of an artist whose work we are disposed to like. Even if it were true that "Gentlemen prefer blondes," they would not necessarily like all blondes to the same degree!

The contribution of structural factors, and especially of Berlyne's collative variables, to liking is quite complex, changing from variable to variable. However, the fact that they make a contribution raises the question of why they are not all listed as intensity variables in our characterizations of the Attribution emotions. Our answer to this question is that familiarity is the only one that appears capable of having an independent effect on intensity, and, as discussed in Chapter 4, this is the criterion that determines whether or not some putative intensity variable will be included in our emotion characterizations. It seems to us that structural factors such as closure and well-formedness constitute aspects of the stimulus object, and as such they influence appealingness directly. This is also our reason for not including complexity as a (potentially) independent intensity variable. Any particular object might be liked or disliked partly as a result of its degree of perceived complexity, but we think, contra Berlyne, that this complexity can be regarded as a property of the object, albeit a higher-order property having to do with relations between properties. This leaves us with Berlyne's remaining collative variables: surprisingness and novelty. The first of these, surprisingness, is already accommodated by our global variable of unexpectedness, in that we view it as influencing the intensity of all emotional reactions. Consequently, we are left only with novelty, and this variable we do regard as capable of having an independent effect, although we have chosen to refer to it as "familiarity."

Although we do not include complexity as an intensity variable, there are a number of tricky issues concerning its relationship to momentary liking, particularly with respect to the way it interacts with the variable that is of concern to us, namely, novelty. The complexity of a stimulus appears to be related more or less monotonically to its interestingness (e.g., Berlyne, 1971) but nonmonotonically to its pleasingness (i.e., in this context, momentary liking). Its contribution to pleasingness appears to interact with other factors, the most important of which, in the present context, is novelty.

Novelty, which we take to be the inverse of familiarity, is a somewhat ambiguous construct. In some studies it has been investigated in terms of the *frequency* of presentation of a stimulus (Berlyne, 1970), and in others in terms of the *discrepancy* between the present and some previously presented stimulus (e.g., Conners, 1964). In the former case, the data suggest that continued exposure leads to increments in liking for more complex stimuli and decrements for less complex stimuli. Thus, novel stimuli are liked better if they are relatively less complex. If the stimuli are complex, they are liked better when they are familiar (less novel). In studies using discrepancy as an index of novelty (while apparently holding complexity constant), the results can be interpreted as showing increments in liking for smaller discrepancies from an adaptation level (i.e., more familiar stimuli) and decrements for larger discrepancies (more novel stimuli). Such findings are, for many reasons, difficult to integrate into a comprehensive picture. First, novelty often interacts with complexity and, no doubt, with many other variables. Second, it is not clear to what extent it has a direct effect on the the degree to which a stimulus is liked as opposed to having an effect through some factor such as interestingness. Third, the function relating novelty to pleasingness may vary from object to object, and is probably nonmonotonic for all objects. Fourth, Berlyne and others argued that such variables all have their effects by causing increases in arousal. Our solution has been to assume that novelty in the sense of discrepancy from similar objects is captured in the appealingness variable, while novelty in the sense of (lack of) familiarity with the same object is captured in our familiarity variable.

In fact, the role of familiarity in liking judgments is one of the few aspects of such judgments that have received considerable attention in the psychological literature. Birch and Marlin (1982), for example, found that children's liking for novel foods increased with the number of times they had been served the food, regardless of whether they had actually eaten any of it. As already indicated, Berlyne (1970) also found evidence that familiarity increases liking, and Zajonc has reported a number of studies demonstrating what has come to be called the "mere exposure" effect (Kunst-Wilson & Zajonc, 1980; Zajonc, 1968). The mere exposure effect suggests that subjects' ratings of how well they like a stimulus increase as the number of prior exposures to the stimulus increases, even under conditions in which subjects are unaware that they have seen the stimulus before. However, other research (e.g., Brickman, Redfield, Harrison, & Crandall, 1972; Mandler & Shebo, 1983) shows that for stimuli that are initially evaluated *negatively*, greater exposure increases the degree to which the stimuli are *disliked*. Thus, at least up to a point, momentary liking is affected by frequency of prior exposure. There is no reason, of course, to suppose that the effect is a linear one. Indeed, it might not even be monotonic. For over a hundred years psychologists have believed that the general function relating various quantitative aspects of stimuli and the affective reaction to them is representable as an inverted **U** (e.g., Berlyne, 1960; Haber, 1958; Wundt, 1874). On the rising portion of such a curve, increased liking is held to result from increases in the independent variable (e.g., unexpectedness, complexity). Ultimately, some optimal level is reached, whereafter increases in the independent variable are held to give rise to reductions in liking. Thus, up to a point, "the more the merrier," after which, "one can have too much of a good thing." We suspect that the contribution of the familiarity variable to momentary liking is of just this kind.

Before leaving these matters, however, let us look at how the concept of optimal level of arousal can explain some instances of the Attraction emotions. Berlyne (1971) assumed that the arousal-potential of a stimulus varied more or less directly with its interestingness or attention-getting potential, but that its pleasingness was associated with an optimal level of arousal. One reason it is difficult to specify even the direction of the effects of the collative variables, then, is that their effects hinge on whether one is currently above or below the optimal level of arousal. Depending on the values of the other variables, increases in the novelty or complexity of a particular stimulus may either increase or decrease the degree to which it is liked.

The optimal level idea is also basic to Eysenck's (1967) conception of introversion-extraversion, in which he explains preferences for sociability, risk-taking, and various other activities on the basis of individual differences in chronic level of arousal. Introverts are hypothesized to be habitually overaroused so that their shy, retiring behavior and their preference for solitary, calm activities stems from their need to reduce external sources of stimulation. In contrast, extraverts are hypothesized to be habitually underaroused so that their outgoing, sociable behavior and their preference for novelty and excitement is part of a search for external sources of stimulation to augment their low internal level of arousal. As a group, extraverts tend to be active people who are more likely to be attracted to smoking, drinking, eating spicy food, going to parties, adopting radical ideas, and engaging in risk-taking because these all move them toward an optimal level of cortical arousal; that is, they are all ways of avoiding boredom and staying awake. Introverts tend to avoid these same experiences because, given that they tend to be chronically overaroused, they find these experiences unappealing. The arousal concept, therefore, does appear valuable for understanding some of the otherwise puzzling individual differences in dispositional liking as well as the effect of certain structural properties of stimuli on their potential appealingness.

Fine-grained Analyses and Emotion Sequences

On several occasions in our earlier discussions of emotion types we noted that the associated tokens should be considered as members of a family of emotions, all of which share the same basic type specification, but whose quality of fit varies according to several factors. Apart from variations in intensity, the two most important of these are the degree to which the semantic focus of a particular token is on some facet other than the experiential aspect, and the degree to which the token is underspecified by the type specification and requires further differentiation. An example of the first (the issue of focus) would be "cowering," which, although listed as a token in the Fear emotions, focuses primarily on a particular kind of fearful behavior. An example of the second (underspecification) would be "grief" in the Well-being emotions. This issue of underspecification is particularly relevant to the presence of "love" as a token in the Liking emotions. While theorists often distinguish different kinds of love (e.g., Lee, 1977; Sternberg, 1986), there appears to be a great deal of structural similarity between them (Sternberg & Grajek, 1984). Accordingly, what we say here is said without regard to distinctions such as those between romantic love and infatuation. In all cases, the momentary experience of love is clearly underspecified by the type specification of LIKING AN APPEALING OBJECT, not merely in the trivial sense that the object is normally constrained to be a human, or at least an animate being, but in terms of its own complex internal structure, which might involve factors like intimacy, passion, and commitment (Sternberg, 1986). Our purpose in raising this topic is only to remind the reader yet again that type specifications (e.g., LIKING AN APPEALING OBJECT) are not intended as *definitions* of emotion words (e.g., "love").

Our specifications of the Attraction emotions impose no constraints on the nature of the appealing or unappealing objects to which they are reactions. This means that the objects of the Attraction emotions are not even restricted to physical ones; they might be psychological objects such as emotional or cognitive states. We have argued elsewhere (e.g., Clore & Ortony 1984; Ortony, 1987) that the proclivity of some cognitive states (e.g., boredom) to be disliked may be a reason for the questionable practice of including them in lists of terms denoting emotions. However, that *emotional* states themselves can be the objects of other emotions, including the Attraction emotions, is more interesting. We have already indicated how this can be in our discussion of Figure 2.2 in Chapter 2. It is not unreasonable to take the next step and to say that (only) the positive emotions are liked, and (only) the negative emotions disliked. Before one can do this, however, one has to be able to explain why, for example, particular experiences of some negative emotions such as fear or anger sometimes seem to be pleasurable. We do not have in mind here cases in which the fact that one experienced a negative emotion is itself construed as a desirable event; it is no mystery why a woman could feel pleased that she got angry with her insufferable boss, this emotion providing her for the first time with the courage to tell him what she really thought. Rather, we have in mind cases like people's apparent liking of the fear associated with riding on a roller-coaster.

There are several ways to view such phenomena. Part of what is going on might be that experiences such as the fear associated with riding on a roller-coaster might be appealing because the pleasurable effects of increases in arousal, as discussed by Berlyne (1971) and Eysenck (1967), outweigh the negative aspects of any genuine fear that is experienced. Such an account would be quite compatible with our overall view, and would predict that people who choose, for example, to take rides on roller-coasters are more likely to be extraverts than introverts in that they are people who are seeking to increase rather than decrease their level of arousal. What would not be compatible with our position would be an attempt to explain the situation by saying that it is the experience of fear itself that is liked. Since we view Fear emotions as *negative* reactions of being displeased, such a reaction cannot *at the same time* be experienced as a *positive* reaction of liking. Whatever the explanation is, it is certainly true that in general we like to be in affectively positive states and dislike being in affectively negative ones. The point of this apparently tautological observation is that it illustrates that emotional experiences themselves (and other experiences, such as aesthetic and religious ones), as opposed merely to the situations that give rise to them, are appraised and reacted to. It also leads to one other observation. When a psychological state is the object of an emotion, there seems no obvious way to decide whether being in that state should be (or is) seen by the experiencer as an event or as an object. If it is conceptualized as an event (e.g., the event of being made afraid), we have to say that any emotion that results as a consequence is a Well-being emotion, whereas if it is conceptualized as an object (e.g., a particular experience of fear) it is an Attraction emotion. This in turn suggests that there are limiting cases in which the distinction between events and objects may be difficult to sustain.

We have now discussed three major classes of emotions that differ from each other in terms of whether one focuses on events, agents, or objects. Something now needs to be said about the interrelations among these classes. We have discussed compound emotions – such as anger – that require a focus on both outcomes and agency at the same time. But we have in mind here another sort of relationship among the classes. According to Heider (1958) and other attribution theorists, one makes causal attributions for the events that one experiences as a matter of course. Often such attributions are made tacitly as part of one's more general understanding of such events but, regardless of whether they are explicit or implicit, the causal attributions for events and actions have important implications for the elicitation of sequences of emotion. When a person is distressed about the undesirable outcome of an event, for example, he is likely to be motivated to determine who or what was responsible. Regardless of whether he finds his own or someone else's action to be responsible, the blameworthiness of the action may also require explanation.

To the extent that one explains an action on the basis of internal traits or dispositions of the actor, these may mediate still other affective reactions. If, for example, one's boss is irritable and says insensitive things, one may experience distress, hurt feelings, self-pity, or one of the other Event-based emotions. But the matter is unlikely to end there. In all probability one will make some causal attribution for this undesirable event. Depending on what features of the situation are salient and what chronic beliefs about oneself and the boss are activated, one might see either the boss or oneself as responsible. Assuming that the boss is seen as responsible, one is then likely to experience not only displeasure (the affective reaction basic to the Event-based emotions), but also disapproval (the affective reaction basic to the Attribution emotions). Thus, because of a pervasive impetus to make causal attributions for significant events, experiencing one of the Event-based emotions will often be the occasion for experiencing one of the Attribution emotions. In addition, the boss's agency in the event is also likely to be the object of causal attributions. If the boss frequently makes hurtful and insensitive remarks, for example, one is likely to see his actions as caused by his personality, and thus experience him as unappealing. Without this attribution there is no necessary reason to assume he would be disliked. If the act were attributed to some external cause, such as pressure from his superiors, then neither disapproval nor dislike should occur. As can be seen from this example, the various branches of the proposed taxonomy tend to be connected via the implicit causal reasoning of the experiencer. The fact that people tend to seek causes for the significant events and actions that they experience means that there is a tendency for there to be, with reference to the depiction in Figure 2.1, a left- to right-movement from Event-focused to Agent-focused to Object-focused emotions.

The tendency for such emotion sequences to take place can be seen in cases of chronic depression. In such cases the nature of one's attributional tendencies may be critical (Beck, 1967; Weiner, 1985). The attribution of the cause of undesirable events to our own agency and the resulting feelings of blameworthiness can be the occasion for further emotional reactions. For example, the act of blaming oneself may be seen as an event in itself, and this, in turn, could give rise to distress or to one of the other Event-based emotions. Moreover, to the extent that we commonly blame ourselves, such blameworthiness may become part of our schema for ourselves and hence a basis for dispositional dislike. Indeed, depressives often report being disgusted with themselves and viewing themselves as thoroughly unappealing (Beck, 1976; Williams, 1984). Since most of us have strongly held goals to be otherwise, this self-hatred is itself an event likely to cause distress. Depressed people, by this analysis, dislike themselves for being dislikable, blame themselves for being blameworthy, and are depressed about being depressed.

Once dislikableness has become a central aspect of the depressive's self-schema, the reasons for the shame and self-dislike may become relatively inaccessible, so that the individual may be left simply feeling dispirited and hopeless without knowing why. This grim attributional path can be contrasted, however, with the likely outcomes of starting with a different causal attribution. If at the outset one finds not oneself but others to be responsible, then one may be able to exit the system more readily. For example, because one is relatively unlikely to have strongly held goals for another person to be admirable, one is less likely to experience as much distress over one's disapproval of them as one is over one's disapproval of oneself. On the other hand, the person of whose actions one disapproves may not be a mere passing stranger in whom one has no personal investment. The person may be one's child, one's spouse, or one's boss, in which case the person may be perceived either as an extension of one's self or as someone with whom one must cope. In such cases one may have strongly held goals for them to act in a praiseworthy rather than a blameworthy fashion and to be likeable rather than dislikable. If so, then blaming them for their actions and concluding that one dislikes them can again be construed as undesirable events and, hence, as occasions for distress, although in such cases it is usually possible to extricate oneself from the situation. At least in principle, one can leave one's spouse, quit one's job, and even distance oneself from one's child in ways that one cannot with respect to one's self, except perhaps by various psychotic disturbances such as depersonalization, amnesia, or multiple personality.

Summary

In addition to the Event-based and Agent-based emotions, there are Object-based emotions that we refer to as Attraction emotions. The two Attraction emotions are characterized by the eliciting conditions of (LIKING) AN APPEALING OBJECT (e.g., love), and (DISLIKING) AN UNAPPEALING OBJECT (e.g., hate). The two variables that are proposed as affecting the intensity of these emotions are the degree to which the object is appealing or unappealing, and the familiarity of the object.

Appealingness is rooted in attitudes that are dispositional likes and dislikes. These dispositions are associated with representations of or categories of objects – one may feel disposed to like dogs and to dislike snakes. Momentary liking (or disliking) thus often derives from how one categorizes an object and what one's disposition is toward objects in that category, as well as from the characteristics of the individual object itself. Familiarity (or novelty) is the one collative variable from Berlyne's work on aesthetic appreciation that appears to be separable from appealingness (apart from surprisingness, which is captured by our global variable of unexpectedness). Familiarity has a complex relationship to momentary liking, but the most likely candidate is an inverted U function.

9   The Boundaries of the Theory

Any theory of emotion, whatever its focus, is likely to be bounded in the sense that there are aspects of the problem that it does not address and is not intended to address. Certainly, this is the case with the theory that we have proposed. We have chosen to focus on the cognitive antecedents of emotions because we think they play a crucial causal role in the experience of emotion. This focus has led us to concentrate on issues relating to the cognition–emotion interface while neglecting a host of other critically important questions. For example, physiology is essential for emotional experience but we have ignored it because it is not relevant to the question of the role that cognition plays in the elicitation of emotions. Nor have we taken a position on the role of facial expression in emotions. Such issues, while certainly important, simply are not ones that we have chosen to address. In this final chapter, we discuss some of the implications of the view of emotion that we have proposed with the goal of trying to show how and where we think they might be relevant to other issues. At the same time, this will give us an opportunity to identify some of the weaknesses in our approach that we ourselves recognize. This in no way, of course, precludes the possibility that there are other weaknesses that we have not recognized.

Emotion Words and Cross-cultural Issues

In discussing emotions, particularly individual ones, it is virtually impossible to extricate oneself from the linguistic complications that arise. We have repeatedly stressed throughout this book that our concern has been with characterizing emotion types rather than with defining English emotion words. To this end, we proposed a set of emotion types characterized in terms of their eliciting conditions. These eliciting conditions are intended as specifications of the necessary, but not always the sufficient, conditions for all the tokens associated with a particular emotion type. Some emotion

172

types (e.g., DISPLEASED ABOUT THE PROSPECT OF AN UNDESIR-ABLE EVENT) have quite a large group of English words associated with them, others (e.g., PLEASED ABOUT THE DISCONFIRMATION OF THE PROSPECT OF AN UNDESIRABLE EVENT) have a very small number of words (in this particular case, just the one word, "relief"), and some (e.g., DISPLEASED ABOUT THE CONFIRMATION OF THE PROSPECT OF AN UNDESIRABLE EVENT) have no English words associated with them. So, although we have often had to talk about individual emotions in terms of the words that are commonly used to refer to them, our focus has been on trying to characterize emotion types in as language-neutral a fashion as possible. Thus, instead of selecting as its theoretical terms particular English emotion words (e.g., "fear"), the theory purports to be a theory about emotions themselves – what we have called "emotion types" – characterized in terms of their cognitive eliciting conditions. Having characterized emotions in this way, it then becomes possible, as a separate enterprise, to investigate the degree to which and the way in which the emotion words in any particular language map onto the hypothesized emotion types. Without the benefit of empirical data, we have distributed about 130 tokens between 22 emotion types. In doing this, we did not feel compelled to assign each token to only one emotion type. To do so would have been contrary to the spirit of our enterprise. To see why this should be, consider words like "perturbed" and "upset." Certainly, the state of being upset seems to be an emotion, but a moment's thought reveals that it is a very general negative state that can be consistent with being distressed, angry, or even ashamed. Thus, the word "upset," from our perspective, is capable of being used to refer to several different emotion types – types that we have tried to characterize independently of the words. In fact, the same problem of lack of specificity of reference is rampant in English emotion words, especially many of the negative terms that we identified as tokens in the Distress emotions. It is almost certain that we have not done a perfect job of distributing tokens among the types; however, this was not our goal. Our goal has been to characterize the principles upon which our approach to emotions is based. The degree to which these principles are valid will have to await empirical results.

In fact, we have conducted a number of preliminary experiments designed to determine how well English emotion words fit into the various emotion categories we have proposed. Before we were able to embark on this project, however, we found it necessary to try to determine some relatively theory-free method of identifying words in English that refer to emotions in the first place. For example, many investigators have included in their lists of emotions (and, in many cases, as basic emotions) terms such as "surprise" (e.g., Ekman, Friesen, & Ellsworth, 1982; Frijda, 1987; Izard, 1977; Tomkins, 1984), about which, in our opinion, a legitimate question can be asked as to whether they refer to *emotions* at all. As we have already indicated, because we do not view surprise as a necessarily valenced reaction, we do not consider it to be an emotion, but this is a theory-laden reason for rejecting it. Clearly, a relatively theory-free reason would be more compelling. One empirical technique that we have used to help isolate emotion words from nonemotion words has been to ask subjects to indicate how confident they are that "feeling *x*" and "being *x*" are emotions when *x* is a putative emotion term (Clore, Ortony, & Foss, 1987). At least for adjectival forms, we have found that terms that are independently rated as good examples of emotions tend to be judged as referring to emotions comparably well in both of these linguistic contexts, whereas nonemotion terms show other patterns. Using this approach, states such as surprise and interest look more like *cognitive* states having to do with various aspects of knowing and believing than they do like emotional states. Starting with a pool of nearly 600 English words that frequently appear in the emotion literature, we were able, using the feel/be distinction, to identify about 270 English words for which we have considerable confidence that they refer to emotions. The excluded words included ones referring to cognitive states (e.g., "surprise," "interest"), ones referring to body states (e.g., "sleepy," "droopy"), and ones referring to objective descriptions and subjective evaluations of people (e.g., "abandoned," "sexy"), which seem to acquire emotional content only if feeling is imported through the use of a linguistic context, as in the phrase "feeling abandoned." A more detailed discussion of this work and of its theoretical underpinnings can be found in Clore, Ortony, and Foss (1987), Ortony (1987), and Ortony, Clore, and Foss (1987).

Our insistence on trying to characterize emotion types has had at least two interesting consequences. First, it resulted in the postulation of two emotion types for which there are no single convenient lexical items in English. Thus, in one instance we found ourselves characterizing an emotion of being DISPLEASED ABOUT THE CONFIRMATION OF THE PROSPECT OF AN UNDESIRABLE EVENT, for which the nearest phrase in English is something like "fears confirmed," and in another we characterized the emotion of being PLEASED ABOUT AN EVENT PRESUMED TO BE DESIRABLE FOR SOMEONE ELSE, which might be glossed as being "happy-for" (someone). Naturally, it would be interesting to discover some language that does have single lexical items for these emotions. A second consequence of trying to characterize emotion types was the recognition of an emotion type that is rarely mentioned in psychological discussions of emotions. The emotion that "fell out" of our analysis was the Fortunes-of-others emotion of being PLEASED ABOUT AN EVENT PRE-SUMED TO BE UNDESIRABLE FOR SOMEONE ELSE (gloating). The fact that our approach leads us to consider recognizable emotions for which our common language happens to have no name, or to which emotion theorists have rarely devoted serious attention, strikes us as being an advantage in that it demonstrates that the method we have employed is one that reduces the extent to which the theory is artificially constrained by the vagaries of linguistic history. We think that an approach to emotion that starts with a set of supposed emotion words and tries to analyze them is less likely to result in as rich a structure as the one we have proposed, and is quite likely to leave out emotions that happen, for whatever historical linguistic reason, not to have readily available lexical representations.

However, we see the main advantage of trying to separate a theory of emotion from the language of emotion as lying in the potential that it provides for developing a theory on a relatively culture-free footing. Thus, at least at the meta-level, we feel comfortable that we have a theory based on culturally universal principles. These principles are that the particular classes of emotions that will exist in a culture depend on the ways in which members of that culture carve up their world. We have suggested that in our culture, the main divisions are between events, the actions of agents, and objects. However, should there be cultures, or other species for that matter, that do not, for example, focus on the actions of agents, then we would predict that they would not, indeed could not, experience Attribution emotions.

We have tried to specify the cognitive antecedents of emotions at a level of description that is, at least in principle, culturally universal in the sense that the specification of the classes of situations that lead to emotions is in terms of psychological constructs for which a reasonable case for universality can be made. These are the constructs of desirability, praiseworthiness, and appealingness, which we think are much more likely to be culturally universal than, for example, descriptions in terms of social constructs such as leisure, work, and social networks (e.g., Argyle, 1987). Thus, for example, we think it more likely that, particularly, a primitive culture will perceive the world in terms of such constructs as the desirability (or otherwise) of an event, than in terms of a difference between work and leisure. Yet, even within cultures that share the three main ways of viewing the world, there remains plenty of room in our theory for cultural and individual differences. Differentiations within these three classes can easily vary from one culture to another simply as a result of the fact that the boundaries between different classes of variable values may be culturally determined. Thus, for example, we proposed the Loss emotions as a subgroup of the Distress emotions that might result from constraining the value of the type of undesirable event to various kinds of losses. If some culture does not consider losses to be salient as undesirable events, there will be a corresponding absence of that class of emotions. In other words, some sources of cultural variation are identical to sources of individual variation – in different cultures, just as for different individuals, different things count as being desirable and undesirable, praiseworthy and blameworthy, and appealing and unappealing.

Emotion Experiences and Unconscious Emotions

For us, the experience is the sine qua non of emotions. One frequent objection to focusing on emotions as experiences flows from the psychoanalytic tradition and its interest in "suppressed" emotions. Interestingly, however, even Freud denied that it made sense to talk of unexperienced emotions (Freud, 1915). In his essay, "The Unconscious," Freud wrote: "It is surely of the essence of an emotion that we should feel it, i.e., that it should enter consciousness. So for emotions, feelings and affects to be unconscious would be quite out of the question" (p. 110). Freud held that the beliefs or cognitions on which emotions are based can be unconscious, and indeed that one of the reasons for maintaining them as unconscious might be to avoid the threat of experiencing certain emotions, but the emotions themselves cannot be unconscious.

The need for an organism to be conscious of its emotions might appear inescapable if one takes a functional view of emotions, treating them as signals to the organism to focus attention on something important with a view to initiating any needed action. However, one might still ask why this function could not be realized directly, without the intervention of a conscious awareness of the emotion. Presumably, the answer would have to be along the lines that the experience of emotions in fact serves crucial information-processing functions. From time to time in the preceding pages we have suggested that the appraisal mechanism need not be conscious. For example, one can be threatened by the prospect of an undesirable event without knowing, or having available to consciousness, exactly what it is that is threatening about the event or in exactly what way the event is undesirable. Let us now imagine that an organism unconsciously registered the eliciting conditions for, say, a Fear emotion, but that the experience of fear were bypassed. If the organism simply tried to initiate an appropriate action, what would that action be? In the absence of conscious awareness of something, either the satisfaction of the eliciting conditions or the corresponding emotion, it is difficult to see how the organism could redirect its processing resources by giving high processing priority (Simon, 1967) to the relevant information in order to discover more about the object of the fear. Under these conditions, the organism would essentially be reduced to behaving with a fixed action pattern, like an automaton. On the other hand, one could view the experiential feels of emotions as shorthand, abbreviated descriptions of the structure of eliciting conditions that serve the purpose of providing relevant affective information. At the same time, they could motivate the cognitive machinery to discover what is going on, thereby at least to some extent giving the organism a chance to respond in a situationally appropriate manner. One does not run away from a bear in the woods, one runs away because one is *afraid* of the bear in the woods. And, in the case of a bear in the woods, running away might well be the most functional solution to the perceived threat. But, without the intervention of consciousness to guide and redirect planning, one would have to assume that the response to all fear situations would be the same, and the result would be a very dysfunctional system. For the investor who fears Wall Street bears, running away would be appropriate only in a figurative sense, and for somebody being threatened by a cheetah, running away is unlikely to be an effective response in any sense at all!

There is one more important cognitive function that the feeling of an emotion has – it is an important way of indexing memory. If an organism experiences a feeling similar to ones experienced in the past, that organism has the potential to respond on the basis of its memory of the success or failure of past responses (see Tomkins's 1979 discussion of what he calls "psychological magnification"). In this way, by taking advantage of the similarities and differences between the current emotion-inducing situation and past ones that led to the same feeling, the organism can *learn* to maximize the effectiveness of its responses. So, emotional experiences can be viewed as signatures (see also Spiro, 1982) for the presence of structured and distinct eliciting conditions, and for indexing memory so that, with the help of reminding mechanisms (Schank, 1982), the organism can potentially respond in the maximally appropriate manner.

Although we have denied the possibility of unconscious emotions, there is one sense in which we think that at least something like an unconscious emotion is possible. We have argued that even if the eliciting conditions of an emotion are satisfied, an emotion will not be experienced if the intensity is not above some threshold. Thus, one might consider such situations at least to be cases of something that could be called a "latent" emotion, although we prefer to think of them as situations involving what we call an "emotion potential" (see Chapter 4 and the section in this chapter on Computational Tractability). In any event, under such conditions it is possible that subsequent to the satisfaction of the eliciting conditions the operative intensity variables change in such a way as to allow the emotion to surface, so that if one does view an emotion potential as a kind of unconscious emotion, it is one that can potentially manifest itself as a normal emotional experience with a change in conditions.

Coping and the Function of Emotions

Emotions don't last for ever. They come, they stay for a while, and they go. Some emotions, such as *relief*, have a relatively short lifespan, others, such as *grief*, last a lot longer. In general, however, in all cases, the person experiencing the emotion has to cope with two distinct things. He or she has to cope, first, with the emotion-inducing situation, and second, with the experience of the emotion itself. There is an extensive psychological literature on coping with stress and emotional situations (e.g., Folkman, Schaefer, & Lazarus, 1979; Wortman & Brehm, 1975). However, our present purposes will not be served by attempting to review this literature, since our goal is merely to make a few quite specific observations on the topic. We shall start our discussion by considering coping with respect to emotion-inducing situations.

As we suggested above, it is reasonable to suppose that one of the functions of emotions is to focus attention on the emotion-inducing event. Thus, one would expect situations that give rise to intense emotions to command more attention than those giving rise to less intense or to no emotions. And, as we also have just discussed, although emotions have cognitive origins, the cognitions that spawn them are not always available to consciousness. Thus, one of the functions of emotions may be to bring into conscious awareness the situations surrounding the emotion so that the organism can take action if it seems to be required. Indeed, it may well be that the function of the physiological concomitants of emotions is both to help focus attention on the situation at hand and to prepare the motor system for action, should action be called for.

If this account is roughly correct, then emotion-inducing situations focus attention on both the situation surrounding the emotion and on the emotion itself, and on occasions, both of these need to be dealt with. In many cases, the function of emotion is to lead the organism to cope with the situation itself, and, to the extent that such coping has already taken place, the intensity of the accompanying emotion may be reduced. This is why *unexpectedness* often has an intensifying effect. When an event happens suddenly, unexpectedly, and without warning, the person experiencing it has no opportunity to prepare for it. The result may be that there is a great deal of cognitive disorganization. This is true both for positive and negative emotions. For example, if a person suddenly learns that a loved one has been killed in an accident, the lack of time provides no opportunity for the person to prepare himself for the situation. Such an event is filled with implications. The person knows this, but has not had any opportunity to work them out in detail. This situation is quite different from the one in which a loved one dies after a long illness. In such a case, the cognitive reorganization has had ample chance to take place and the person is much better able to cope with the actual news of the death. The same is true for the case in which a person discovers that her name has been randomly drawn from a list of millions to win a million dollars in some product promotion campaign. The event was totally unexpected and the fortunate winner has had no opportunity to prepare herself for it – she doesn't know what to do, what to say, how to reorganize her life, and so on. She needs time to "think it through." If, however, she had anticipated it, she would have had the chance to do this thinking, so that the announcement of her winning would have required much less cognitive reorganization.

This means that prior warning, in allowing time for coping, is likely to result in some muting of emotion relative to what might be predicted in cases of higher unexpectedness. Indeed, as was discussed in Chapter 6 in the context of research reported in Breznitz (1984), the time course of fear when subjects are told that they will receive an electric shock at some time in the future shows an initial high intensity followed by a decline until the time for the shock approaches, at which point fear starts to increase again. The initial emotional reaction is intense because there has been no opportunity for the subject to cope with the anticipated situation – the unexpected news is alarming and gives rise to the emotion of shock. As the subject starts to cope with the anticipated situation the shock subsides. Notice, however, that there is another sense of coping in which preparation may not help. This is the sense in which the person, while trying to engage in the cognitive reorganization demanded by the situation, comes to believe that he cannot achieve this reorganization. Again, to use the fear example, as the time for the electric shock approaches and it becomes more salient, subjects may begin to realize that there is nothing (more) they can do to offset or cope with the anticipated negative situation. This is one of the ways in which depression and the associated states of helplessness and hopelessness arise.

So, failure to cope is likely to intensify the emotion in at least the following two ways: first, failure to cope because of insufficient time (i.e., due to the unexpectedness of the event) will result in more intense emotion, and second, failure to cope due to inability (even given enough time) will result in more intense emotion. Care has to be taken here, however, in separating out the *intensifying* effects of failure to cope and the emotion-inducing effects. Failure to cope, especially of the second, inability, type is likely not only to intensify emotions, but also to generate emotions. Despair may be born of fear when resignation sets in because the person comes to believe that he has no control over the situation.

When a person is in an emotional state, his being in that state is as much a situation as any other. Consequently, as discussed in the last sections of Chapter 2 and of Chapter 8, a person in an emotional state may experience additional emotions as a result of it. This means that the question of coping can arise as much for emotions themselves as it can for the situations that give rise to them. A person may be unable to cope with his joy, or his anger, or his fear. Interestingly, the English language has a number of expressions that imply an inability to cope with emotions themselves. We speak of people as "crying with joy," "out of control," "beside themselves," and so on. Here we have an interesting phenomenon. One would think that if an inability to cope with a situation intensifies the resulting emotion, then in cases where the emotion is positive, as in hearing the news about the million-dollar win, the joy would be more intense. We have argued that in some cases the failure to cope is due to the unexpectedness, and in such cases it seems reasonable to take the position that the intensity of the resulting (positive) emotion might be increased – unexpected pleasures are more pleasing than expected ones. But, perhaps the other kind of failure to cope does not enhance the intensity of positive emotions. There is something counterintuitive about proposing that inability to cope enhances positive emotions. One would think that people would find such failure aversive, regardless of its cause. In extremely positive situations in which there is an inability to cope, it might be that two things are going on: a high level of arousal that amplifies the intensity of all active emotions *and* some elements of negative emotion as a result of the coping failure. When people cannot cope with positive emotions they often behave in a manner that has many similarities with the behavior associated with the experience of negative emotions (we have already noted how they can "cry" with joy). It would make good sense to discover that the mechanisms associated with distress and other negative emotions are activated because of the negative construal of the inability to cope, even while the positive emotions are the ones that are predominantly experienced. Interestingly, such highly arousing situations *are* often accompanied by cognitive states which themselves can occasion negative reactions, states such as a sense of confusion and disorientation. Such symptoms are particularly noticeable in cases of intense relief. The profusion of tears shed by the near and dear on the return of their loved ones who had been held hostage in Iran or Lebanon is testament to this fact.

In the case of positive emotions, the inability to cope seems to pose something of a paradox – a paradox that we hope our discussion has at least partly resolved. The result is an intensification of the entire *emotional experience* even though some of this is realized through the combined effects of the positive emotions and the negative consequences of the inability to cope with them. In the case of negative emotions, failure to cope with the emotions themselves is easier to understand. The grief is made worse because the person doesn't know what he is going to do and how to handle the new situation.

In our discussion of the Prospect-based emotions we noted the role of proximity – the closer some feared event seems to be, the more intense the fear. Proximity may be influential not only because increases in proximity render the anticipated event psychologically more real, but also because the reduced intervening time between the experience and the anticipated situation entails less time for the psychological preparation that is required by the situation. Coping, therefore, is an important aspect of emotional experience. It is, of course, closely related to the degree of control a person perceives himself as having – the more control a person has, the more will he be able to cope. Yet the two are not identical. A person may have no control over the expected death of a loved one, yet believe that he or she can deal with the situation when it arises.

The main point of the observations we have made here is to suggest that there may be a cycle in which emotion-inducing situations lead not only to emotions themselves, but also to a need to cope with the emotions to which they give rise. The extent to which a person does cope, or thinks he can cope, in turn influences not only the intensity of the emotions that arise, but in some cases creates new, additional emotions, along with new demands on the coping mechanisms.

Computational Tractability

At the beginning of this book we mentioned that one of our goals was to lay the foundation for a computationally tractable model of emotion. It is therefore fitting, perhaps, that we conclude by reviewing the proposals we have made in light of this goal. We shall do this by presenting some examples of the kind of formalisms that might be derived from our emotion characterizations and discussing how they might contribute to some of the goals of Artificial Intelligence (AI), and how the methods of AI might help us to evaluate, modify, and improve the account of the emotions that we have offered.

Before we proceed with our discussion, we should clarify what we take to be the issue here and, in particular, what we take not to be the issue. Our interest in emotion in the context of AI is not an interest in questions such as "Can computers feel?" or " Can computers have emotions?" There are those who think that such questions can be answered in the affirmative (e.g., Frijda & Swagerman, 1987; Sloman & Croucher, 1981), however, our view is that the *subjective experience* of emotion is central, and we do not consider it possible for computers to experience anything until and unless they are conscious. Our suspicion is that machines are simply not the kinds of things that can be conscious. However, our skepticism over the possibility of machines having emotions certainly does not mean that we think the topic of emotion is irrelevant for AI; on the contrary, we think it is an important and much neglected topic in the field. There are many AI endeavors in which the ability to understand and reason about emotions or aspects of emotions could be important. Obvious examples include natural language understanding, cooperative problem solving, and planning.

If computers are going to be able to reason about emotions, the first thing that will be needed is a system of rules and representations about the elicitation of emotions. We think that the emotion characterizations that we have proposed can provide the basis for a first step in this direction. The simplest of these rules will be those for the Well-being emotions. One might associate two main rules with each emotion. For example, for Joy emotions, one of these two rules might be something like Rule (1) below:

(1)   IF DESIRE $(p, e, t) > 0$
        THEN *set* JOY-POTENTIAL $(p, e, t) =$
          $f_j [\, | \, \text{DESIRE} \, (p, e, t) \, |, \, I_g \, (p, e, t)]$
        Where $| \, \text{DESIRE} \, (p, e, t) \, |$ is the absolute value of a function that
        returns the degree of desirability that a person, p, assigns to some
        perceived event, e, at time, t, under normal conditions, and where
        $I_g \, (p, e, t)$ is a function that returns the value of the combined effects
        of the global intensity variables.

The left-hand side of this rule is basically just a statement of the eliciting conditions for Joy emotions (see Chapter 5); it merely specifies the condition that some event be desirable. Specifically, the rule asserts that if the desirability of some event, e, in working memory is positive, then the value of a function called JOY-POTENTIAL should be set to the value returned by a function, $f_j [\, | \, \text{DESIRE} \, (p, e, t) \, |, \, I_g \, (p, e, t) \,]$, that represents the combined effects of the variables postulated as influencing the intensity of Joy emotions. The first argument of the function, f_j, which is a function that is specific to Joy emotions (hence the subscript, j), is the absolute value of the desirability of the event, e, for the experiencing person, p, at time t. The second argument, I_g (p, e, t), represents the contribution to intensity made by the global variables in response to the event.[1] Note that the DESIRE function is a function that computes desirability in the technical sense in which we have used it throughout this volume; it does not refer to the degree to which the person wants the event but to the accumulated beneficial consequences of the event when it returns a positive value, and to the accumulated harmful consequences of the event when it returns a negative value.

The rule for Distress emotions would be the same as Rule (1) except that the value of the DISTRESS-POTENTIAL function is only set if the DESIRE function returns a negative value. JOY-POTENTIAL and DISTRESS-POTENTIAL are definitely *not* the same thing as the emotions of joy and distress. Such *emotion-potentials* serve two purposes. First, they can serve a sort of empathetic role by allowing the inference that joy and distress are possible emotions under the current conditions – an intelligent conversation program might use the activation of joy-potential as the basis for a question like "Was what happened sufficiently important to make you feel happy?" Second, they invoke other rules (e.g., Rule 2, below) that check whether the intensity of the reaction is sufficient to activate the emotion, and, if so, set the intensity of the emotion in question.

A crucial component of the account of emotion that we have presented in the preceding chapters is that in order for an emotion to be experienced, the intensity of the reaction has to be above some threshold value. The main purpose of the emotion-potential functions is to allow for the computation of the magnitude of the reaction without prejudice as to whether or not an emotion ensues. Up to this point, we have only shown how it might be possible to formalize the elicitation of an emotion-potential. In order to determine whether any emotion in fact ensues, and if so, with what intensity, we shall need rules such as Rule (2):

(2)   IF JOY-POTENTIAL (p, e, t) > JOY-THRESHOLD (p, t)
        THEN *set* JOY-INTENSITY (p, e, t) =
            JOY-POTENTIAL (p, e, t) − JOY-THRESHOLD (p, t)
        ELSE *set* JOY-INTENSITY (p, e, t) = 0

---

1 We shall not elaborate here on how the global variables (e.g., sense of reality, proximity, and unexpectedness) might be represented because such an excursion would take us too far afield.

Rule (2) checks to see whether the current value of JOY-POTENTIAL exceeds the threshold (i.e., JOY-THRESHOLD) required to establish a Joy emotion. In this way, if a Joy emotion is a possibility, and the variables hypothesized to affect the intensity of Joy emotions give rise to a value that exceeds the current threshold (i.e., the threshold for person p at time t), it activates the Joy emotion, by setting JOY-INTENSITY, for p, with respect to event, e, starting at time, t to the discrepancy from the threshold. Otherwise, the value of JOY-INTENSITY is reset to zero, indicating that p definitely does not experience joy in response to event e at time t. The need for this last step will become clear later. However, we should point out right here that although we are not proposing to directly compound the effects of different events that give rise to JOY-POTENTIAL into JOY-INTENSITY, setting the intensity to zero does not result in all trace of the potentially emotion-inducing event being lost because the current value of JOY-POTENTIAL is preserved. We are assuming that when the value of JOY-INTENSITY exceeds its default value of zero, it is tantamount to asserting the truth of a predicate, JOY, which means that the system is postulating the existence of a feeling of joy in p about event, e, initiated at time t. The structure of the rule for Distress emotions would be identical to Rule (2) except that it would employ a distress-specific function, f_d, instead of the joy-specific function, f_j.

In an AI context, there are important beneficial side-effects that result from distinguishing between emotions and emotion-potentials. The distinction would make it relatively easy for a natural language-understanding system to deal with certain mood effects, as would be required, for example, to make sense of sentences like "John was in a wonderful mood that morning. When his children were obnoxious at breakfast, it didn't bother him at all." One might suppose that obnoxious children at breakfast would bother John if he were not in a good mood, and certainly that they would if he were in a bad mood. This knowledge can be fairly easily represented under the present proposal. The effect of the first sentence would be to *raise* the threshold value for many of the negative emotions, and lower it for positive ones. The result would be that, for example, anger could now only be activated with a higher value of the function that combines its intensity factors, and even then, the resulting anger would be less intense than would be the case if the threshold were at its default value. This is because the intensity of an emotion is determined by the difference between the magnitude of the effects of its intensity variables and its current threshold value, as illustrated in Rule (2).

The distinction between emotions and emotion-potentials also provides a mechanism for solving some other traditionally difficult problems in natural language understanding. In particular, it makes it relatively easy to solve the pragmatic inference problems surrounding denials. Suppose a text starts with the sentence "John was not afraid as he entered the court room." Human language understanders spontaneously make the pragmatic inference that the situation was one in which one might have expected John to be afraid. In the system we propose, this can be handled by allowing FEAR-POTENTIAL to be activated while setting its value below that of FEAR-THRESHOLD. In other words, what the system would do is exactly what the pragmatic inference licenses, namely it would recognize that a potentially fear-inducing situation existed which, in fact, did not give rise to fear.

It would be a relatively simple matter to augment rules such as Rule (2) to select one or more appropriate English language tokens that roughly reflect the current intensity. Thus, for example, if the value of JOY-INTENSITY is relatively low, it might select tokens such as "pleased" and "glad." If very high, it might select "ecstatic" or "euphoric." The effects of these tokens could, of course, be modified through the use of qualifying adjectives, however, that is a detail we shall not discuss here. A reasonable mapping between lexical items and intensity ranges for different emotion types could easily be achieved through the use of an empirically derived intensity map.

Having dealt with a very simple case, we can now outline the sort of rules we anticipate for a Prospect-based emotion such as fear.

(3)   IF PROSPECT (p, e, t) AND DESIRE $(p, e, t) < 0$
THEN *set* FEAR-POTENTIAL $(p, e, t) =$
$f_f [\,|$ DESIRE $(p, e, t) \,|,$ LIKELIHOOD $(p, e, t),$ $I_g (p, e, t) \,]$

(4)   IF FEAR-POTENTIAL $(p, e, t) >$ FEAR-THRESHOLD (p, t)
THEN *set* FEAR-INTENSITY $(p, e, t) =$
FEAR-POTENTIAL $(p, e, t) -$ FEAR-THRESHOLD (p, t)
ELSE *set* FEAR-INTENSITY $(p, e, t) = 0$

Rule (3) indicates that when it is true that p entertains the prospect of e at time t (indicated by the predicate, PROSPECT), and if p considers e to be undesirable at time t, then the potential for fear will be triggered. In other words, it specifies the eliciting conditions for Fear emotions (see Chapter 6). As with Rule (2), the magnitude of the emotion-potential is determined by the intensity variables hypothesized to influence the intensity emotion – in the case of fear, by the absolute value of the desirability of the event, the subjective likelihood that it will be realized, and the contribution of global factors. Rule (4) then determines whether the magnitude of FEAR-POTENTIAL exceeds the current threshold for Fear emotions, and if so it

sets the intensity of fear to the difference between the current value of
FEAR-THRESHOLD and the just set value of FEAR-POTENTIAL. Otherwise, it resets the value of FEAR-INTENSITY to zero to represent the fact
that p did not experience fear in response to event, e, at time, t.

With these rules for fear in hand, we can now consider the the more
complex rules for relief :

(5)   IF FEAR-POTENTIAL $(p, e, t) > 0$ AND DISBELIEVE (p, e, t_2)
        AND $t_2 \geq t$
        THEN *set* RELIEF-POTENTIAL $(p, e, t_2) =$
           f_r [FEAR-POTENTIAL (p, e, t), EFFORT (p, e),
           REALIZATION (e, t_2), $I_g (p, e, t_2)$]

(6)   IF RELIEF-POTENTIAL $(p, e, t_2) >$ RELIEF-THRESHOLD (p, t_2)
        THEN *set* RELIEF-INTENSITY $(p, e, t_2) =$
           RELIEF-POTENTIAL (p, e, t_2) − RELIEF-THRESHOLD (p, t_2)
        AND *reset* FEAR-POTENTIAL $(p, e, t_2) =$
           f_f [| DESIRE (p, e, t_2) |, LIKELIHOOD (p, e, t_2), $I_g (p, e, t_2)$]
        ELSE *set* RELIEF-INTENSITY $(p, e, t_2) = 0$

Several features of these rules warrant discussion. First, however, notice
that the left-hand side of Rule (5) is rather different from those that we
have discussed so far. It involves three conjoined conditions. One is that
FEAR-POTENTIAL (p, e, t) be greater than zero. The reason that RELIEF-
POTENTIAL depends upon FEAR-POTENTIAL rather than upon the emotion itself (FEAR-INTENSITY) is that a suspicion that something undesirable might be going to happen could give rise to FEAR-POTENTIAL
without sufficient intensity to exceed the FEAR-THRESHOLD, yet the subsequent disconfirmation might still lead to relief. In other words, if the
potential for fear exists, then, necessarily, the potential for relief exists.
The second conjunct in the left-hand side of Rule (5) is the predicate
DISBELIEVE (p, e, t_2). The DISBELIEVE predicate has to be treated lo-
cally to the knowledge representation. That is, it is true just in case p
believes that e is no longer a possibility. Should it subsequently turn out
that p was wrong, and that e does or did indeed transpire, the associated
emotion of relief, if it was activated as a result of Rule (6), will have been
activated nonetheless, even if, in some objective sense, it was inappropriate. Finally, the third conjunct involves the introduction of a second time
parameter, t_2. The constraint on this parameter is that t_2 not be before t as
indicated by the clause $(t_2 \geq t)$ in the rule. Usually, but not necessarily, t
precedes t_2 so that RELIEF-POTENTIAL at time, t_2, can only arise if there
was some FEAR-POTENTIAL at time, t.

The right-hand side of Rule (5) is also relatively complicated, although
the principle it embodies is the same as for comparable rules we have

already discussed, namely, it sets the value of the emotion-potential to equal the value of a relief-specific function, f_r, whose value is determined by the variables hypothesized to affect the intensity of relief. In the particular case of relief however, these variables are complicated by the fact that they involve the embedded contribution of fear variables, represented by FEAR-POTENTIAL (p, e, t). The other variables are the *effort* expended with respect to the event (i.e., in attempting to prevent it), the degree to which the event was *realized*, and the global intensity variables. A fully worked out account of the contribution of effort to the intensity of relief would probably have to exploit the distinction between instrumental and non-instrumental effort discussed in Chapter 4. However, a detailed analysis of how this distinction might be incorporated into the kinds of rules we are sketching is beyond the scope of the present discussion. The other new parameter introduced in Rule (5) – realization – is intended to reflect the fact that some relief-inducing events may be feared events that were to some degree (i.e., partially) realized (see Chapter 4).

The first part of the right-hand side of Rule (6) is essentially the same as for the other emotions in that it sets the intensity of the emotion to the difference between the level of the emotion-potential and the emotion threshold. However, there is a clause in this rule that has no counterpart in any of the other rules we have proposed, namely that which resets the value of FEAR-POTENTIAL. The new value that gets assigned is the same as gets assigned by Rule (3), but the value that gets returned will now depend upon the current values (i.e., at time t_2) of the intensity factors (i.e., upon DESIRE (p, e, t_2), LIKELIHOOD (p, e, t_2), and $I_g (p, e, t_2)$). This is probably something of an oversimplification. However, it is a reasonable first approximation. Finally, the rule stipulates that if the threshold for a Relief emotion is not exceeded, then the intensity of relief is set to zero. Notice that, for technical reasons, the parameter, e, for RELIEF is the same as for FEAR even though, at an intuitive level, people fear some particular event but are relieved, not about the event, but about the *absence* of the event. However, as long as we interpret RELIEF as being PLEASED ABOUT THE DISCONFIRMATION OF THE PROSPECT (OF E) (see Chapter 6), this is perfectly consistent.

These rules are beginning to become rather complicated, so we shall briefly discuss an example to illustrate how they work. Suppose that p is walking alone along a dark street in an unsavory part of town and he hears quickening footsteps behind him. It occurs to him that perhaps he is going to be mugged (i.e., he entertains the prospect of an undesirable event at time t). By Rule (3), a value for FEAR-POTENTIAL will now be computed. Let us suppose now that p has a high fear-threshold so that when Rule (4) fires FEAR-INTENSITY gets set to zero. Now, let us add a little excitement: a police car comes screeching to a halt alongside the man behind p, and after a scuffle and a few gun-shots, the man lies dead on the sidewalk. With p's curiosity piqued, he inquires as to what happened and learns that the man was a dangerous, armed, escaped murderer, looking for money, food, and shelter. The police tell p that he would certainly have been brutally attacked had they not arrived when they did. This new situation, at time t_2, is sufficient to cause Rule (5) to fire because we still have FEAR-POTENTIAL for p from time t with respect to a mugging event, but now, at time t_2, p knows that the event cannot happen (i.e., the DISBELIEVE predicate is TRUE). The result of Rule (5) firing is that RELIEF-POTENTIAL now gets computed on the basis of the values of the intensity variables that led to p's prior FEAR-POTENTIAL, and the values of the other variables affecting the intensity of relief (effort, realization, and current values of the global variables). If this value exceeds RELIEF-THRESHOLD, then p will experience a Relief emotion. We can now see the point of the second action that results from Rule (6), the resetting of FEAR-POTENTIAL. The new value will be given by the values of the variables at time t_2, and we assume that this value is now lower than it was before, at least in part because of the reduction of the contribution of the likelihood variable to zero. Notice that if FEAR-POTENTIAL remains above zero, Rule (4) can fire again. Interestingly, if one were to allow the threshold for fear to lower as a result of what happened, it would now be possible for p to experience retrospective fear, even though he was not scared initially.

As a final example of the kinds of rules that might be developed, we shall consider how we might approach the Attribution emotions by looking at the rules for an Appreciation emotion such as admiration. The emotions, of course, will involve rather different intensity variables because they are based on the praiseworthiness of an action evaluated in terms of standards, rather than on the desirability of events evaluated in terms of goals.

(7)   IF PRAISE $(p, a, d, t) > 0$ AND NOT $(a = p)$
        THEN *set* ADMIRATION-POTENTIAL $(p, a, d, t) =$
            f_a [$|$ PRAISE (p, a, d, t) $|$,
            DIFF $(a, a\text{-}type, d, d\text{-}type)$, I_g (p, a, d, t)]
        Where PRAISE (p, a, d, t) is a function that returns the degree of
        praiseworthiness that a person p, assigns to some agent's a, deed d, at
        time t, under normal conditions.

(8)   IF ADMIRATION-POTENTIAL $(p, a, d, t) >$
        ADMIRATION-THRESHOLD (p, t)
        THEN *set* ADMIRATION-INTENSITY $(p, a, d, t) =$
        ADMIRATION-POTENTIAL (p, a, d, t)
        $-$ ADMIRATION-THRESHOLD (p, t)
        ELSE *set* ADMIRATION-POTENTIAL $(p, a, d, t) = 0$

Again, the first of these rules, Rule (7), essentially represents the eliciting conditions for Appreciation emotions (see Chapter 7). Thus, the function PRAISE (p, a, d, t) represents the degree of praiseworthiness assigned to some agent's action. Rule (8) resets the intensity level relative to the current threshold, with its value ultimately depending on some (admiration-specific) function, f_a, of the two variables identified in the emotion characterization as being the local variables together with the effects of the global factors. The two local variables are PRAISE (p, a, d, t), and DIFF (a, a-*type, d, d-type*). This latter function is intended to represent the "deviation of the person's action from person/role-based expectations," given the current context, including beliefs about the agent's role, etc. The four arguments it takes are the action or deed, d, of the agent, a, and the *type* of deed, *d-type*, one might expect of that *type* of agent, *a-type*. As we have discussed elsewhere, something like this is necessary in order to capture the intuition that one is likely to admire different people to different degrees for performing the same act because of who or what they are.

Our purpose in laying out the kinds of rules we have just reviewed is to show that our emotion characterizations do, in principle, have sufficient specificity to be developed into a formal system. We think that our discussion in Chapter 3 provides the necessary framework for computing functions such as DESIRE and, more speculatively, PRAISE. Notions such as THRESHOLD are easy to represent and, if allowed to change as a function of context, provide considerable power and flexibility. We certainly do not want to suggest that it is a trivial matter to implement a formalism of the kind that we have outlined – all manner of issues remain to be spelled out in detail before this would be possible. For example, it will be necessary to determine the nature of the kinds of emotion-specific functions featured in Rules (1), (3), (5), and (7) and to experiment with the weights to be assigned to the intensity variables (see Chapter 4) for different emotions. Another important question we have completely ignored concerns the time course of the functions that will be used. Clearly it will be necessary to associate some sort of decay function with emotions and emotion-potentials, but we are nowhere near knowing what these functions might look like and whether there need to be many or just one.

The rules we have proposed appear to offer a mechanism that could deal with the creation of moods resulting from a number of individual events none of which produced sufficient intensity to give rise to an emotion. The simplest example to present is for joy: All that one would need to do would be to allow JOY-THRESHOLD to start to fall as the sum of the values returned by the JOY-POTENTIAL function started to rise. In this way, if the person, p, were to experience a series of events that were potentially joy-inducing the probability of later ones resulting in a Joy emotion would increase, essentially as a result of a simulated mood effect in which several minor desirable events lead to a "good" mood, thus making it easier to experience a Joy emotion. Finally, the issue of conflict resolution will have to be dealt with – some sort of precedence rules will be required to determine under what conditions multiple rules can fire, and under what conditions choices have to be made – and what choices they would be – when the left-hand sides for several rules are satisfied.

Exactly what control mechanisms would be required to develop a working system along the lines we have suggested remains as a research problem. However, we think that we have shown that the potential is there, and we see many advantages in exploring the issue further. Apart from the relevance of emotions to a number of subareas in AI, we think that the AI enterprise itself can be beneficially exploited by emotion theorists. The possibility of implementing a formal model of the cognitive bases of emotions in a computer system raises the prospect of being able to experiment with some of the parameters of the model in ways which are impossible in the real world or in the psychological laboratory.

Summary

In this book we have not attempted to review either the theoretical or empirical literature on emotion. Nor have we focused on any of the research designed to test the proposals we have discussed. Instead, we have proceeded on the assumption that progress in psychological research on emotion can be attained through an analysis of the cognitions that underlie emotions. To this end, we raised and proposed provisional answers to two primary questions – "What is the cognitive structure of the emotional system as a whole?" and "What is the cognitive structure of individual emotions?" In the process of treating these questions, we have had to address many other subsidiary questions as well, although in many cases our answers were more implicit than explicit. One of the inescapable questions in such an enterprise is, of course, "What are emotions?" Our answer to this question emerged from pretheoretical research done earlier on the structure of the affective lexicon. That research is detailed elsewhere (Clore, Ortony, & Foss, 1987; Ortony, Clore, and Foss, 1987), and was not discussed here. In those reports it was proposed that emotions are internal, mental states that vary in intensity and that are focused predominantly on affect. By "affect" we simply mean evaluative reactions to situations as good or bad. However, the point of this definition was primarily to distinguish emotions from other kinds of affective conditions.

In this book we went beyond such a loose relatively theory-independent characterization of what an emotion is, proposing instead that emotions are *valenced reactions to events, agents, or objects, with their particular nature being determined by the way in which the eliciting situation is construed.* Saying that emotions are valenced reactions required us to examine the nature of the reactions and the source of the valence. This raised the question of how people arrive at evaluations, and of what it is about situations and about the people doing the evaluating that determines how they are evaluated. We presented only an outline of an answer to the first of these questions in our treatment of knowledge representation and the cognitive psychology of appraisal (Chapter 3). There, we sketched some of the structural considerations relevant to the question of how such appraisals might be computed. We believe that the development of a more detailed answer to that question represents the most significant challenge for cognitive scientists in the study of emotion. Most of this book was devoted to answering the second of the subquestions – namely, what it is about persons and situations that determines how situations are evaluated. The qualitative nature of the affective reaction depends in the first instance on what aspect of a situation is evaluated: an event, its agent, or an object. Depending on which of these is the focus of attention, the primary affective reactions include being pleased or displeased, approving or disapproving, and liking or disliking. In particular, the reaction of being pleased or displeased reflects one's perception of the consequences of events as desirable or undesirable. Desirability is computed on the basis of the implications an event appears to have for one's goals. The reaction of approving or disapproving reflects one's perception of an agent's action as praiseworthy or blameworthy. Praiseworthiness is computed on the basis of the standards, principles, or values implicated by the action. Finally, the affective reaction of liking or disliking reflects one's perception of objects (including persons, things, ideas, experiences, etc.) as appealing or unappealing with respect to one's attitudes towards them.

This general conception constituted the basis of our answer to one of the overarching questions with which we began. The structure of the overall emotional system can be represented as groups or families of emotion types that share the same eliciting conditions. These types are differentiated forms of more general affective reactions to events, agents, and objects. To the second overarching question, concerning the cognitive structure of individual emotions, there were as many answers as there are emotion types to be analyzed. The answers were presented in Chapters 5 through 8, in which the specifications for 22 emotion types were presented. Each of these are differentiated forms of one of the more general affective reactions on the basis of such features as whether the situation is positive or negative and whether it concerns the self or another. Although we did not focus on questions about the function of emotions, our general approach has been to characterize the distinct emotions in terms of the psychological situations that they represent. That approach suggests the view expressed above and also by others that the function of the emotions is to represent in a conscious and insistent way (through distinctive feelings and cognitions) the personally significant aspects of construed situations.

Until a great deal more empirical research has been conducted, we cannot know whether our tentative answers to the questions we have addressed in this book are pointing us in the right direction. Presumably, future research and analysis and the comments of critics will require us to alter some of the proposals that have been made. Our major goals have been to group emotion types together in spaces in terms of similarities and differences in their eliciting conditions, and to specify the variables that govern the intensity of each emotion type. We generally found, when it came to a consideration of the intensity issue, that the emotions that we had grouped into the same space on the basis of similarity of eliciting conditions turned out to be influenced by the same set of intensity variables. The fact that this was possible at all strikes us as an encouraging sign because it suggests that different aspects of the system converge on the same answers. The result is that we are *happy* about the consequences of our efforts, we are *pleased with ourselves* for what we have done, and we *like* the end result! At the same time, we would be the first to acknowledge that others, having different goals, different standards, and different attitudes, could have a quite different view of our efforts so that, in principle, they could experience *distress, reproach*, and *dislike*. We hope not; but time alone will tell.

References

Abelson, R. P., & Sermat, V. (1962). Multidimensional scaling of facial expressions. *Journal of Experimental Psychology, 63*, 546–554.

Abelson, R. P. (1983). Whatever became of consistency theory? *Personality and Social Psychology Bulletin, 9*, 37–54.

Adams, J. S. (1965). Inequity in social exchange. In L. Berkowitz (Ed.), *Advances in experimental social psychology* (Vol. 2). New York: Academic Press.

Angyal, A. (1941). Disgust and related aversions. *Journal of Abnormal and Social Psychology, 36*, 393–412.

Argyle, M. (1987). *The psychology of happiness*. New York: Methuen.

Arnold, M. B. (1960). *Emotion and personality*. New York: Columbia University Press.

Aronson, E. (1968). Dissonance theory: Progress and problems. In R. P. Abelson, E. Aronson, W. J. McGuire, T. M. Newcomb, M. J. Rosenberg, & P. H. Tannenbaum (Eds.), *Theories of cognitive consistency: A sourcebook* (pp. 5–27). Chicago: Rand McNally.

Aronson, E., & Mills, J. (1959). The effect of severity of initiation on liking for a group. *Journal of Abnormal and Social Psychology, 59*, 177–181.

Averill, J. R. (1975). A semantic atlas of emotion concepts. *JSAS Catalog of Selected Documents in Psychology, 5*, 330 (Ms. No. 421).

Averill, J. R. (1982). *Anger and aggression: An essay on emotion*. New York: Springer-Verlag.

Beck, A. T. (1967). *Depression: clinical experimental, and theoretical aspects*. New York: Harper & Row.

Beck, A. T. (1976). *Cognitive therapy and the emotional disorders*. New York: International Universities Press.

Berlyne, D. E. (1960). *Conflict, arousal, and curiosity*. New York: McGraw-Hill.

Berlyne, D. E. (1970). Novelty, complexity and hedonic value. *Perception and Psychophysics, 8*, 279–286.

Berlyne, D. E. (1971). *Aesthetics and psychobiology*. New York: Appleton-Century-Crofts.

Birch, L. L., & Marlin, D. W. (1982). I don't like it; I never tried it: Effects of exposure to food on two-year-old children's food preferences. *Appetite, 4*, 353–360.

Block, J. (1957). Studies in the phenomenology of emotions. *Journal of Abnormal and Social Psychology, 54*, 358–363.

Bower, G. H. (1981). Mood and memory. *American Psychologist, 36*, 129–148.

Bowlby, J. (1980). *Attachment and loss*. Vol. III. *Loss*. New York: Basic Books.

Brewer, W. F., & Lichtenstein, E. H. (1981). Event schemas, story schemas, and story grammars. In J. Long & A. Baddeley (Eds.), *Attention and performance, IX* (pp. 363–379). Hillsdale, NJ: Erlbaum.

193

Brewer, W. F., & Lichtenstein, E. H. (1982). Stories are to entertain: A structural-affect theory of stories. *Journal of Pragmatics, 6*, 473–486.

Breznitz, S. (1984). *Cry wolf: The psychology of false alarms*. Hillsdale, NJ: Erlbaum.

Brickman, P., & Campbell, D. T. (1971). Hedonic relativism and planning the good society. In M. H. Appley (Ed.), *Adaptation-level theory*. New York: Academic Press.

Brickman, P., Redfield, J., Harrison, A. A., & Crandall, R. (1972). Drive and predisposition as factors in the attitudinal effects of mere exposure. *Journal of Experimental Social Psychology, 8,* 31–44.

Bridger, W. H., & Mandel, J. J. (1964). A comparison of GSR fear responses produced by threat and electrical shock. *Journal of Psychiatric Research, 2*, 31–40.

Bush, L. E. (1973). Individual differences in multidimensional scaling of adjectives denoting feelings. *Journal of Personality and Social Psychology, 25*, 50–57.

Campos, J. J., & Barrett, K. C. (1984). Toward a new understanding of emotions and their development. In C. E. Izard, J. Kagan, & R. B. Zajonc (Eds.), *Emotions, cognition, and behavior* (pp. 229–263). New York: Cambridge University Press.

Cantor, J. R., Bryant, J., & Zillman, D. (1974). Enhancement of humor appreciation by transferred excitation. *Journal of Personality and Social Psychology, 30*, 812–821.

Carroll, J. S. (1978). The effect of imaging an event on expectations for the event: An interpretation in terms of the availability heuristic. *Journal of Experimental Social Psychology, 14*, 88–96.

Chapman, D. (1985). *Planning for conjunctive goals* (Tech. Rep. No. 802). Cambridge, MA: MIT AI Lab.

Cherfas, J. (1986). Grub that's hard to swallow. *Radio Times*, November 22–28, p. 22.

Cialdini, R. B., Borden, R. J., Thorne, A., Walker, M. R., Freeman, S., & Sloan, L. R. (1976). Basking in reflected glory: Three (football) field studies. *Journal of Personality and Social Psychology, 34*, 366–375.

Cialdini, R. B., & Richardson, K. D. (1980). Two indirect tactics of image management: Basking and blasting. *Journal of Personality and Social Psychology, 39*, 406–415.

Clark, M. S. (1982). A role for arousal in the link between feeling states, judgments, and behavior. In M. S. Clark and S. T. Fiske (Eds.), *Affect and cognition* (pp. 263–289). Hillsdale, NJ: Erlbaum.

Clore, G. L. (1985). The cognitive consequences of emotion and feeling. Paper presented at the American Psychological Association, Los Angeles.

Clore, G. L., & Byrne, D. (1974). The reinforcement-affect model. In T. L. Huston (Ed.), *Foundations of interpersonal attraction*. New York: Academic Press.

Clore, G. L., Foss, M. A., Levine, S., & Ortony, A. (in preparation). The Prospect-based emotions: Tests of proposed eliciting conditions.

Clore, G. L., & Ortony, A. (1984). Some issues for a cognitive theory of emotion. *Cahiers de Psychologie Cognitive, 4*, 53–57.

Clore G. L., Ortony, A., & Foss, M. A. (1987). The psychological foundations of the affective lexicon. *Journal of Personality and Social Psychology, 53*, 751–766.

Collins, A. M., & Loftus, E. F. (1975). A spreading activation theory of semantic processing. *Psychological Review, 82*, 407–428.

Conners, C. (1964). Visual and verbal approach motives as a function of discrepancy from expectancy level. *Perceptual and Motor Skills, 18*, 457–464.

Crosby, F. (1976). A model of egoistical relative deprivation. *Psychological Review, 83*, 85–113.

Dahl, H., & Stengel, B. (1978). A classification of emotion words: A modification and partial test of de Rivera's decision theory of emotions. *Psychoanalysis and Contemporary Thought, 1*, 261–312.

Davis, J. A. (1959). A formal interpretation of the theory of relative deprivation. *Sociometry*, 22, 280–296.

Davitz, J. R. (1969). *The language of emotion*. New York: Academic Press.

Dawson, M. E. (1973). Can classical conditioning occur without contingency learning? A review and evaluation of the evidence. *Psychophysiology, 10*, 82–86.

de Rivera, J. (1977). *A structural theory of the emotions*. New York: International Universities Press.

Ekman, P. (Ed.) (1982). *Emotion in the human face*. New York: Cambridge University Press.

Ekman, P., Friesen, W. V., & Ellsworth, P. (1982). Research foundations. In P. Ekman (Ed.), *Emotion in the human face* (2nd ed., pp. 1–143). New York: Cambridge University Press.

Elliott, R. (1969). Tonic heart rate. *Journal of Personality and Social Psychology, 12*, 211–218.

Engen, T., Levy, N., & Schlosberg, H. (1958). The dimensional analysis of a new series of facial expressions. *Journal of Experimental Psychology, 55*, 454–458.

Epstein, S. (1967). Toward a unified theory of anxiety. *Progress in Experimental Research and Personality, 4*, 1–89.

Eysenck, H. J. (1967). *The biological basis of personality*. Springfield, IL: Chas. S. Thomas.

Fainsilber, L., & Ortony, A. (1987). Metaphorical uses of language in the expression of emotions. *Metaphor and Symbolic Activity, 2*, 239–250.

Feather, N. T. (1967). Attribution of responsibility and valence of success and failure in relation to initial confidence and task performance. *Journal of Personality and Social Psychology, 7*, 129–144.

Fillenbaum, S., & Rapaport, A. (1971). *Structures in the subjective lexicon*. New York: Academic Press.

Fishbein, M., & Ajzen, I. (1975). *Belief, attitude, intention and behavior: An introduction to theory and research*. Reading, MA: Addison-Wesley.

Fiske, S. T. (1982). Schema-triggered affect: applications to social perception. In M. S. Clark & S. T. Fiske (Eds.), *Affect and cognition* (pp. 55–78). Hillsdale, NJ: Erlbaum.

Fiske, S. T., & Pavelchak, M. A. (1986). Category-based versus piecemeal-based affective responses: Developments in schema-triggered affect. In R. M. Sorrentino & E. T. Higgins (Eds.), *Handbook of motivation and cognition: Foundations of social behavior* (pp. 167–203). New York: Guilford.

Folkman, S., Schaefer, C., & Lazarus, R. S. (1979). Cognitive processes as mediators of stress and coping. In V. Hamilton & P. M. Warburton (Eds.), *Human stress and cognition: An information processing approach* (pp. 265–298). London: Wiley.

Forgas, J. P., & Moylan, S. (1987). After the movies: the effects of mood on social judgments. Manuscript, University of New South Wales.

Freud, S. (1915). The Unconscious. In E. Jones (Ed.), *Collected papers of Sigmund Freud: Vol. IV*. New York: Basic Books.

Frijda, N. (1987). *The emotions*. New York: Cambridge University Press.

Frijda, N., & Swagerman, J. (1987). Can computers feel? Theory and design of an emotional system. *Cognition and Emotion, 1*, 235–257.

Gerard, H. B., & Mathewson, G. C. (1966). The effects of severity of initiation on liking for a group: A replication. *Journal of Experimental Social Psychology, 2*, 278–287.

Gray, J. A. (1982). *The neuropsychology of anxiety*. Oxford: Oxford University Press.

Greer, D. L. (1983). Spectator booing and the home advantage: A study of social influence in the basketball arena. *Social Psychology Quarterly, 46*, 252–261.

Griffitt, W., & Veitch, R. (1971). Hot and crowded: Influences of population density and temperature on interpersonal behavior. *Journal of Personality and Social Psychology, 17,* 92–98.

Grings, W. W., & Dawson, M. E. (1978). *Emotions and bodily responses: A psychophysiological approach.* New York: Academic Press.

Haber, R. N. (1958). Discrepancy from adaptation level as a source of affect. *Journal of Experimental Psychology, 56,* 370–375.

Heider, F. (1958). *The psychology of interpersonal relations.* Hillsdale, NJ: Erlbaum.

Helson, H. (1964). *Adaptation-level theory.* New York: Harper.

Hiatt, L. R. (1978). Classification of emotions. In L. R. Hiatt (Ed.), *Australian aboriginal concepts* (pp. 182–187). Canberra: Australian Institute of Aboriginal Studies.

Homans, G. C. (1974). *Social behavior: Its elementary forms.* New York: Harcourt Brace Jovanovich.

Iran-Nejad, A., & Ortony, A. (1985). Quantitative and qualitative sources of affect: How unexpectedness and valence relate to pleasantness and preference. *Basic and Applied Social Psychology, 6,* 257–278.

Isen, A. (1984). Toward understanding the role of affect in cognition. In R. Wyer & T. Srull (Eds.), *Handbook of social cognition* (pp. 174–236). Hillsdale, NJ: Erlbaum.

Isen, A., Shalker, T., Clark, M., & Karp, L. (1978). Affect, accessibility of material in memory, and behavior: A cognitive loop? *Journal of Personality and Social Psychology, 36,* 1–12.

Izard, C. E. (1972). *The face of emotion.* New York: Appleton-Century-Crofts.

Izard, C. E. (1977). *Human emotions.* New York: Plenum.

James, W. (1884). What is an emotion? *Mind, 9,* 188–205.

James, W. (1890). *The principles of psychology.* New York: Holt.

Johnson, E. J., & Tversky, A. (1983). Affect, generalization, and the perception of risk. *Journal of Personality and Social Psychology, 45,* 20–31.

Jones, E. E., & Davis, K. E. (1965). From acts to dispositions: The attribution process in person perception. In L. Berkowitz (Ed.), *Advances in experimental social psychology,* Vol. 2, New York: Academic Press.

Kahneman, D., & Tversky, A. (1982). The simulation heuristic. In D. Kahneman, P. Slovic, & A. Tversky (Eds.), *Judgment under uncertainty: Heuristics and biases.* New York: Cambridge University Press.

Kahneman, D., & Miller, D. T. (1986). Norm theory: Comparing reality to its alternatives. *Psychological Review, 93,* 136–153.

Kearney, G. E. (1966). Hue preferences as a function of ambient temperatures. *Australian Journal of Psychology, 18,* 271–275.

Kelley, H. H. (1967). Attribution theory in social psychology. In D. Levine (Ed.), *Nebraska symposium on motivation,* Vol. 15 (pp. 192–238). Lincoln: University of Nebraska Press.

Koffka, K. (1935). *Principles of gestalt psychology.* New York: Harcourt, Brace.

Konečni, V. J., & Sargent-Pollock, D. (1976). Arousal, positive and negative affect, and preference for Renaissance and 20th-century paintings. *Motivation and Emotion, 1,* 75–93.

Kunst-Wilson, W. R., & Zajonc, R. B. (1980). Affective discrimination of stimuli that cannot be recognized. *Science, 207,* 557–558.

Lang, P. J. (1984). Cognition in emotion: concept and action. In C. E. Izard, J. Kagan, & R. B. Zajonc (Eds.), *Emotions, cognition, and behavior* (pp. 167–191). New York: Cambridge University Press.

Lazarus, R. S., Averill, J. R., & Opton, E. M. (1970). Toward a cognitive theory of emotion. In M. Arnold (Ed.), *Feeling and emotion.* New York: Academic Press.

Lazarus, R. S., Kanner, A. D., & Folkman, S. (1980). Emotions: A cognitive-phenomenological analysis. In Plutchik & H. Kellerman (Eds.), *Emotion: Theory, research, and experience, Volume 1: Theories of emotion* (pp. 189–217). New York: Academic Press.

Lee, J. A. (1977). A typology of styles of loving. *Personality and Social Psychology Bulletin, 3*, 173–182.

Leventhal, H., & Tomarken, A. J. (1986). Emotion: Today's problems. In M. R. Rosenzweig & L. W. Porter (Eds.), *Annual review of psychology*. Palo Alto, CA: Annual Reviews.

Levi, L. (Ed.) (1975). *Emotions: their parameters and measurement*. New York: Raven Press.

Lyons, W. (1980). *Emotion*. Cambridge: Cambridge University Press.

McCarty, D., Diamond, W., & Kaye, M. (1982). Alcohol, sexual arousal, and the transfer of excitation. *Journal of Personality and Social Psychology, 42*, 977–988.

McCloskey, M. (1983). Naive theories of motion. In D. Gentner and D. Gentner (Eds.), *Mental models* (pp. 299–324). Hillsdale, NJ: Erlbaum.

McDougall, W. (1926). *An introduction to social psychology*. Boston: Luce and Co.

Mandler, G. (1975). *Mind and emotion*. New York: Wiley.

Mandler, G. (1982). The structure of value. In M. S. Clark & S. T. Fiske (Eds.), *Affect and cognition* (pp. 3–36). Hillsdale, NJ: Erlbaum.

Mandler, G. (1984). *Mind and body*. New York: Norton.

Mandler, G. (1985). Scoring goals. *The Journal for the Integrated Study of Artificial Intelligence, Cognitive Science and Applied Epistemology, 2*, 25–31.

Mandler, G., & Shebo, B. J. (1983). Knowing and liking. *Motivation and Emotion, 7*, 125–144.

Mansueto, C. S., & Desiderato, O. (1971). External vs. self-produced determinants of fear reaction after shock threat. *Journal of Experimental Research in Personality, 5*, 30–36.

Martin, L. L. (1983). *Categorization and differentiation: a set, re-set, comparison analysis of the effects of context on person perception*. Unpublished Ph.D. dissertation, University of North Carolina at Greensboro.

Merton, R., & Rossi, A. S. (1957). Contributions to the theory of reference group behavior. In R. Merton (Ed.), *Social theory and social structure*. New York: Free Press.

Mineka, S. (1979). The role of fear in theories of avoidance learning, flooding, and extinction. *Psychological Bulletin, 86*, 985–1010.

Mowrer, O. H. (1960). *Learning and behavior*. New York: Wiley.

Nisbett, R., & Ross, L. (1980). *Human inference: Strategies and shortcomings of social judgment*. Englewood Cliffs, NJ: Prentice-Hall.

Norman, D. A. (1981). Twelve issues for cognitive science. In D. A. Norman (Ed.), *Perspectives on cognitive science* (pp. 265–295). Hillsdale, NJ: Erlbaum.

Oatley, K., & Johnson-Laird, P. N. (1987). Towards a cognitive theory of emotions. *Cognition and Emotion, 1*, 29–50.

Ortony, A. (1987). Is guilt an emotion? *Cognition and Emotion, 1,* 283–298.

Ortony, A., & Clore, G. L. (1981). Disentangling the affective lexicon. In *Proceedings of the Third Annual Conference of the Cognitive Science Society*. Berkeley, California.

Ortony, A., Clore, G. L., & Foss, M. A. (1987). The referential structure of the affective lexicon. *Cognitive Science, 11*, 341–364.

Ortony, A., & Partridge, D. (1987). Surprisingness and expectation failure: What's the difference? *Proceedings of the Tenth International Joint Conference on Artificial Intelligence* (pp. 106–108). Los Altos, CA: Morgan Kaufmann.

Ortony, A., & Radin, D. I. (in press). SAPIENS: Spreading Activation Processor for Information Encoded in Network Structures. To appear in N. Sharkey (Ed.), *Review of Cognitive Science*. Norwood, NJ: Ablex Publishing Corporation.

Ortony, A., Turner, T. J., & Antos, S. J. (1983). A puzzle about affect for recognition memory. *Journal of Experimental Psychology: Learning, Memory, and Cognition, 9*, 725–729.

Parducci, A. (1965). Category judgment: A range-frequency model. *Psychological Review, 72*, 407–418.

Parducci, A. (1968). The relativism of absolute judgments. *Scientific American, 219*, 84–90.

Panksepp, J. (1982). Toward a general psychobiological theory of emotions. *The Behavioral and Brain Sciences, 5*, 407–467.

Petry, H. M., & Desiderato, O. (1978). Changes in heart rate, muscle activity and anxiety level following shock threat. *Psychophysiology, 15*, 398–402.

Piers, G., & Singer, M. B. (1953). *Shame and guilt: A psychoanalytic and cultural study.* Springfield, IL: Charles C. Thomas.

Plutchik, R. (1962). *The emotions: Facts, theories, and a new model.* New York: Random House.

Plutchik, R. (1980). A general psychoevolutionary theory of emotion. In R. Plutchik & H. Kellerman (Eds.), *Emotion: Theory, research, and experience, Volume 1: Theories of emotion* (pp. 3–31). New York: Academic Press.

Pyszczynski, T. (1982). Cognitive strategies for coping with uncertain outcomes. *Journal of Research in Personality, 16*, 386–399.

Ravlin, S. B. (1987). *A computer model of affective reactions to goal-relevant events.* Unpublished master's thesis, University of Illinois, Urbana.

Roseman, I. (1984). Cognitive determinants of emotions: A structural theory. In P. Shaver (Ed.), *Review of personality and social psychology: Vol. 5. Emotions, relationships, and health* (pp. 11–36). Beverly Hills: Sage.

Rozin, P., & Fallon, A. E. (1987). A perspective on disgust. *Psychological Review, 94*, 23–41.

Rule, B. G., Dyck, R., & Nesdale, A. R. (1978). Arbitrariness of frustration: Inhibition or instigation effects on aggression. *European Journal of Social Psychology, 8*, 237–244.

Runciman, W. G. (1966). *Relative deprivation and social justice: A study of attitudes to social inequality in twentieth-century England.* London: Routledge & Kegan Paul.

Russell, J. A. (1980). A circumplex model of affect. *Journal of Personality and Social Psychology, 39*, 1169–1178.

Schachter, S., & Singer, J. (1962). Cognitive, social, and physiological determinants of emotional state. *Psychological Review, 69*, 379–399.

Schank, R. C. (1982). *Dynamic memory.* New York: Cambridge University Press.

Schank, R. C., & Abelson, R. (1977). *Scripts, plans, goals, and understanding.* Hillsdale, NJ: Erlbaum.

Scherer, K. R. (1984). On the nature and function of emotion: A component process approach. In K. R. Scherer & P. Ekman (Eds.), *Approaches to emotion* (pp. 293–318). Hillsdale, NJ: Erlbaum.

Schwarz, N., & Clore, G. L. (1983). Mood, misattribution, and judgments of well-being: Information and directive functions of affective states. *Journal of Personality and Social Psychology, 45*, 513–523.

Shaver, K. G. (1985). *The attribution of blame.* New York: Springer-Verlag.

Sherman, S. J., Ahlm, K., Berman, L., & Lynn, S. (1978). Contrast effects and their relationship to subsequent behavior. *Journal of Experimental Social Psychology, 14*, 340–350.

Simon, H. A. (1967). Motivational and emotional controls of cognition. *Psychological Review, 74*, 29–39.

Sloman, A., & Croucher, M. (1981). Why robots will have emotions. *Proceedings of the Seventh International Joint Conference on Artificial Intelligence*, 197–202.

Spector, A. J. (1956). Expectations, fulfillment, and morale. *Journal of Abnormal and Social Psychology, 52*, 51–56.

Spielberger, C. D. (1972). Anxiety as an emotional state. In C. D. Spielberger (Ed.), *Anxiety: Current trends in theory and research*, Vol. 1. New York: Academic Press.

Spiro, R. J. (1982). Subjectivity and memory. In J. F. Le Ny & W. Kintsch (Eds.), *Language and comprehension.* The Hague: North Holland Publishing Company.

Spinoza, B. de. (1677/1986). *Ethics and On the correction of the understanding*. Translated by A. Boyle. London: Dent.

Steck, L., & Machotka, P. (1975). Preference for musical complexity: Effects of context. *Journal of Experimental Psychology: Human Perception and Performance, 1*, 170–174.

Stefik, M. (1981). Planning and metaplanning. *Artificial Intelligence, 16*, 141–170.

Sternberg, R. J. (1986). A triangular theory of love. *Psychological Review, 93*, 119–135.

Sternberg, R. J., & Grajeck, S. (1984). The nature of love. *Journal of Personality and Social Psychology, 47*, 312–329.

Stouffer, S. A., Suchman, E. A., DeVinney, L. C., Star, S. A., & Williams, R. M. (1949). *The American soldier: Adjustment during army life*, Vol. 1. Princeton: Princeton University Press.

Strongman, K. T. (1978). *The psychology of emotion*. New York: Wiley.

Suls, J. M., & Miller, R. L. (1977). *Social comparison processes: Theoretical and empirical perspectives*. Washington: Hemisphere Corp.

Tomkins, S. S. (1979). Script theory: Differential magnification of affects. In H. E. Howe, Jr., & R. A. Dienstbier (Eds.), *Nebraska symposium on motivation*, Vol. 26. Lincoln: University of Nebraska Press.

Tomkins, S. S. (1980). Affect as amplification: Some modifications in theory. In R. Plutchik & H. Kellerman (Eds.), *Emotion: Theory, research, and experience, Volume 1: Theories of emotion* (pp. 141–164). New York: Academic Press.

Tomkins, S. S. (1984). Affect theory. In K. R. Scherer & P. Ekman (Eds.), *Approaches to emotion* (pp. 163–195). Hillsdale, NJ: Erlbaum.

Turner, T. J. (1987). *The role of standards of reference in the experience of anger*. Unpublished Doctoral Dissertation, University of Illinois, Urbana.

Tversky, A., & Kahneman, D. (1973). Availability: A heuristic for judging frequency and probability. *Cognitive Psychology, 5*, 207–232.

Tversky, A., & Kahneman, D. (1974). Judgment under uncertainty: heuristics and biases. *Science, 185*, 1124–1131.

Upshaw, H. S. (1969). The personal reference scale: An approach to social judgment. In L. Berkowitz (Ed.), *Advances in experimental social psychology*, Vol. 4 (pp. 315–371). New York: Academic Press.

Verinis, J. S., Brandsma, J. M., & Cofer, C. N. (1978). Discrepancy from expectation in relation to affect and motivation: Tests of McClelland's hypothesis. *Journal of Personality and Social Psychology, 9*, 47–58.

Walster, E., Walster, G. W., & Berscheid, E. (1978). *Equity: Theory and research*. Boston: Allyn & Bacon.

Watson, J. B. (1930). *Behaviorism*. Chicago: University of Chicago Press.

Wegner, D., & Vallacher, R. (1981). *Implicit psychology*. New York: Oxford University Press.

Weiner, B. (1985). An attributional theory of achievement motivation and emotion. *Psychological Review, 92*, 548–573.

Weiner, B., & Graham, S. (1984). An attributional approach to emotional development. In C. E. Izard, J. Kagan, & R. B. Zajonc (Eds.), *Emotions, cognition, and behavior* (pp. 167–191). New York: Cambridge University Press.

Wertheimer, M. (1923). Untersuchungen zur Lehre von der gestalt. II. *Psycholog. Forschung, 4*, 301–350.

Wicker F. W., Payne, G. C., & Morgan, R. D. (1983). Participant descriptions of guilt and shame. *Motivation and Emotion, 7*, 25–39.

Wierzbicka, A. (1986). Human emotions: Universal or culture-specific? *American Anthropologist, 88*, 584–594.

Wilensky, R. (1978). *Understanding goal-based stories*. Unpublished doctoral dissertation, Yale University, New Haven, CT.

Wilensky, R. (1983). *Planning and understanding*. Reading, MA: Addison-Wesley.

Williams, J. M. G. (1984). *The psychological treatment of depression*. New York: Free Press.

Woodworth, R. S. (1938). *Experimental psychology*. New York: Holt.

Wortman, C. B., & Brehm, J. W. (1975). Responses to uncontrollable outcomes: An integration of reactance theory and the learned helplessness model. In L. Berkowitz (Ed.), *Advances in experimental social psychology,* Vol. 8. New York: Academic Press.

Wundt, W. (1874). *Grundzuge der physiologischen psychologie*. Leipzig: Engelmann.

Zajonc, R. B. (1968). Attitudinal effects of mere exposure. *Journal of Personality and Social Psychology, 9,* 1–27.

Zajonc, R. B. (1980). Feeling and thinking: Preferences need no inferences. *American Psychologist, 39,* 117–123.

Zanna, M. P., & Cooper, J. (1974). Dissonance and the pill: an attribution approach to the study of the arousal properties of dissonance. *Journal of Personality and Social Psychology, 29,* 703–709.

Author Index

Abelson, R. P., 6, 12, 39, 41, 42
Adams, J. S., 102
Ahlm, K., 161
Ajzen, I., 163
Angyal, A., 159
Antos, S. J., 5
Argyle, M., 175
Arnold, M. B., 6, 11, 12, 27, 48
Aronson, E., 32, 73
Averill, J. R., 6, 12, 26, 30n

Barrett, K. C., 28
Beck, A. T., 170
Berlyne, D. E., 163–6, 168
Berman, L., 161
Berscheid, E., 102
Birch, L. L., 165
Block, J., 6
Borden, R. J., 79
Bower, G. H., 5, 162
Bowlby, J., 62
Brandsma, J. M., 64
Brehm, J. W., 178
Brewer, W. F., 131
Breznitz, S., 63, 117, 179
Brickman, P., 161, 165
Bridger, W. H., 62
Bryant, J., 66, 67
Bush, L. E., 30n
Byrne, D., 162

Campbell, D. T., 161
Campos, J. J., 28
Cantor, J. R., 66, 67
Carroll, J. S., 118
Chapman, D., 43
Cherfas, J., 159
Cialdini, R. B., 79, 136
Clark, M. S., 5, 162
Clore, G. L., 9, 13, 16, 30, 31, 32, 66, 111,
    112, 116, 127, 162, 163, 167, 174, 190

Cofer, C. N., 64
Collins, A. M., 38
Conners, C., 165
Cooper, J., 67
Crandall, R., 165
Crosby, F., 102
Croucher, M., 182

Dahl, H., 30n
Davis, J. A., 102
Davis, K. E., 159
Davitz, J. R., 6
Dawson, M. E., 7, 62
de Rivera, J., 7
Desiderato, O., 117
DeVinney, L. C., 102
Diamond, W., 67
Dyck, R., 140

Ekman, P., 7, 8, 26, 27, 32, 174
Elliott, R., 117
Ellsworth, P., 8, 27, 174
Engen, T., 6
Epstein, S., 12
Eysenck, H. J., 166, 168

Fainsilber, L., 8
Fallon, A. E., 160
Feather, N. T., 64
Fillenbaum, S., 15
Fishbein, M., 163
Fiske, S. T., 160
Folkman, S., 6, 12, 48, 178
Forgas, J. P., 162
Foss, M. A., 9, 13, 16, 30, 31, 32, 112, 116,
    127, 174, 190
Freeman, S., 79
Freud, S., 176
Friesen, W. V., 8, 27, 174
Frijda, N., 1, 10, 11, 27, 61, 174, 182

Gerard, H. B., 73
Graham, S., 27
Grajek, S., 167
Gray, J. A., 27
Greer, D. L., 40n
Griffitt, W., 162
Grings, W. W., 7

Haber, R. N., 166
Harrison, A. A., 165
Heider, F., 23, 69, 71, 77–9, 98, 135,
    169
Helson, H., 161
Hiatt, L. R., 144
Homans, G. C., 102

Iran-Nejad, A., 32
Isen, A., 5, 162
Izard, C. E., 27, 174

James, W., 4–5, 7, 27
Johnson, E. J., 5
Johnson-Laird, P. N., 27
Jones, E. E., 159

Kahneman, D., 65, 71, 74, 118, 122, 153
Kanner, A. D., 6, 12, 48
Karp, L., 5, 162
Kaye, M., 67
Kearney, G. E., 160
Kelley, H. H., 159
Koffka, K., 77
Konečni, V. J., 160
Kunst-Wilson, W. R., 165

Lang, P. J., 10
Lazarus, R. S., 6, 12, 48, 178
Lee, J. A., 167
Leventhal, H., 1
Levi, L., 7
Levine, S., 16
Levy, N., 6
Lichtenstein, E. H., 131
Loftus, E. F., 38
Lynn, S., 161
Lyons, W., 6

McCarty, D., 67
McClosky, M., 10
McDougal, W., 27
Machotka, P., 160
Mandel, J. J., 62
Mandler, G., 6, 12, 40, 48, 159, 165
Mansueto, C. S., 117
Marlin, D. W., 165
Martin, L. L., 66

Mathewson, G. C., 73
Merton, R., 102
Miller, D. T., 65, 153
Miller, R. L., 96, 105
Mills, J., 73
Mineka, S., 27
Morgan, R. D., 142
Mowrer, O. H., 12, 27
Moylan, S., 162

Nesdale, A. R., 140
Nisbett, R., 71
Norman, D. A., ix, 5

Oatley, K., 27
Opton, E. M., 6
Ortony, A., 5, 8, 9, 13, 16, 30, 31, 32, 38,
    65, 111, 112, 116, 126, 127, 142, 167,
    174, 190

Panksepp, J., 27
Parducci, A., 161
Partridge, D., 65, 126
Pavelchak, M. A., 160
Payne, G. C., 142
Petry, H. M., 117
Piers, G., 144
Plutchik, R., 7, 26, 27, 32
Pyszczynski, T., 117n

Radin, D. I., 38
Rapaport, A., 15
Ravlin, S. B., 36, 52
Redfield, J., 165
Richardson, K. D., 79
Roseman, I., 7, 28
Ross, L, 71
Rossi, A. S., 102
Rozin, P., 160
Rule, B. G., 140
Runciman, W. G., 102
Russell, J. A., 6

Sargent-Pollock, D., 160
Schachter, S., 6
Schaefer, C., 178
Schank, R. C., 39, 41, 42, 177
Scherer, K. R., 25, 32
Schlosberg, H., 6
Schwarz, N., 5, 66, 162
Sermat, V., 6
Shalker, T., 5, 162
Shaver, K. G., 54
Shebo, B. J., 165
Sherman, S. J., 161
Simon, H. A., 177

Singer, J., 6
Singer, M. B., 144
Sloan, L. R., 79
Sloman, A., 182
Spector, A. J., 64
Spielberger, C. D., 12
Spinoza, B. de, 29
Spiro, R. J., 177
Star, S. A., 102
Steck, L., 160
Stefik, M., 43
Stengel, B., 30n
Sternberg, R. J., 167
Stouffer, S. A., 102
Strongman, K. T., 1
Suchman, E. A., 102
Suls, J. M., 96, 105
Swagerman, J., 182

Thorne, A., 79
Tomarken, A. J., 1
Tomkins, S. S., 27, 32, 174, 177
Turner, T. J., 5, 17, 140
Tversky, A., 5, 71, 74, 118, 122

Upshaw, H. S., 161

Vallacher, R., 99
Veitch, R., 162
Verinis, J. S., 64

Walker, M. R., 79
Walster, E., 102
Walster, G. W., 102
Watson, J. B., 27
Wegner, D., 99
Weiner, B., 27, 170
Wertheimer, M., 77
Wicker, F. W., 142
Wierzbicka, A., 8
Wilensky, R., 43, 44
Williams, J. M. G., 170
Williams, R. M., 102
Woodworth, R. S., 32
Wortman, C. B., 178
Wundt, W., 166

Zajonc, R. B., 5, 165
Zanna, M. P., 67
Zillman, D., 66, 67

Subject Index

action tendencies, 10–11
action types, 79, 189
activation: as a dimension of emotions, 6–7; in goal structures, 38–9
adaptation levels, 161
admiration (*see also* Appreciation emotions), 23–4, 79, 136, 145–6, 147, 150n, 188–9
affective reactions, *see* valenced reactions
agents: actual, 23, 78, 136, 140, 153; definition of, 18, 78; formal, 23, 78, 136, 140, 153
anger (*see also* self-anger), 12, 24, 26–8, 67–8, 103, 124, 146–9, 151–3, 184
Anger emotions, 148, 151–3; intensity variables for, 148
anticipatory excitement (*see also* Hope emotions), 112, 116
anxiety, 12, 15, 111, 112, 114n
appealingness, 20, 45, 48, 56–8, 81, 157–67, 175, 176; and value of attitudes, 56–8
appraisal, ix, 6, 12, 34–58, 48, 65, 176
Appreciation emotions, 145–6, 189; intensity variables for, 79–81, 145
apprehension, 62, 111, 112
approving, 19–20, 23, 45, 56, 57, 78, 87, 134–7, 145, 147–8, 151
arousal, 6, 7, 12, 51, 65–8, 165, 166, 168, 180; and appraisal 6, 7, 12; as a dimension of emotions, 6, 7; as information, 66–8; and introversion–extraversion, 166, 168
arousal variable, 65–8
artificial intelligence, 2, 17–18, 181–90
attentional focus, 18, 20–4, 48, 83, 85, 89, 134, 169, 175; alternation of, 51–3; and compound emotions, 134, 139, 147–9; as determining different emotions, 20–4, 101, 103, 123, 131, 169; as a function of emotions, 176, 178; and organization of emotions, 18–24

attitudes, 3, 46–7, 56–8, 103, 156, 163; and schemas, 158–60, 162–3, 170
Attraction emotions, 19, 20, 23–4, 56–8, 81, 156–68; intensity variables for, 56–8, 81, 157, 163–6
Attribution emotions, 19, 20, 23, 53–6, 77–81, 134–46; intensity variables for, 53–6, 77–81, 137–42, 146
availability heuristic, 118
aversion, 157

balance principle, 98–9
basic emotions, 7, 25–9, 127, 149, 173
being displeased, 19–23, 28, 56, 70, 86–93, 99, 102–3, 106, 109–13, 119–21, 147–8, 151
being pleased, 19–23, 70, 86, 88, 92–3, 99, 104, 106–7, 109–16, 118–22, 130, 147–8, 151
blameworthiness, *see* praiseworthiness

causal attributions, 134, 152, 169–70
cognitive anesthesia, 62, 63
cognitive dissonance, 73
cognitive states, 32, 113, 116, 131, 167, 174, 180
cognitive unit, 23, 77–9, 135–6
cognitive-unit variable, 77–9, 135, 137, 140, 148
collative variables, 163–6
compassion, 93
compound emotions, 24, 25–6, 28–9, 146–54
computational tractability, 2, 53, 181–90
consciousness, 4, 70–1, 121, 176–8, 182
contempt, 103, 135, 145–6, 151
contentment, 86, 89
contrition, 106–7
coping, 132, 178–81
cultural and individual differences, 2, 8, 18, 55, 75, 139, 144, 159, 166–7, 175–6

delight, 86, 89
depression, 87, 170, 179
deservingness variable, 76–7, 94–5, 96, 99, 101
desirability, 4, 20–3, 48–53, 86–107, 110–32, 175–6, 182–5; and value of goals, 45, 48–53
desirability variable, 20, 48–53, 70, 86–95, 112–16, 119–20, 121–3; and relation to other variables 56, 65–73, 96, 101, 115–16, 117n, 125–7
desirability-for-other variable, 75–6, 92–5, 99–105
desirability-for-self variable, *see* desirability variable
desire, 5, 39
despair, 132, 180
disappointment, 12, 21, 22, 53, 71–4, 122, 123–5, 130, 150n; retrospective, 124–5
Disappointment emotions, 122–5; intensity variables for, 71–5, 122–5
disapproving, 19–20, 23, 45, 56, 67, 87, 134–7, 142, 145–8, 151, 154, 169–70
disgust, 4, 157, 160, 170
disliking, *see* liking
Disliking emotions, 157–68; intensity variables for, 81, 157–66
dissatisfaction, 87
distress, 4, 21–2, 32, 78, 85–91, 128–32, 147, 169–70, 173, 180
Distress emotions, 85–91, 127, 128–31, 173, 184; intensity variables for, 87, 89–90
dread, 111, 112, 114, 118
dreams, 61

ecstasy, 86, 89, 185
effort, 53–4, 71–3, 123–4; 138; instrumental contrasted with noninstrumental, 73
effort variable, 71–3, 123–4; relation to other variables, 53–4, 72–3
elation, 4, 86
eliciting conditions, 3–4, 15–16, 32, 87, 172, 177
embarrassment, 135, 137, 138, 142, 144
emotion, definition of, 13
emotion groups, 13, 15–16, 19–25, 68–81; local variables for, 68–81
emotion potentials, 61, 81, 178, 182–9
emotion sequences, 25, 32, 67–8, 170
emotion specifications, 86–8, 91, 103, 104
emotion theories, 5, 7, 12 cultural aspects of, 175–6; role of behavior in, 10–11; role of language in, 8–9, 103, 137, 144; role of physiology in, 11–12; role of self-reports in, 9
emotion thresholds, 61, 81–3, 113, 183–9

emotion tokens, 2, 8–9, 17, 70, 87–8, 103, 167, 172–3
emotion types, 2, 8–9, 15–25, 88, 91, 116, 167, 172–4
emotion words (*see also* emotion tokens), 1, 6, 116, 172–6
emotion-inducing situations: and attentional focus, 20–1, 178; construal of, 1, 3, 4, 12; emotions as, 32, 167–8, 180; recollections of, 61
emotions: competition between, 121, 131, 147, 190; differentiation of, 1, 12, 19–23, 29; dimensional characterization of, 6–7; duration of, 123, 178; experience of, 10, 176–8, 182; and learning, 177; as valenced reactions, 3, 18, 19, 29–32
empathy, *see* Good-will emotions
envy, 99, 101, 102
euphoria, 86, 185
evaluation (*see also* appraisal): attitudes-based, 44–7, 56–8; from different perspectives, 50, 54; goal-based, 35–44, 48–53; standards-based, 44–7, 53–6
event types, 64
Event-based emotions, 19–23, 48–53, 68–77, 85–107, 109–32; intensity variables for, 48–53, 68–77
events: definition of, 18; desirable and undesirable aspects of, 51–3
expectation-deviation variable, 79–81, 140–1

facial expressions, 7
familiarity variable, 81, 163–6
fear, 8–10, 12, 21, 22, 62–3, 70, 71, 109–18, 122, 128, 144, 168, 176–7, 179, 185–8; retrospective, 109, 124–5, 188
Fear emotions, 112–18, 125, 131, 185–8; intensity variables for, 70–1, 112–18
fears-confirmed, 22, 119–21, 128–9, 174
Fears-confirmed emotions, 119–21; intensity variables for, 71–5, 119–21
feeling guilty, 106, 137, 142–3
feeling offended, 148, 153
feeling vindicated, 106
feelings, as information, 66–7, 163
folk theories, 9–10, 144
Fortunes-of-others emotions, 19, 22–3, 92–107; intensity variables for, 75–7, 94–7
fright, 15, 111, 112
frustration, 56, 66–7, 122, 153

gloating, 19, 23, 75, 76, 99, 103–5, 175
Gloating emotions, 99, 104–5, 175; intensity variables for, 75–7, 99–100, 104–5

goal structure, 34–47, 48–53; dynamic na-
    ture of, 37–8, 43; types of links in, 35–
    8; virtual nature of, 34–5
goals, 3, 39–44; all-or-none, 44, 74–5; differ-
    ent kinds of, 39–42; duration of, 42–3;
    focal, 50; implicit and explicit, 39, 42–
    3; partially-attainable, 44, 74–5
Good-will emotions, 92–9; intensity vari-
    ables for, 93–7
gratification, 24, 147, 148, 153
Gratification emotions, 148, 153; intensity
    variables for, 148
gratitude, 24, 147, 148–9
Gratitude emotions, 148–51; intensity vari-
    ables for, 148
grief, 22, 87, 90–1, 178, 181

happiness (*see also* joy); 87, 90, 127
Happy-for emotions 93–9; intensity vari-
    ables for, 75–7, 93–7
hate, 24, 157
homesick, 87, 91
hope, 12, 21, 22, 70–1, 83, 110, 112–17,
    120; retrospective, 109, 124–5
Hope emotions, 112, 112–17, 125, 131; in-
    tensity variables for, 70–1, 112–17
hopefulness, 83, 115–16
hopelessness, 132, 170, 179

Ill-will emotions, 92, 99–105 intensity vari-
    ables for, 100–1
indignation, 145
individual differences, *see* cultural and indi-
    vidual differences
intensity, 13, 16–17, 20, 24–5, 34, 48–58,
    59–83, 177, 178, 180, 182–9
intensity variables, 16, 20, 48–58, 59–83;
    central, 20, 48–58; and computational
    modeling, 182–90; criterion for, 59, 80,
    81, 94; global, 16, 25, 60–8; local, 16,
    24, 68–83; weights on, 81–3
interest, 174
interestingness, 164–6
interests, 23, 34, 41–4, 46, 47, 82, 94–5,
    150, 152
introversion–extraversion, 166, 168

jealousy, 99, 101, 102
joy, 21–2, 85–91, 128–31, 147, 180, 182–4
Joy emotions, 86–90, 127, 128–31, 182–4;
    intensity variables for, 87, 89–90

knowledge representation, 6, 34–47, 52,
    158–60, 182; relevant subpart of, 39,
    47; structure of, 34–8, 50

likelihood variable, 70–1, 73, 114–16
liking, 19–20, 23, 76; dispositional, 24, 56–
    8, 76, 97–9, 158–60; momentary (*see
    also* Attraction emotions), 24, 97–9,
    158
Liking emotions, 157–68; intensity variables
    for, 81, 157–66
liking variable, 76, 96–9
loneliness, 87, 91
Loss emotions, 90–1, 107, 154, 176
love, 24, 157, 167
lovesick, 91

mixed emotions, 26, 51–2, 101
mood, 162, 184, 189–90
motives, 11, 34, 49

natural language understanding, 183–5
non-emotional states, 29–32
Norm theory, 65, 153
novelty, 81, 163–6
numbing (*see also* cognitive anesthesia), 62

objects, definition of, 18–19
obsessiveness, 41, 138
optimal-level theory, 166–7

phobias, 63, 118
physiology, 7, 11–12, 65–8
pity (*see also* Sorry-for emotions), 21, 76,
    78, 83, 93, 95–8, 104
praiseworthiness, 20, 53–6, 134, 138–40,
    169, 175, 176, 189; and control, 54; and
    effort, 53–4; and intention, 54, 140; and
    responsibility, 54, 139; and value of
    standards, 45–6, 55–6
pride, 23, 77–9, 105, 135–41, 147, 153
Pride emotions, 78, 137–41, 144; intensity
    variables for, 77–81, 137–41
Prospect-based emotions, 19, 22, 70, 109–25;
    intensity variables for, 68–75, 112–24
proximity variable, 62–4, 116–18, 181

realization variable, 74–5
reference group, 102, 161
regret, 87, 91, 154
relative deprivation, 102, 105
relief, 12, 21, 72, 121–5, 128–31, 178, 186–
    8; retrospective, 110, 124–5
Relief emotions, 121–5, 186–8; intensity
    variables for, 71–5, 121–5
remorse, 24, 147, 148, 154
Remorse emotions, 148, 154; intensity vari-
    ables for, 148
reproach, 56, 145–6, 147, 154

Reproach emotions, 78, 145–6; intensity variables for, 79–81, 145–6
resentment, 21, 75, 99–103
Resentment emotions, 99–103; intensity variables for, 75–7, 99–105
resignation, 116, 131–2

sadness (*see also* distress), 22, 87
Satisfaction emotions, 118–21; intensity variables for, 71–5, 119–21
Schadenfreude (*see also* gloating), 23, 104
self, 23, 77–9, 92, 94n, 100–2, 104–7, 135, 140, 153; as agent, 135–6, 138–40, 153; own model of, 45, 141, 170; theoretical conceptualization of, 23, 77–9, 135, 140
self reports, 9
self-anger, 124, 148, 154
self-pity, 78, 106, 169
self-reproach, 23, 77–9, 135–43, 147, 154
Self-reproach emotions, 137–44; intensity variables for, 79–81, 137–42
sense of reality variable, 60–2
shame, *see* self-reproach
shock, 87, 125–7, 128
social comparison, 96, 105, 161
Sorry-for emotions, 93–9; intensity variables for, 75–7, 93–7
spreading activation, 38–9
standards, 3, 44–7, 53–6, 134–5; implicit, 47, 55; relation to goals, 46, 47, 150, 152
subjective importance, 3, 51–2, 65; and arousal, 51

surprise, 32, 125–7, 131, 174; pleasant, 125–7, 129–30; unpleasant, *see* shock
suspense, 131
sympathy (*see also* Sorry-for emotions), 93, 95–7

tastes (*see also* attitudes), 46, 56–8, 158–9
terror, 111
type specifications, *see* emotion specifications

unappealingness, see appealingness
undesirability, *see* desirability
unexpectedness, 32, 64–5, 79–81, 164, 178–9
unexpectedness variable, 64–5; different manifestations of, 64, 79–81; distinguished from likelihood, 64–65
unhappiness (*see also* distress), 87, 90
upset, 87, 173

valence, as a dimension of emotions, 6–7
valenced reactions, 3, 13, 18–24, 60, 156
value: of goals, 45, 48–53; inheritance of, 47, 55; intrinsic, 46, 55–6, 57, 72; and social norms, 138–9; of standards, 45–6, 55–6
vicarious emotions, 61, 131

Well-being emotions, 19, 22, 85–90, 168, 182–4; intensity variables for, 89–90
worry, 112